CHICAGO PUBLIC LIBRARY
HAROLD WASHINGTON LIBRARY CENTER

R0019037268

SF   Young, Carrie.
315.2
.W4   Green broke
Y68

THE CHICAGO
PUBLIC LIBRARY

COP. 1

FOR REFERENCE USE ONLY
Not to be taken from this building

BUSINESS/SCIENCE/TECHNOLOGY
DIVISION

© THE BAKER & TAYLOR CO

GREEN BROKE

Carrie Young

Dodd, Mead & Company
NEW YORK

Copyright © 1981 by Ahdele Carrine Young
All rights reserved
No part of this book may be reproduced in any form
without permission in writing from the publisher
Printed in the United States of America

1 2 3 4 5 6 7 8 9 10

Library of Congress Cataloging in Publication Data

Young, Carrie.
  Green broke.

  1. Welsh pony. 2. Ponies—Legends and stories.
3. Farm life—Ohio. 4. Young, Carrie. I. Title.
SF315.2.W4Y68   636.1'6   80-27963
ISBN 0-396-07953-9

BST

R

In this narrative based on my twenty years on a pony farm, I have reconstructed situations and incidents as I remember them, using somewhat of a novelized form. Some of the characters are composites, and names have been changed.

C.Y.

For Lee and Felicia

Contents

GREEN
BROKE

1

Exodus from Split-Level Land

I give *Business Week* magazine full credit—or full blame—depending on whether I have had a good day or a bad day on the farm.

I wouldn't be out here if, in the spring of 1956, the March 24 issue of *Business Week* hadn't landed on our city coffee table, containing an article that told in rather glowing terms—for this staid publication, at least—how almost anyone, even city folks, perhaps *especially* city folks with a little spare cash to invest, could realize a tidy profit by getting in on the latest rural rage: *breeding ponies.* All you needed, the article exuded, were forty acres of not-the-best grassland and a lean-to that you might very well, if you were handy, throw up yourself, in which to shelter a few mares and a stallion, and you had yourself a business that could easily net you $5,000 on a $15,000 investment *the first year.*

I remember as if it were yesterday the film that formed over Witt's eyes as he read me snatches of this exciting story. He no longer saw the spanking new split-level house in which we were at that very moment luxuriating—the house of our dreams, with the splendid fieldstone fireplace of which he was so proud. He forgot about the $1,120.47 he had just paid a nursery to landscape our quarter acre in a South Metropolis suburb. He forgot it included a hundred—yes, a *hundred*—of his favorite rosebushes. He

1

forgot about the $393.00 he had paid Sears Roebuck to install the charming cedar picket fence to hold in our two small children, Stoyer and Liz. He forgot about everything except that damned forty acres and a lean-to.

I was patient with him. My woman's intuition told me that, like male menopause, the symptoms would disappear if treated with sympathy and kindness.

I sacked my woman's intuition forever when, less than two years later, the film was not only still over Witt's eyes, but he had his forty acres and a lean-to. Only it wasn't *exactly* forty acres and a lean-to. It had become a rather more expensive *fifty* acres—$55,000 expensive, to be exact —because it included an eight-room house, a barn, three other outbuildings, and a creek running dead center through the place, with a bridge, which never comes cheap. And, of course, two pony mares and a stallion, to the tune of $3,300.

Now, more than twenty years later, I never know whether to laugh or cry when I think of the water that has passed both over and under the bridge. Not only the floods, but the droughts; the bottom falling out of the pony market just as we had ponies to sell; the stray animals that would never take no for an answer; and the hard fact that Witt had swept me off my feet with his smooth talk of the idylls of farm living—and then handed me the broom.

What actually landed me out here was that, back in 1956, my defenses were low because I thought it would never come down to the wire. Not even when Witt took off from work at his public relations office in South Metropolis one afternoon and drove a hundred miles down into the hills of Highland County to a pony sale did I think he was really serious. He returned ablaze with the news that fat little old Shetland mares without papers (he had already picked up some fancy barn talk) were selling for $300 to $500. And people were so wild for ponies, he said, that they would buy anything on four legs that whinnied.

I asked him what, in the name of sweet reason, he knew about raising ponies.

"What is there to know?" Witt answered loftily. "You breed some mares to a stallion, and you sell off the colts. That's all there is to it."

So he began to look for his forty acres, and soon he realized the problem. Even if he found the acreage, and even if he were able to throw up a lean-to (with the carpentry skills Witt possessed, it might as well have been a Greek Revival mansion), how was he going to drive fifteen or twenty miles back and forth every day to take care of his ponies, in addition to looking after his public relations business?

It didn't take much perception to know what his next line of thinking was going to be: a whole farm; a live-on farm, that is. I tried to head it off. I reminded him that I had grown up on a wheat farm in North Dakota and that if I swallowed hard I could still taste the dust. "A woman would have to be off her clock to want to go back to anything remotely resembling a setup like that," I said, "when she's already got a vernal oasis like this." I reminded him that I didn't know a thing about ponies, either, or horses, for that matter.

"And just what about *you*, if you level with yourself?" I asked. "You grew up on a farm here in Ohio and you know darned well you never owned a pony or a horse, and what's more you've always told me how you hated farm work, hated to plow corn, and you couldn't wait to get off the farm and into a city job—and you never looked back."

Witt smiled that saintly little smile that always means I don't really know what I'm talking about, and then he muttered something about after all he was born in a log cabin near Greenville, and men born in log cabins don't easily forget their roots, and then he picked up the evening paper and started to circle all the farm for sale ads with a big red pencil.

Even in 1956, it was easier to find a flea named Freda in a collie's coat than it was to find a forty-acre inhabitable farm within an hour's driving distance of downtown South Metropolis.

Every weekend, for a year and a half, we packed the children into the car and set out looking for farms. The more we looked, the more convinced I was that we'd never find one. I insisted on the right of refusal if the house had one of those closed, dark stairways to the second floor, with a door at the bottom of the stairs, which has always given me claustrophobia. This automatically got me out of some dillies, because Witt was apt to fall in love with almost every farm we looked at, no matter how terrible it was.

One farm for which he developed a sizable passion had the tallest, ugliest house I thought I had ever seen. It had a scrolled purple cornice and a skinny blue tower, which loomed straight up to the heavens like a weird, wild bird poised for flight. The house was modernized just to the unfortunate point where you felt you couldn't afford to tear it all out and start over again. There was half a bath. The assumption was that the other half was not needed, because there was still the old privy out back. Half the living room had been remodeled, with a big new picture window and flashy paneling on either side. The other half was pure Victorian. Half the kitchen was modernized: on one side were bright new cabinets and a new electric range; on the other side the old white cabinets still hung, with sagging doors and chipping paint, along with the old black coal-burning range.

The habit of hanging onto things must have run in the family, because in the barn manure lay four feet high at the barn door, rising to a crest of at least six feet at the far end of the wall, against which the cows stood balancing themselves so that they wouldn't plummet down the slope and out the door. Witt thought the entire farm was lovely except for the manure, which, in fact, he said, might turn out to be a gold mine; we could package it and sell it for fancy fertilizer.

The murky closed stairway running up to infinity just barely squeaked me out of that one.

Another farm that almost became ours had a charming old colonial pink-shuttered house, which had been professionally decorated. We very nearly signed the papers on this one, but at the last moment we became unaccountably wary and had an appraiser look it over first. He reported that the house was so structurally weak that only a prayer and two cunningly placed jackposts kept it from falling into the basement.

These were the good farms. Dozens and dozens of others we just drove past or around and viewed the shambles; and even Witt had to admit we didn't have the money or the know-how to fix them up. If Witt had been handy and could have done his own carpentry, plumbing, and electrical work, I suppose we might have been able to whip one of these farms into shape. Witt did pride himself on being ambidextrous, which meant, I had come to learn, that he could pound an equally crooked nail with either hand.

In the summer of 1957, I took Stoyer with me to Alamo, North Dakota, to visit my parents. Witt took a week off from his public relations business to stay home and take care of baby Liz. They were supposed to be mowing the lawn and trimming a hundred rosebushes, but instead they must have been out in wet diapers stumping the farm circuit. Witt's first words to me when we stepped off the plane were, "By God, I'd like to see you turn this one down. The stairway is open!"

A real estate agent took us out the next day to see the farm Witt had come up with in my absence. We drove out from South Metropolis, fifteen miles through wooded suburbs that gave way to farms and fields lush with tasseled corn and thick soybeans; and then we turned off on a country road, where heavy woods suddenly snugged up to us on both sides. Abruptly we came to a clearing and saw the farm high on a hill, nestled against a tree-fringed horizon. The buildings were shaded by giant maple trees whose silver-tipped leaves shimmered in the sun. The prettiest creek I had ever seen ran below the farm at the foot of the hill. The water was curling over and lazying along a wide, flat limestone bed, sparkling clear in the late afternoon sun. Short, brilliant lime-green grass grew flush to the water.

We crossed an old wooden bridge that rattled under the automobile tires and took the curved, graveled lane up the hill to the farm buildings, which, I had to admit to myself, were rather cozily fixed. They were all close together, all connected by a black-topped driveway and set off by a board fence; and all were painted a fresh, blinding white. The barn, with green sloping roof, faced broadside out to the driveway, making a right angle with the corncrib and two smaller sheds. As we got out of the car, Witt gave me a defiant look.

The house was an unusual-looking New England colonial with a portico that faced out toward the road. The back of the house, which faced the driveway, was built up like a saltbox with two stories.

The real estate agent told us that the original house had burned down in 1943, but the seven lovely old silver maple trees now towering over the house had survived, although they still wore great black scars from the blaze. The small one-and-a-half-story house, which had replaced the old one, had been remodeled several years ago by a new owner, who had put on a full second story, the portico in front, a gabled back porch, and a large garage connected to the house by a sheltered patio. The old barn had also burned down, around 1929, and had been rebuilt. Only three of the original buildings remained: the corncrib, the old smokehouse (now a toolshed), and one other small shed with a concrete floor.

When we went inside the house and took the *open* balustraded stairway up to two tremendously airy bedrooms with sloped ceilings and dormered cubbyholes, so perfect for our two children, I felt all my bastions slipping from me. Witt smiled at me, the smile of a winner.

We went back down to the living room and I looked out of the front windows and saw the clipped green meadow below, saw it roll pleasingly down to the creek, saw it come up again on the other side of the water and slope up to the road. A strange thing happened to me. I found myself sketching in tiny red ponies grazing and frolicking all over the grass, and I laughed at the sight. And then Witt startled me by whispering in my ear, "That's a view you could live with forever, isn't it?"

Along with the farm went fifty acres, half of them tillable and lying behind the farm buildings. The other half lay in front along the road and would make ideal pony pasture, with the stream providing fresh water and with trees of every description to protect the ponies from the wind, hot sun, and cold rains. Sycamores, wild cherry trees, willows, and poplars grew in profusion along the creek bed. On every hillside stood full-blown old Osage orange trees, with hawthornes, wild crab apples, honey locusts, cedars, and an occasional dogwood mixed in. A few giant oaks towered over everything.

The next day we made the realtor an offer, with our split-level in South Metropolis thrown in on the deal.

We went through an agonizing week during which the owner of the farm drove past our house a dozen times every day in his pickup, sizing up our house, trying to decide whether or not to accept our offer. He finally decided to take it, and he was the kind who, when he decided to move, wanted to *move*, so exactly two weeks later we switched places with him.

I will never forget the day we moved. The furniture truck led the procession out of the city and onto the country roads, followed by Witt in the station wagon with baby Liz up front in the car seat, and four-year-old Stoyer darting excitedly from window to window in the back seat. I brought up the rear in our old blue '54 Ford, and I thought as I drove along on that hot August morning, "This is the only time in my life I will have all of my family and all of my possessions rolling out on parade before me." For an instant, I thought I knew how a pioneer woman must have felt as she crossed the Oregon Trail, and then I laughed as I thought how she would have scorned the comparison.

I carried my baby girl into the kitchen of the farmhouse at the same moment the former lady of the house was bringing her baby boy out. As she was crossing the kitchen, her baby burped up a little of his milk and it landed on the floor. The woman impatiently ripped off a paper towel from the roller above the counter, mopped up the milk with one flick, and continued on as if she couldn't wait to leave. She had had two years of it, and it was obvious that this was enough for her. I wondered uneasily how she could leave this seemingly beautiful spot and take her two small sons back into the city just when they should be growing up to enjoy the farm. I wondered how I would feel in two years, or five, or ten, or twenty—if I lasted that long.

The next morning, just at dawn, as the sun was trying to break through the lacy locust trees that lined the eastern edge of our brand-new farm, a huge truck came rolling over the bridge with a clanking rattle that got us out of bed like a shot, and a fat, florid man with a handlebar moustache informed us he knew for a fact that our septic tank hadn't been cleaned for so long that if we didn't let him do it in the next five minutes the entire house would erupt like Mount Vesuvius. He held his nose for effect. He relieved the innocent Witt of $118 for the job, completed so hastily that his truck was clank-clanking back over the bridge again before the sun had climbed over the barn. We learned later that the going rate was $35. It was a portent of things to come.

2

Witt Goes Hunting for Pony Seed

The children took to farm living overnight. They acquired an enormous black puppy named Holbein, who grew up to be the fiercest and the most gullible registered German shepherd in the county. The three of them made a racetrack out of the black-topped surface that connected the house and farm buildings. Stoyer hooked up his big coaster wagon to his tricycle and tied Liz's tiny wagon on behind it. Liz piled all of her teddy bears in the small wagon, seated herself in the big wagon, and Stoyer pulled the whole shooting match on his tricycle, with Holbein riding herd. They were soon going at such breakneck speed around the corners that teddy bears flew in all directions, to the peril of the cat and any ducks that had strayed up from the pond.

I was embroiled those first weeks in a canning caldron of tons of tomatoes from a garden I hadn't even planted, while the Concord grapes nagged me, lying lush and ripe on their picket fence, and the peaches and apples in the orchard fell from the trees for want of plucking. All the while Witt, sticking single-mindedly to the purpose for which we had come, was out looking for pony seed.

Finding good pony stock in 1957 was not easy. The pony business was booming out of sight. The small equines had

9

gained steadily in popularity in the decade after the war ended. The Shetland pony market, in particular, had gone hog-wild. Spectators at auction sales watched, open mouthed, as buyers coolly bid anywhere from two to ten thousand dollars for tiny registered Shetland stallions that stood no higher than a man's waist, and for squat little mares to go with them. If a pony was red or golden, with a snowy white mane and tail, and if he was under forty inches, the price went even higher. The ambience was gold rush. To add to the excitement, at least one highly publicized Shetland stallion sold for $60,000. Prices in five figures were not uncommon for highly touted animals that had cleaned up the ribbons in the numerous show-rings sprouting up all over the country.

A small farmer, or almost anyone else who had several acres of land, driving home from one of these heady auctions, would find himself thinking, "Why shouldn't I get in on some of this easy money?" So he'd go to the next auction and pay an awesome price he probably couldn't afford for a Shetland stallion and several mares, thinking he would quadruple his investment in just a few years when he had built up his herd and could begin to sell off his foals. What he didn't know was that the inflated prices had been started by the big breeders, who had come up with the wonderful gimmick of bidding up their ponies for each other at the auctions into whopping four and five figures, instead of trading or doing business with each other at a fair price in their own barns.

It started like this: a breeder had used the same stallion for a few years and he needed new blood. So he located another breeder in the same situation. But instead of making a simple trade, they took their stallions to an auction, and each bid (or had someone else bid for him) an enormous preset figure for the other's stallion. Neither was out of pocket for any money. But the news was out that ponies were selling like solid gold hotcakes. It didn't take long for this gimmick to mushroom, and it lasted for years. It lasted until hordes of small breeders had built up their herds to where they could start to sell off their foals and get their investments back, only to find that the Shetland market was bust. The show was over. The ironic part about it was that the small breeders were not the only ones who suffered. The big breeders, too, were ultimately the victims of their own gimmickry. They had actually begun to believe that there was a permanent market for Shetland ponies out there other than each other; that the "sucker sales" could go on forever. They, too, were finally left with huge herds they couldn't sell.

Even in late 1957 a careful observer—and Witt was one of them—could see that the auctioneers at the local sales were having to huff and puff and turn slightly purple in order to maintain the astronomically high bids for a Shetland pony. But this didn't discourage Witt, because he had been reading in the pony magazines about a new breed of pony—one that he was convinced would soon overtake the Shetland in popularity.

This was the Welsh mountain pony. And Witt made up his mind—although he had never seen one—that this was the breed of pony we were going to raise. From what he had read, Witt said, here was a pony big enough to be of some use other than as an expensive toy for men to pass from hand to hand, as the Shetland had become. The Welsh pony stood up to a man's chest instead of to his waist. And, according to the literature and photographs he obtained from the American Welsh Pony Society, the Welsh pony looked somewhat like an exquisite small Arabian horse; he made a great mount for older children, he could jump like a deer, and he had an incredibly smooth gait as well, making him a good harness pony. As an added attraction, he was something new. Although he'd roamed the hills of Wales since the time of the Romans, the average American had never heard of him. Witt believed that the Shetlands were bottoming out, and that the Welsh were coming on like gangbusters, and he wanted to be in at the start.

Witt learned that Welsh ponies in small numbers, less

than five hundred, had been steadily imported from Wales since the end of the war, and that there were several thousand ponies from this foundation stock registered in the American Welsh studbook. He telephoned or wrote letters to all of the breeders he could run down, most of them in the East and several in the Midwest. The rush on the pony market in general had already caught up with them, and most of them had nothing for sale. He finally found an eastern breeder who, having been hit by drought and low on pasture, was willing to part with a two-year-old stallion out of one of her prize imported Welsh mares. Witt immediately sent her a check for eight hundred dollars for the stallion, sight unseen, and told her he would come to Maryland immediately to pick him up. He felt pretty smug about it. We had lived on the farm less than a month.

The Maryland trip should have given Witt some indication that raising ponies was more than "breeding some mares to a stallion and selling off the colts," but if it did, he wasn't ready to admit it. To make the trip, he purchased an ancient one-pony trailer and persuaded Chris Lauzier, his associate from his public relations office and also a stranger to anything equine, to accompany him. They rolled jauntily down the lane one crisp September morning, the tiny trailer careening dizzily on its tucked-under wheels behind the station wagon. It turned out that the two of them were like two Red Riding Hoods in the woods. They lost the trailer in the middle of Columbus. It plunged crazily down a residential street, narrowly missing women, children, and dogs. A curb finally stopped it, but not without damage. They spent six harrowing hours in Columbus before they could find a welding shop with the equipment to repair it.

They reached Baltimore in the middle of the night, couldn't find lodging, slept in the car until morning, then wearily located the pony farm, where Witt learned the hard way exactly how big a Welsh pony is. His stallion wouldn't fit into the trailer unless he stood catty-corner. Even then it was a tight squeeze. The woman who had sold him the stallion pointed out to him that the trailer had obviously been constructed to haul just one Shetland. She said she would not let her beautiful pony go in this humiliating fashion unless Witt and Chris promised to take him out and exercise him every three or four hours on their way home. This they promised to do. But at the first rest stop, as they were getting ready to back the stallion out of the trailer for his exercise, they had suddenly stared at each other and realized at the same frightening moment that neither of them knew how to reload the stallion into the trailer. So they drove wildly home all that day and into the night, without even stopping for a cup of coffee. They arrived home at four in the morning, managed to back the trailer (another skill they didn't possess) halfway into the barn, and only then did they have the temerity to untie the stallion and let him step back out of the trailer. They were both shaking worse than the autumn leaves that skittered along the driveway.

That was enough pony hauling for Witt to last him a lifetime. He couldn't wait to sell the trailer for half of what he'd paid for it, and we never again owned another trailer, nor did we ever again haul another pony ourselves.

I was not disappointed when I went out to the barn the next morning to get a good look at our future herdsire. For sight unseen, I didn't think Witt had done too badly. Stalwyrt Beau was running around the barnyard doing a considerable amount of whickering and no worse for having stood catty-corner over five hundred mountainous miles in a trailer made for a Shetland. He had an enchanting burnished coat of iron gray, a glittering mane and tail the color of an antique coin, huge eyes set far apart in his head, and a jaw that meant business. I noticed he had rubbed his halter off on a fence post. I wondered uneasily if Witt knew how to get it back on. I certainly didn't.

I broached the matter to him several times in the next few

days, but he said he had no time for such unimportant trifles, because he had to redouble his efforts to find several mares to mate with his new stallion. His luck was running high, because he soon learned of an Ohio breeder who had just brought in several dozen Welsh ponies off a boat from Wales, and was willing to sell a few of the fine imported mares that did not fit into his own breeding program. Witt went to see the mares and purchased a three-year-old in foal for fifteen hundred dollars and a yearling for a thousand. The seller graciously agreed to deliver them, a stipulation vital to clinching the deal, at least on Witt's part. A few days later, the biggest horse van I had ever seen, big enough to haul six horses or twelve ponies, pulled into the driveway, with our two Welsh mares rattling around alone in it. And Egrett and Widowbird, fresh from the hills of Wales, took their places on the other side of the barn from Beau.

Egrett looked so much like Beau that she could have been his twin, except that she was fatter and squatter and had an even bolder eye—an eye and a spirit, we came to learn, that could quail almost any other animal on earth. Widowbird, the yearling, was a tall pink roan, with a smaller, softer eye, and skittish. Soon after they arrived, I noticed they had both hung their halters on iron fence posts in the barnyard. Again, I wondered uneasily if Witt knew how to get them back on. Because I certainly didn't.

3

In Training

*T*wo mares and a stallion. We were in the pony business.

We named our fifty acres Lillehesten, which translates roughly out from the Norwegian as littlehorse.

This next fact is hard to believe, but I will swear to its truth on my grandfather's Norwegian Bible: two years went by, and we were never able to get the original halters back on those three ponies. If we had known which end of the halter was up and which down, it might have helped. We never could figure out which piece went over the nose and which under the chin.

Witt didn't worry about it for one minute. Why, he said airily, did we *ever* have to lay a hand on the ponies? It had been working perfectly well to *chase* them in and out. He pointed out that we had been chasing them in and out of the barn, in and out of their stalls, in and out of the pastures, and it was working just fine.

But when I projected myself into the years ahead and saw us with sixty ponies of all ages, and still chasing, somehow it didn't look right to me. "What about when one of them gets sick?" I asked. "What are you going to do then? And what about when the time comes that we'll have ponies to sell? How can you sell a pony you can't catch?"

15

I reminded him that we were supposed to be in the pony business to make money. "We should have gotten at least half our investment back by now, according to that damned article in *Business Week*," I said.

"We will just worry about all of those minor things when the time comes," Witt answered soothingly. "Meanwhile we are getting along fine as things are."

So slowly that it was almost painless, it had begun to come over me that the pony business was not going to be Witt's ticket. I knew it wasn't my ticket, either. But I also knew something else. If we didn't get those ponies halter trained pretty soon we were going to be in trouble. Egrett had already had two foals, a chestnut filly she'd conceived in Wales, now a yearling, and a fiery black colt sired by Stalwyrt Beau, neither of which had had the touch of a human hand. And she was growing another one. We were going to have a farm full of broncos before we knew it. And not a cowboy in sight.

One evening when Witt came home from work I told him I'd placed a classified ad for a part-time pony trainer. A waste of money and altogether unnecessary, he replied, but if I wanted to fool with it, he wouldn't stop me.

Three persons answered the ad: two men and a fifteen-year-old girl. I decided to give one of the men a try—the one who said he shoed horses for a living and did some training on the side. Just before he arrived, I went out to the barn and put Egrett, Widowbird, and Beau in stalls in opposite corners of the barn. The stalls hadn't been made for ponies, but were really sheep pens, about four feet high and compartmented with open boards, with gates leading from one pen to the other. I chased Egrett's suckling colt into the pen next to his mother, where he could see her and touch her, yet be out of the way. The yearling filly I stashed away behind the barn. She would have to wait until another time. I had no more than finished my arrangement than the trainer drove in.

He was a fat-cheeked man with just a little tobacco juice running out of the side of his mouth and a great deal of tobacco juice running down the driver's side of his pickup truck. I gave him the three halters and showed him the three ponies. He told me to "get back in the house, lady," and he'd have those ponies haltered before I could boil water.

I could have boiled enough water to stew an elephant before he came out of the barn and rang the doorbell. He had one halter over his arm, and he was sweating.

"That swayback mare—that potty gray—she'll try to get the best of you, but she knows when she's licked," he said. "And the stud, that's like taking mush from a kid. But that she-bitch of a roan, you can have her." He pitched the halter at me and spat tobacco juice viciously into my flower bed.

"Egrett isn't swaybacked. She has a classic short Welsh back and I'm surprised you didn't admire it. I'm also surprised that Widowbird got the better of you. She seems a mild sort of thing to me."

"There's your halter, lady, help yourself. But watch you don't step on all them boards and nails she strewed around when she leapt out of her pen and into the next one. You owe me nine dollars, three for each of them ponies. To make up for not haltering the squaw, I trimmed up the stud's feet real good. He'll go like grease for you now. You'll see."

By the next morning Stalwyrt Beau had hung his halter neatly on an iron fence post on his side of the barn. Egrett had ground hers in the dust of the barnyard she shared with Widowbird, and Widowbird was running around in circles and shying at the halter every time she came within smelling distance of it. Rather than have my classified ad go for a total loss, I thought I might as well have the second man who called have a go at my three recalcitrants.

He turned out to be a cocky man who walked on his heels and toed out, a hotshot racer of harness horses who had been in the money all over the country and carried a batch of newspaper clippings to prove it. He said his name was

Demetrius but not to get too excited about it, because everyone called him Speed. He said he was just cooling his heels in Peatville for a few days while his wife was in the hospital awaiting a baby, an indulgence on his part he considered a waste of time when he could be burning up the tracks. But his in-laws, I surmised, had given him some kind of ultimatum about being in residence for the birth, their clout stemming from a slight matter of their owning the harness horses.

I gave Speed the three halters and showed him the ponies. I had taken the precaution of putting Widowbird in a corner stall with two solid walls. Speed strutted around the barn, looked tolerantly down at the ponies as if they were kittens and remarked that this was hardly enough work for him to start on but, what the heck, he had nothing better to do until his kid showed up. Then, without warning, from a stance in the middle of the barn, he made a flying leap and landed in Beau's stall. Suddenly he was a tiger stalking his prey. He cornered Beau and in one flash of his hand over the stallion's head he had him haltered. He was so fast I didn't even see the strap going into the buckle. Without a word, he vaulted back into the middle of the barn and made another flying leap into Egrett's stall. Egrett gave him about three minutes of very fast footwork around the pen before he had her fast.

This was turning into quite a show for my benefit. Again Speed vaulted back into the middle of the barn, ran across and threw himself over the gate into Widowbird's stall. Widowbird whinnied in terror and climbed the wall. Then she came down hard and climbed the other wall. Speed scrambled, not so gracefully, back over the gate and into the center of the barn. He sat down on a bale of hay. He became thoughtful. He studied his hands. He turned them over and he caressed the palms, one with the other, and he flexed the fingers in and out.

"See these hands? If a finger was to get broke or hurt I couldn't feel the reins no more. A driver has got to have sensitive hands. Don't get me wrong. I could halter that mare in a minute. She's nothing, she's no-account, if I went to do it. But I just can't take no chances. Not in my business."

Now I knew the anxiety that Arthur Rubinstein and Van Cliburn had to live with. I told Speed I understood. I asked him how much I owed him. This sent him into a fresh study. He finally shook his head and said there was no possible way he could put a mere hourly wage on the kind of skill he possessed and therefore he would have to conclude I didn't owe him anything. I wished him luck with his baby and we parted friends.

It wasn't until Egrett and Beau again lost their halters that the truth finally hit me. This routine would go on forever. What I needed was not someone to train the ponies, but someone to train me to handle the ponies. And when the children were old enough, I could teach them. But these men with their strong-arm methods. I couldn't do that. I could never wrestle down a pony. There must be a gentler way. Gentle. That was it. That fifteen-year-old girl. I'd give her a call.

Yes, she'd love to come and work four hours a day for seventy-five cents an hour. No, transportation was no problem, it was only fifteen miles and her mother could easily bring her and come for her; besides, in a month she'd be sixteen and could drive herself. Experience? Grief, yes. She'd had her own ponies and horses for *years*, had, as a matter of fact, trained them all from the ground up. Would tomorrow be too soon?

After hearing all that, I expected a girl with some heft to her. I was a bit taken aback to see a short wisp of a girl jump out of a station wagon the next morning. She had bright, bouncy hair the color of Dijon mustard, round brown eyes behind shell-pink harlequins, and freckles on top of freckles. She was wearing jeans, sneakers, and a white T-shirt that labeled her, front and back, as Dutch.

She extended an incredibly tiny hand and said, "Hi! You know that name I gave you over the telephone? You can forget about that and call me, like, Dutch?"

As we walked toward the barn I noticed that her jeans pockets were bulging, and I soon learned with what: lumps of sugar and carrots. She said, "I hope you won't get impatient if, you know, it takes me a few days with the ponies? For awhile it looks like I'm not getting anywhere and then, like, things start breaking?"

She moved through the barn without squeaking a straw underfoot and peered intently at each pony through her harlequins. "The best thing going for you with a spooky pony," she said in a whisper voice, "is never to make any sudden movements. Like, if you even put your hand up real fast, whoosh, you've lost a day's training?"

I told Dutch I thought Egrett and Beau had been well trained by former owners and were just bluffing us while they could still get away with it, but that Widowbird was the real problem; that she'd probably been manhandled all the way from Wales to Ohio without benefit of previous halter training; and after that I'd made the mistake of letting two strange men terrorize her in as many days.

"What the poor thing needs," Dutch said, "is, like, a whole lot of sitting? Now what I need is another pony to throw in with her to give her confidence and also, like, to make her jealous?"

Egrett's yearling filled that bill perfectly. Our first foal, we had proudly named her Lillehesten Mourning Dove. All of the ponies subsequently born on the farm carried our farm name, not from pomposity, but for convenience. Otherwise we would have had to come up with original names that didn't duplicate the thousands already in the studbook registries.

Mourning Dove had never been touched either, but she'd never been frightened, and she wasn't spooky. Dutch opened the rear barn doors wide and let Widowbird and

Mourning Dove walk in and out from the barnyard at will. She knelt for hours at a time on the straw-covered barn floor, sugar lumps and carrots in hand. I was often out there with her because I was determined to learn her method of operation. I saw quickly that it was based on *quid pro quo*. *I'll give you a lump of sugar if you'll let me touch your nose. I'll give you a carrot if you'll let me stroke your neck. I'll give you a handful of oats if you'll put your nose in the halter. Good girl!*

Mourning Dove, at the end of several days, decided that wearing a halter was more than a fair trade for sugar and carrots and, having learned where the goodies were hidden, was nuzzling Dutch for more, but Widowbird was still leery, and hung back in the barnyard. Finally, the attention Mourning Dove was getting was just too much for her, and she began to walk halfway into the barn with Mourning Dove and lay her ears back and shove just at the moment when the younger filly was curling her lips over the tidbit. Soon Widowbird was wearing a halter, too. Dutch was right. Things, had, like, started to break.

Now Dutch needed a helper to walk behind the mares and urge them along as they learned to lead, and I needed the experience, so we worked together for several hours a day all summer long. I learned how to groom the ponies so that their manes and tails glistened, how to tie them up with a slipknot, loosely at first, gradually tightening the rope each day until they had learned not to struggle. I learned how to pick up their feet and clean out their hooves. The day I learned how to longe them on a rope so that they would run around me in a circle, I felt almost as hotshot as Speed. We found that Egret and Beau had, indeed, been bluffing. When put through their paces, they responded well. Now there was only one pony left to be trained: Egret's suckling colt.

We always say that Hector was born with his ears laid back. Foaled black with a tiny star in his forehead, he was a handsome colt. He had great bold eyes in a beautifully chiseled head, and fine limbs. Just as mean boys are euphemistically referred to by doting relatives as "all boy," we'd tell visitors who watched him cut up that he was "all colt." From the first hour Hector was born, he gave Egrett a hard time. He kicked, climbed, bit, and rode her all day long—when he wasn't running away from her across the creek and making her clatter across the stones after him.

Firm in the belief that there are no mean ponies, only people who make them that way, Dutch approached Hector with an open mind and her usual gentle gesture. Sitting with him in the pen right next to Egrett, where he could see and touch his mother through the boards, she spent days tempting him with handfuls of tender crimped oats. Every time she approached him he laid his ears back and backed up to her with his rear. After he had forced her to hop into his hay manger to escape his back legs, he would back off and stick his head through the wooden partition to try to reach his mother's teats.

Hector's behavior finally got to Dutch. She started walking around the barn looking grim, not caring whether she squeaked a straw underfoot or not. One day she brought a horseshoer with her, a neighbor of hers whom she was in the habit of bringing on occasion to trim up the ponies' hooves. After he had finished his job, she asked him, ever so sweetly, "Oh, Mr. Clatterbuck, I wonder if you'd mind putting this halter on that foal for me. My hands are so small he just, like, keeps slipping out of them?"

A hard-nosed individual, Mr. Clatterbuck had not more than five minutes ago proclaimed that he had never seen the sixteen-hand horse he couldn't throw and shoe bottoms up. He grumped in exasperation that she would ask him to do anything so simple. Impatiently he grabbed the halter and went in the stall with Hector. There ensued a violent struggle with such squealing, grunting, and cursing that Dutch and I stepped out of the barn and put our hands to our heads. Just when it seemed the barn was going to cave in, the noise stopped and there was only heavy breathing, then a fit of coughing. We stepped back in the barn. Mr. Clatterbuck was sitting on a bale of hay trying to draw a ragged breath and light a cigarette at the same time. Hector was standing in the middle of his pen, also heaving in and out, but wearing a halter.

I glanced at Dutch, wondering if she would feel guilty about the difficult situation in which she had put Mr. Clatterbuck. Not at all. She acted fast. She grabbed up a rope and snapped it on Hector's halter before the colt knew what had hit him, and she tied him up so tight he couldn't move. None of that gradùally-getting-used-to-a-slack-rope stuff for him. And then she ran her hands over him and brushed him all over. Those two finally reached an uneasy truce. But they never liked each other. In fact, whenever I saw Dutch working Hector, I always thought they both looked as if they had their ears laid back.

Dutch was about the luckiest thing that had happened to me since we moved to the farm. Not only was she good with the ponies, but Stoyer and Liz were crazy about her. On a hot day we'd knock off work and all take off for the swimming pool a couple of miles down the road. The children were awed because Dutch could swim the entire length of the pool and back without touching bottom. She soon taught four-year-old Liz to swim, and one day as we were sitting around the pool we got the idea, I don't remember whose it was, that she should teach me to ride a horse.

She and I had been trying to train Widowbird for a riding pony, but she was much too skittish. Dutch had mounted her several times, but Widowbird had walked around as if she were treading on eggs, ready to explode if anyone even hissed in the distance. The thing to do, Dutch said, was for me to come to her place and she'd teach me to ride on one of her horses. I was gung-ho. But none of this loose Western riding for me. Dutch's parents had treated her to English riding lessons when she was a child, and she said she'd teach me the whole bit—how to hold the reins draped over the correct fingers just so, the cantering and the posting, the leading with the right leg around the corners—the entire business.

I sent away to Miller's in New York for an Olympia forward-seat saddle, a pair of Marlborough riding boots, flared riding breeches with goatskin patches, a checked riding shirt with matching choker and, of course, a stock pin; and to set it all off, a plaited kangaroo calfskin riding crop. I'll say this for myself, I stopped short of a hunt coat and cap.

Eight Saturdays in a row, when Witt was at home to stay with the children, I donned my livery, threw my saddle in the car, checked to be sure I hadn't forgotten my riding crop, and drove to Dutch's place. Along with a lot of ponies, she had two horses, a spirited palomino she called Duchess, and an aged white mare named Maiden—the perfect one for me. Maiden was at least fifty feet high and when I had finally managed to scale her heights and was seated in my forward-seat saddle I was so queasy I avoided looking all that way down to the ground. After eight weeks, I was neither cantering nor posting, I was just staying on, and one thing I could never remember was to keep my heels down in the stirrups.

This continued lack of riding form on my part nonplussed Dutch. She'd sail past me doing figure-eights with the beautiful Duchess, at the same time shouting at me, "KEEP THEM HEELS DOWN!" Mounted on a horse, Dutch changed instantly from genteel quiet to tomboy raucous. I was impelled to correct her grammar, and I'd answer, "Keep *those* heels down, Dutch!" She'd shout back, "I GOT MY HEELS DOWN. YOU'RE THE ONE, LIKE, NEEDS TO KEEP THEM HEELS DOWN."

The only time Maiden ever worked up any real enthusiasm for carrying me was when I'd turn her around to go back to the barn, and then she'd really fly, to my utter peril.

One day we'd been riding in a stubbled field where the ground was still soft from a hard rain. I was just sitting on Maiden, resting a minute to catch my breath. Maiden was resting, too, and when she shifted her weight from one back leg to the other, it sank down in the earth a couple of inches, and I fell off and knocked myself cold. When I came to, a minute later, my equestrian ambitions had vanished. I retired my saddle and gave Liz my stock pin. But the plaited kangaroo calfskin riding crop has served me well. To this day, I use it to chase ponies in and out of the pastures.

Dutch helped me with the ponies every summer until she was eighteen. One day at the county fair she was admiring a quarter horse tied in a box stall in one of the barns, and the owner of the horse, a boy named Dan, showed up.

From then on her attention span went down to nil. She started carrying a clipboard to remind herself what she had to do in the barn and even then she couldn't remember. I knew the situation was serious when, turning crimson, she consulted me on the wretched condition of her hands and asked me if there was anything she could do to keep them from perspiring when they were, like, being held? I told her I didn't think a little sweat was going to come between her and true love, and I showed her how to file her nails into exquisite little points. I like to think that helped the course of events. At any rate, the boy named Dan succumbed to her blandishments, hands and all, and he gained a wife and I lost the only pony trainer I ever had.

But by then I could almost get by without one. Dutch had left me the gift of her gentle touch, and it would stand me in good stead in the years to come.

4

The Ducks

I have never been exces-
sively fond of two-legged feathered creatures that live mostly
on the ground. I prefer my birds high in the sky where they
can be seen and admired—where they do not have to be
fraternized with. This standoffishness on my part stems
from my childhood in North Dakota, where my sister Fran
and I spent many a hot summer chasing my mother's
turkeys out of the neighbor's wheat fields. Chasing a turkey
is like trying to chase someone who has just come out of the
anesthetic after having a tooth pulled. Fran and I came to
hate those birds. One of the happiest moments in our
childhood was the day our mother sold out her last turkey.

So it was not surprising that Witt and I had our first
argument over the ducks even before we had moved out to
the farm. A few days before we moved, Witt had gone out to
the farm auction, when the former owner sold his livestock,
machinery—everything he didn't want to take with him
back into the city. When Witt came home he mentioned
casually that he had acquired a pair of setting ducks for our
first farm animals.

"Setting ducks!" Already I didn't care for the sound of it.

Yes, Witt said, the former owner had sold at auction at
least thirty or forty ducks that he had chased up from the

farm pond in the woods, but that a pair of female ducks were sitting on clutches of eggs underneath the corncrib and had secreted themselves so far beneath that they could not be reached, let alone moved.

"If they could neither be reached nor moved," I said, "then that makes them an intrinsic part of the farm—like the fences—so I suppose you didn't have to pay anything for them."

"No," said Witt, "I paid five bucks apiece for them."

"Was it *your* idea to buy this pair of invisible setting ducks?" I asked.

"No," Witt replied, already fed up with the turn the conversation was taking. "The guy came up to me and asked me if I didn't want to buy them. Just a little private transaction between the two of us. He said we really need ducks out there to eat the moss off the farm pond. They eat it like crazy and it keeps the water clear without our having to put chemicals in it.

"He said the ducks are no work at all and we should by all means keep them down on the pond all winter long. He says they don't get cold because they waterproof their own feathers with the oil secreted from a gland at the base of their tails."

"A likely story," I said.

Witt had had enough. "The trouble with you," he said rather vehemently, "is that I don't think you like ducks!"

It was just a few days after we took possession of the farm that a white Pekin duck waddled out from under the corncrib trailed by a dozen yellow ducklings. The next day a black-and-white Muscovy duck emerged from the other side of the corncrib with another waddle of ducklings. Our duck population had gone from zero to twenty-five in nothing flat. Stoyer and Liz went wild over the fluffy babies. I felt somewhat meanspirited over the hard time I had given Witt about his duck purchase.

For the first twenty-four hours all was serene in duck

camp, each mother duck sticking to her own underside of the corncrib and keeping close watch on her brood as a good duck should. But soon it became evident that even two matriarchs in a duck commune was one matriarch too many. The white Pekin duck was an indefatigable quacker, and the Muscovy duck quacked not at all. The white duck was an empire builder to boot; she saw herself as the great white mother. She "kuk-kuk-kukked" all day long, calling and cajoling and pleading until she had weaned all of the ducklings away from the Muscovy duck except three stubborn loyalists. On the second night the white duck settled down on her side of the corncrib like a bloated blimp, trying to spread her wings around twenty ducklings that were popping and slipping out from under her in all directions. The Muscovy duck, with the look of one who's been had, was sitting, very flat, under her side of the corncrib, warming her triplets, with room to spare.

Both mother ducks, however, quickly tired of the vicinity of the corncrib, and soon became sloppy mothers as well. They ranged farther and farther into the back hayfield, quit counting heads, failed to heed cries of distress from ducklings that had strayed too far from the flock. It seemed that every time I was dressed to go somewhere, I would come out to the car, only to hear pitiful cries from an abandoned duckling that had got himself trapped under the corncrib and couldn't find the way out. This meant a trip back into the house to remove my street clothes, pull on jeans so that I could crawl under the corncrib and rescue the duckling. Covered with dirt and cobwebs, I'd take a shower, get dressed again, only to come out to the car and hear another distress signal. One memorable day I went through this routine three times before I escaped out of hearing distance. I lived for the day the mother ducks would decide it was time to take their broods down to the farm pond in the woods— and keep them there—and when the day came, I thought my troubles were over.

There is no more charming sight than a pair of ducks swimming on a pond followed by several dozen ducklings, in single file, that are getting their feet wet for the first time. In just a few minutes, the ducklings realize they are born to swim, and then the bobbing, weaving, diving and general hell-raising begins. The children and I watched them for hours.

For the rest of that summer and into autumn, the ducks remained in the woods, swimming on the pond, eating algae and insects, the ducklings growing so rapidly that by Thanksgiving they were three-quarters grown. The Muscovy drakes were already as large as their mother. Some of them were brilliantly colored in dark shades of black, blue, green, and chestnut. The white Pekins were smaller, and not nearly so aggressive.

Our first snow came early in December that year with suddenly falling temperatures and a bitter wind. Witt came home early and burst into the house shouting, "We've got to get those poor ducks up from the pond and into the corncrib or they'll freeze to death!"

I reminded him that the former owner had told us never to take the ducks from the pond—to leave them there the year round. "Remember what he said about the oil from their own glands waterproofing and insulating them, or something like that?"

"All hogwash!" Witt replied. "They'll never survive the winter down there."

We spent several frantic hours shooing squawking ducks out of the woods and up the long hill from the farm pond. As darkness and more snow fell we had every duck locked up in one side of the corncrib. Witt filled flat pans of water for them, and spread cracked corn all over the floor. He looked smug. The next morning, he got up a half hour early so he would have time to feed the ducks as well as the ponies before he went to work.

When the weather turned warm and the snow melted, I

suggested we let the ducks go back down to the woods and the pond again.

"What?" Witt said. "And have to go through all that work again in a day or two? We'll keep them up here in the corncrib until the weather stabilizes."

And there they remained until spring. The only redeeming feature about having them in a side of the corncrib was that the wood slats on the raised floor were placed far enough apart so that some of the duck manure fell through to the ground. The bevy of twenty-five ducks made such a horrendous squawk that you could hear them in the house with the windows closed on a quiet day. The Muscovies, who retained flight tendencies, roosted on the rafters, and the white Pekins perched on the floor. When we opened the door to feed them, a hurricane of flying feathers exploded in the air, along with enough garbled croaking to make the tower of Babel seem like a mausoleum. Witt became possessively fond of those birds. I could look out of the kitchen window and see him standing at the door of the corncrib, laughing and chattering companionably with the ducks as he tossed in handful after handful of corn.

The first balmy day in April, we spent all one Sunday morning chasing the ducks back down to the pond. I was amazed to see how they had grown. The colored Muscovy drakes had outgrown the Pekin drakes by at least two pounds and outshone them both in size and plumage. On the other hand, the white females were larger and more aggressive than the Muscovy females. It was a beautiful sight to see: two dozen full-grown ducks of white and colored plumage swimming on the pond and devouring great mouthfuls of algae—a wonderful clean-up process that would clear the water, as the man had said, and make it sparkling.

When I came out to the kitchen early Monday morning to make Witt's breakfast, I glanced out the window and saw a full convention of ducks squatting all over the driveway and looking expectantly at the door of the corncrib. By the appearance of the asphalt, which was peppered with green droppings, they had been there all night.

"The moral of the story," I told Witt grimly, "is always believe a former duck owner when he tries to give you good advice."

Witt thought it was a terrific joke. After having a good laugh, he swiftly got in his car and went to work. I enlisted Stoyer's help. He was only five but big for his age. I gave him a small bamboo pole and took one at least twelve feet long myself, which we had found in the toolshed. They had been left there by the former owner (probably to chase ducks). Between the two of us we managed to herd the ducks back down the long hill to the woods and into the pond. Then I walked back up the hill and hosed off the driveway.

The next morning I would rather not have looked out the window, because I had a hunch what I was going to see: the full team of ducks in dress uniform exercising their rights to the driveway. Again Stoyer and I chased them back down the hill and into the woods, and again I spent half a day cleaning the asphalt.

After a week of this, I hated those ducks. I hated them when I went to bed at night and I hated them even worse when I woke up in the morning because I knew they'd had all night to desecrate the driveway while I slept. Not only that, but the Muscovy drakes—huge, ugly-brilliant, imposing creatures—struck such fright into three-year-old Liz when they came walking toward her on the driveway that she came screaming into the house and wouldn't go out for the rest of the day. One drake was bigger and bolder than all the rest, so striking that Stoyer named him Captain Hideous. He had a lustrous black breast, a ring of white around his neck, and shimmering plumage of purplish green and slate blue. With a comblike crest and angry carunculated skin over head and face, he looked like the meanest pirate an imaginative boy could conjure up. When Captain Hideous put one foot on the driveway, Liz fled in terror.

Witt insisted that the ducks' preoccupation with the driveway was temporary and that they must be given some time to adjust to living on the pond and in the woods again; and it was true, as the summer wore on, that they came up to the house less frequently. Again, several female ducks produced hatches, but this time from nests in the woods. When another autumn rolled around, between thirty-five and forty ducks were swimming more or less peacefully on the pond.

As winter came on, I tried to convince Witt to leave the ducks on the pond; but no, with the first snow, back they went into the corncrib. Coddled for another winter in the snug, dry comfort of the corncrib, those ducks never wanted to set foot in water again. The previous summer, whenever Stoyer and I had chased them down to the pond, they had had the decency not to show their faces up at the house again until the next morning. But now—just as we were dragging breathlessly back up to the top of the hill after having chased them down with our bamboo poles, we would hear a taunting noise from above. Looking up, we'd see the full team of Muscovy ducks flying low over our heads, squawking and gaggling as they beat us up to the driveway. Utterly frustrated and outraged, I generally shouted back up at them.

"All right for you, you blatherskites. Push that line too far and we'll make canard à l'orange out of you yet!"

Meanwhile, the white Pekin ducks, who didn't like to fly, were sneaking up the back way on foot through the hayfield and coming in behind the farm buildings! With a pincer movement like this, they had us coming and going.

When I suggested selling the ducks, Witt said it was out of the question: they were here before we were, they not only had squatting rights, but seniority rights.

I saw nothing but green-asphalted summers ahead.

And then something began to happen that just goes to show, if you wait long enough and do nothing at all, the winds will shift.

The ducks began to disappear in the night.

Witt was sure it was the foxes. He and Stoyer had seen several in the fields that summer. Strangely, we never heard any commotion in the night; but the flock of ducks kept shrinking. Witt took to sleeping with a flashlight in hand. Whenever he heard even a leaf rustle outside our window at night, he leaped up and ran outside to reconnoiter. He never saw anything but bland, blinking duck eyes staring at him from the driveway and from the low-hanging branches in the silver maple trees around the house. But the next morning another duck would be gone. I asked him once what he would have done if he had encountered the enemy. He had no weapon other than his flashlight.

"I just want the satisfaction of catching the bastards red-handed," he said. "When the time comes, I'll think of something, you can be sure of that." Spoken like a true public relations man.

Whoever or whatever was getting the ducks preferred Pekin over Muscovy. The white ducks were going the faster. Soon we had only a dozen left. One night I was reading the classifieds, and I noticed an ad that read: "Wanted, twelve white ducks to swim on pond." I showed the ad to Witt. "Sell them," he said grimly.

By the time the portly, middle-aged man and his wife came out to see them, we had only seven white ducks left, but the couple took them anyway. They were having difficulty finding white ducks. They had a summer cottage with a pond, and said they loved to sit on the back porch of an evening and watch the ducks swim.

The paucity of white duck did not deter the thief in the night. He took Muscovy instead. Every morning when Witt counted ducks the air was blue with imprecations. When we were down to nineteen ducks, Witt came home from work one evening and said he had met a man at lunch that day who was sponsoring a family of displaced persons from Western Europe. He had paid their passage and was helping them get settled on a farm near Greenville. The man was soliciting donations in kind for the family.

Witt looked at me, dead sober, and asked, "Would you mind very much if I gave them the rest of our ducks? They want poultry."

I murmured that it would be hard, but if it was for a good cause I guessed I could stand it.

Witt turned away to hang up his coat, and spat out to himself, "Better the DPs than the foxes, by God!"

The displaced person and his sons came the next Saturday morning with a pickup truck and crates. They massacred the English language, but they were sophisticated duck catchers. They cornered them in a box stall in the barn and in record time they crated up all of the remaining ducks and drove away with them. There was only an occasional muted squawk as the pickup rolled down the lane toward the road.

I waited a decent interval—until Witt left for work on Monday morning—and then I hosed down the driveway for the last time.

We never did hear how the displaced family got along with the Muscovies, nor did we hear anything of the seven white ducks, until years later. Through a book review club I met again the woman who had bought the white ducks, and we became friends. One evening at a club meeting, we had just heard a review of *Jonathan Livingston Seagull*. We were drinking tea and eating blueberry cobbler, but it was hard to come down from the clouds. My friend turned to me and said, "Remember those white ducks you sold us out at your farm years ago? Those were the strangest ducks. They wouldn't stay on the pond. It was almost as if they were allergic to water. We had to sell them."

"Didn't you ever wonder," I replied, "why *we* wanted to sell those ducks?"

Her eyes flew open, and we both burst out laughing. Time heals most wounds.

5

Building Up the Herd

*T*he Welsh pony market was holding strong several years after we'd gone into the pony business, and Witt became impatient because we had nothing to sell. Egrett in two successive years had come forth with a filly and a colt, which we felt we must keep for breeding stock, but the skittery Widowbird had been barren. Most mares come in heat every eighteen to twenty-one days during the spring and summer months and can then be bred. But Widowbird seemed to be in a constant, tenuous state of heat. She teased Beau into thinking she was going to bestow her favors on him, but at the crucial moment she'd buck and try to kick his teeth in. After his front end was tattooed with the print of her hooves, Beau finally took the position, "I may be dumb but I'm not stupid," and he refused to go near her, entice as she would.

We called two veterinaries out at different times to see if they could figure out what was wrong with her, but Widowbird could smell a vet before his automobile had turned in the lane. She gave him the same treatment she had given Speed. No D.V.M. could ever lay a hand on her. Witt said we might as well write Widowbird off as a dead loss, and we'd better think about buying another mare. Since business commitments were keeping him tied to his office, he

36

suggested that I go East that fall, attend the annual meeting of the Welsh Pony Society convening in Baltimore, then go to the Maryland pony breeder's sale that was being held at nearby Timonium. There, he said, I could buy another fine registered Welsh mare in foal. When I demurred, thinking secretly that all another mare meant was more work for me out at the barn, he cagily pointed out that it would be a splendid opportunity for me to visit my sister Fran in Washington, D.C., who had married and produced three daughters in the eight years since I'd seen her. I snapped at the bait, and agreed to make the trip.

When a cab dropped me off at the Timonium sale barn on a humid autumn evening to the sound of a hundred ponies nickering plaintively into the night air, it occurred to me that I had never in my life bid on anything at auction. When I was a child, my mother had taken me with her to the apron auctions at her Ladies' Aid. They were fun because the auctioneer always tried on all the frilliest aprons and made a fool of himself. But I hadn't learned anything about bidding from my mother. She followed a no-risk policy at these affairs. She always bought back her own apron.

"Here I have no apron to buy back," I reflected shakily, "and the risk is somewhat greater." Witt had said he was certain I could buy a mare in foal for $1,200 or less, but if I saw something really sensational I could go to $1,500. This sounded like a lot, he said, but if the mare was carrying a filly—and there was a fifty percent chance she was—then we would, in effect, be getting two mares for one.

Auctions where "flesh" is on the block, unlike auctions of inanimate objects, which are often cool and calculating, have a feral quality that is at once exciting and repulsive. Animals and men take their cues from each other, each in turn inciting the other to varying degrees of frenzy. Visceral sights, sounds, and smells filled the sale barn at Timonium that evening and my stomach began to churn. Sitting high up in the bleachers where I could see and feel the thumping, throbbing, sweating mass of ponies and people below, I began to sway dizzily, and I wondered whether I could last out the sale. I had planned to arrive early enough so that I could carefully examine the Welsh mares in their stalls, but the taxi had become ensnarled in Baltimore traffic, and I had had only a few minutes to look over the ponies before the sale began. I had decided there were only two bred mares with pedigrees that would mesh with Beau's. I would bid on these if I could muster up the nerve.

Welsh ponies were selling like untarnished gold nuggets at a fire sale that night, and pony after glistening pony was run smartly through the ring and hammered down by the auctioneer before my unpracticed ear could unravel the gobbledegook. It took me only a few minutes to realize, however, that Witt had underestimated the amount I must pay to get a good Welsh bred mare. When one of the two mares I had spotted earlier was led into the ring, I had no more than wet my lips to enter the fray than the bidding had zoomed well over the two thousand dollar mark. The same thing happened when the second mare came in.

I was enormously relieved. I had been expunged from the bidding by prohibitive prices, and now cut loose from my mission with impunity, I could sit back and enjoy the rest of the sale.

The relief was so great, in fact, that I became drowsy. It had been a long, heady day: the flight from Ohio early that morning; a joyful reunion with my sister and all those new children; champagne cocktails at the luncheon meeting with the Welsh breeders at a Baltimore hotel.

I was swaying dreamily to the auctioneer's singsong, when something caught my eye and my head snapped up. A girl was running dramatically into the ring with the most dazzling pony I had ever seen: a tawny chestnut mare with enchanting yellow dapples dancing and glittering over her body. Her luxuriant mane shone blindingly white under the harsh barn lights, and her tail shimmered and flowed behind her like a wedding veil. Great amber eyes that matched her dapples flashed through incredible white eyelashes. Her limbs were as fine as antique spoon silver.

All my life I have heard tales of persons who lost their heads at auctions. I had never believed them until it happened to me. I was hypnotized. My lips opened and I found myself bidding, once, twice, and yet a third time. And then the bidding stopped. For a moment the barn seemed eerily quiet, and then the auctioneer banged down his gavel. The mare was mine for one thousand dollars. My head cleared, and I drew a long gasping breath. I gazed one last time at my mare as she was being led out of the ring. She was beautiful beyond description. There was no doubt of that. There was only one thing wrong.

She was a Shetland pony.

As this stunning fact washed over me, I shivered and tried to shake it off, like a dog shakes off water when he comes up the bank after swimming in the creek. I didn't have time to think about it now. I had other things to do. From the moment an animal is sold at auction, its keeping and care is the responsibility of the buyer. I followed my mare out of the barn and back to the stalls. I prevailed upon the seller to take the mare back home for several days and keep her for me until I could send a truck for her. Then I went around to the cashier's booth and wrote a check.

Back in my room long after midnight, I understandably tossed about for a way to break the news to Witt that the mare I had purchased was not a Welsh mare. When pressed to the wall, I do not have the most undevious mind in the world. I concocted a good variety of reasons why I had come up with a Shetland. *She was all we could afford and I didn't want to come home empty-handed. . . . She was so beautiful and all the Welsh were* dogs. *. . . I have the inside track that Welsh are on their way* out. *. . . Boy, are we lucky we learned in* time. *. . . You don't know this, but Shetlands are* rebounding. *. . .*

But whatever I conjured up as my end of the conversation, the only reply I could ever come up with at his end was, "You bought a *what?*"

Wearily I picked up the telephone. I knew he was waiting for my call. May as well give it to him straight.

"I lost my head and bought a Shetland mare."

As I heard Witt's voice it seemed to reverberate from peak to peak over the Appalachian Mountains that separated us. I held the receiver away from my ear. I really didn't need the telephone to hear him.

"You bought a *what?*"

When Dulcet Pandora backed daintily out of a trailer and twirled around on our driveway, the children had been hanging on the fence for hours waiting for her. I had made a deal with a young neighbor, Normal Hayes, and his bride Melody, who owned a horse trailer, to make the trip to Baltimore to fetch her. It would be a sort of honeymoon trip for them, and they had taken their time on the road.

In the meantime, Stoyer, seven, and Liz, four, had worked themselves up into a frenzy of anticipation. They had always been a little frightened of our Welsh ponies, too spirited and too large for them to consider as pets, but Pandora's name alone gave them visions of a pony cut down to their size. Now, when they finally saw her, I knew she exceeded their wildest expectations. Their eyes became as round as bright coins, their hands reached out awesomely to touch her gloriously silky mane and tail, to stroke the unreal yellow dapples that seemed to ripple under her tawny skin.

Watching their joy, I suddenly felt very guilty. I had obtained this pony on a selfish impulse, not consciously thinking of my children at all. Without realizing it, I had brought home the touchstone pony of every child's dream. I knew at that moment what I came to learn was true in the following years when we had ponies to sell: that parents seldom buy ponies for their children. They buy them for themselves. They pretend they're for their children, but in reality they are buying the ponies they themselves never had as children.

After fourteen trips to the barn that night for one more look at Pandora, each time returning with bigger stars in their eyes, Stoyer and Liz finally dropped into bed exhausted, undoubtedly, I thought, with yellow dapples dancing in their heads. Witt went back out to the barn to turn out the lights for the last time, and when he came in he reported that the children had bedded Pandora down with so much straw that she was floating in it right up to her white eyelashes.

As he reached up to put the flashlight back on the shelf, Witt muttered something to himself that I couldn't quite hear. It sounded like, "To hell with it. Kids that happy ought to be worth something."

I didn't ask him to repeat it. I wasn't going to crowd my luck. But Witt never again mentioned the fact that I had creamed our breeding program by introducing Shetlands.

At the giddy moment when I had outbid everyone in the sale barn for Pandora, I was oblivious of the premium that was riding with her; for Pandora was carrying the foal of a much-beribboned Shetland stallion, a legendary blazing-red pony on whom I have never laid eyes to this day. At least I had done one thing right. I had secured a bred mare, albeit the wrong breed. When Stoyer and Liz learned that Pandora was expecting, they became so euphoric that I had to sit on them the rest of the winter and on into spring to keep them from floating through the roof. On May Day Pandora foaled an exquisite tiny filly so red that the children named her Poinsettia, because she reminded them of the brilliant color of the Christmas flower.

It soon became apparent that Poinsettia was going to be just as gorgeous a pony as Pandora, even outranking her mother in the eyelash department, but the sad fact was that our beautiful two-for-one mares enhanced our breeding program not at all, because Witt was right when he had predicted that Shetlands were bottoming out. In the next year, the Shetland pony market began to collapse like an overinflated blimp with a slow leak. I may have purchased one of the last thousand-dollar Shetlands. Many breeders holding huge herds tried to jettison their animals at the sales before it became widely known that the market was crumbling. This brought prices down even faster. By year's end it was almost impossible to get a hundred-dollar bill— much less a thousand—for the finest pedigreed Shetland pony.

Since I had already shot our wad and we had no more money to spend on getting another Welsh mare, I felt a certain amount of guilt. I began to look at Widowbird in a new light. Surely there must be some way we could get her into production. I stewed around about it all that summer, but did nothing, letting another good breeding season go past, until I finally decided to consult yet a third veterinary about her barren condition.

Doctors of veterinary medicine, we soon learned after moving to the farm, are for the most part a peculiar breed, more interesting and fun than your average stuffy M.D.

They are also the cross you must bear if you raise animals.

The first vet we ever called to the farm had steadied his nerves so thoroughly with good bourbon before he arrived that the only sensible thing to have done was to pour him back into his car and head him in the direction of home. Instead, I let him check over Egrett's brand new foal, which had arrived that morning, the first one born on the farm and a grand occasion for us. He pronounced the foal fine as frog hair, and when I excitedly asked him what we had come up with—a filly or a stud colt—he laughed foolishly and replied, "To tell you the truth, I didn't look."

I never again called a veterinary for a routine foaling. I obtained a book entitled *Veterinary Handbook*, which I read from cover to cover. I kept a widenecked bottle of iodine in which to dip the umbilical stump and I had a can of Crisco handy for balling out a constipated foal. If the foal was nursing and the mare had lost her afterbirth I took it as a good sign and left well enough alone.

Another D.V.M. whose services we used over a period of time, an excitable redhead, had always tilted a few before he got here, too. A frustrated broncobuster, this one, he always insisted on lassoing any recalcitrant pony who declined to be examined or medicated; but he usually ended up entangled in his own rope on the floor of the barn, while the pony escaped out the door to the far corner of the pasture, refusing to be caught again until the red demon had departed the farm. When he had tried to lasso Widowbird, she not only escaped the noose but flattened the vet and leaped over him lengthwise on the way out. He said as she passed over his face he counted himself lucky for her long stride. I'm sure he tilted more than a few on his way home that day.

Then I discovered Dock, who, to my immense relief, was a teetotaler. Dock was a hawk-nosed man in his late fifties, with a head of heavy soot-colored hair and a salt-and-pepper mustache he never found time to trim. Dock's trademark was the "instant diagnosis." Before he had both feet in your barn, he'd say, "There's a clean case of colic if I ever seen one!" Dock eschewed all esoteric devices such as fever thermometers and stethoscopes, relying instead on feeling the pony's neck and putting his ear against the pony's belly. If he heard something rumbling, this was bad news. If he didn't hear any rumbling at all, that seemed to be even worse. If Dock told you a pony was going to make it, you could count on it; but if he clucked his tongue hard against the roof of his mouth, you'd better not get your hopes up. In fact, Dock's opinions had such a high degree of accuracy that other, more inexperienced veterinaries often consulted him on difficult cases.

Dock wasn't much interested in piling up worldly goods for himself. Sometimes you'd take a cat or dog into his office, and he'd say disgustedly, "Sheesh! I can't charge you

nothing. This here critter's fitting to cure up his own self."
And he'd send you home, your animal and your money
intact. But the loveliest thing about Dock was that he always
came when you needed him—not six hours later. One of the
first things we learned about sick ponies was that if you wait
to get them treated until tomorrow, or even this afternoon, it
may be too late. Other vets I called were usually just leaving
their offices to go out on cases much more serious than
mine. But when I called Dock I knew that by the time I had
climbed into my gum boots, run a pail of warm soapy water
and carried it out to the barn, haltered my sick pony and
secured a rope on him, Dock would be driving up the lane.

Another thing about Dock—you could walk into his office,
which was a converted pantry in the rear of his old Victorian
Gothic house, and get all sorts of free advice about any
four-legged creatures you happened to have on the place—
often with sample pills to take home to try out on specula-
tion. "That old cat sounds like she's got hairballs in her all
right. Choke a thimble of this petroleum jelly down her ever'
few days."

So when I decided to go into town to talk to Dock about
Widowbird that October morning, I was secretly hoping for
one of his instant absentee diagnoses, perhaps with a potion
to put in her feed or water, that would miraculously bring my
refractory mare full blaze into heat.

As five-year-old Liz and I drove down the lane, turned onto
the road, and looked across the creek and up the hill at our
farm, I thought, if we ever decide to leave this place, it will
never be in autumn. The tree-fringed horizon against which
the farm nestled was a golden arc, still bathed in morning
haze, and the farm itself was softly lit with the incandescent
brilliance of sassafras trees glowing through the pale yellow
of the silver maples that towered over the farm buildings.
The giant sycamore at creek's edge was shedding its mottled
leaves, and they glittered as they fell to blanket the front
meadow where half a dozen ponies grazed contentedly.

All along the country roads leading into town, trees I had never even noticed before suddenly stood out in all their blazing beauty, like dowdy women turned Cinderellas at a ball. Every farm, no matter how drab, had at least one spreading maple or oak that had transformed it, for several weeks at least, into country-calendar beauty.

Anyone who had grown up in North Dakota during the dust bowl years, as I had, could never take an Ohio autumn for granted.

Dock was straightening out his pantry shelves when Liz and I walked into his office. He looked so cozy fussing around in a long rubber apron, I wondered why more vets didn't think of converting old pantries into offices. The floor-to-ceiling shelves on two sides were perfect for his supplies and medicines, and the built-in-pastry board in between, with a window over it through which he could look across the yard to the shed where he had his kennels, made a good examining table. He had many of his medicines in Smucker jelly jars with the labels still attached. He had them coded, because I came to know that the tiny red bladder pills for cats were always in the strawberry jam, and the big, bloated worm capsules for dogs in the elderberry jelly. There were many instant sassafras-tea bottles with red liquids in them, whether the original tea or some other potion I do not know.

Dock listened to me recount the story of Widowbird—how she was constantly in heat but never enough to be bred; how she was making a timid stallion out of Stalwyrt Beau; how two other vets had given up on her. I said there was no use calling him out and putting him through that, too. Did he have any ideas?

But Dock knew when to stick to his guns. "I lay you odds that there Widowbird mare needs a hormone shot. But I give her the wrong kind, with them nerves of hers, she'll be over in the next county for you. Say I could get next to her with a needle, which you know I can't—no way. I still wouldn't do it. Not unless I can get into her pelvis to see how the land lays."

I had to agree that Dock was right. Liz and I started to go out the screen door, which was torn in shreds from cat and dog claws, when he remarked, as an afterthought, "Few years ago over on the Catwalk Bend an old fella had a flitty mare like yours he wanted bred the worst way. Happened he was a fair carpenter. Built a tight stall around his horse so she couldn't maneuver in any direction. He cut me a dandy hole in the gate behind her so I could reach my arm through and examine her pelvis. I ended up giving that old mare a whale of a hormone shot."

"How exciting. Did the mare come in heat?"

"You better believe it. Come roaring into heat." Dock held up a jelly glass to the sun and squinted through it. "Mare never did conceive. Started jumping fences instead. Old fella had to get rid of her."

"Oh," I said, rather deflated. "We don't have any fair carpenters around our place anyway."

But I couldn't get Dock's story out of my mind, and I thought about it all the time Liz and I were buying the groceries. On the way home, we saw Normal Hayes high up on a ladder against his barn wall, sign painting, and on an impulse I turned in his lane. Normal was just putting the finishing touches to bold white letters that ran all the way across his high red barn. HAYES ACRES. NORMAL & MELODY HAYES. When he saw us his long thin frame descended rather precipitously down the ladder. I was surprised to see that his place had been considerably spruced up. He had lived alone here for a few years after his mother died, before marrying the young, blond Melody. His red pickup truck, parked in front of the barn, was also emblazoned with fresh white lettering that said: HAYES ACRES. NORMAL & MELODY HAYES.

As we got out of the car, he daubed at his thinning hair with a paint-stained handkerchief, waved his hand at all the lettering and said a little sheepishly in his slow drawl,

"Melody's idea. She's been keeping me busy since I got a few days layoff from the motor works. I suppose you seen the mailbox when you drove in."

I said, no, as a matter of fact, I hadn't, because the barn lettering had blinded me as I turned off the road.

"She's got our life stories on both sides of that mailbox," Normal said. "More'n they'll ever squeeze on my tombstone, I can tell you that. But look at it this way: If I wake up some morning and don't remember who I am, I can always look out the window and find out in a hurry."

I told him my troubles with Widowbird and asked him what he thought about building a tight stall for her so Dock could examine her. He said he thought it might just work, and promptly offered to build it for me himself. He was no "finish" carpenter, he said, but for that kind of job, "fair to middling" would do as well.

Then he beckoned me well out of earshot of the house and said in a low voice, "You'd be doing me a favor, at that. I'm fearsome of heights, and it's been some kind of hell up there painting those cussed letters the last few days. Melody don't know it. Us being fresh married and all, I didn't want her to think she hooked up with a yellow stripe.

"And this morning," he continued miserably, "I seen her eyeing the silo. You can see for yourself it goes straight up to glory. If I have to paint our damn names around that, I'll be permanent wall-eyed."

Normal said he was due back at the factory by week's end, and if he had the excuse of gainful employment for the next few days, he might be able to stall off the silo job indefinitely. He said he'd be over at my place first thing in the morning. As we were leaving, he stuck his head in the back window of the car. "You can't blame Melody for wanting to crow a little," he said laughing. "You know, she went from Hicks to Hayes, and she thinks it's some improvement."

I found plenty of old lumber the former owner had left behind in the corncrib, and after measuring Widowbird on all sides I decided to build her stall against the outside wall of the small shed we used as a doghouse for Holbein. This shed was fenced into the back barnyard, so it would be a good place to get Widowbird in and out of. Normal, entering into the spirit of the thing, built a stall so tight that she would have only a few inches to spare on all sides. He made the stall low enough in front so that her head and neck would go over the top board and we would be able to tie her head down with ropes to thick brass rings attached to iron stakes pounded in the ground. This way her chest would be flat against the front of the stall, and there would be no way she could move back and forth. Normal made a hinged gate with a sturdy slide bar in the back, in which he left a hole about two feet square, through which Dock could extend his arm and do the pelvic exploration.

Now all we had to do was to teach Widowbird to come in and out of the stall. It would have been easier to teach an earthworm to crawl in and out of a piece of elbow macaroni. Dutch was working here that summer, and she and I tried to lure Widowbird in with her daily ration of oats. The first day she craned her neck into the back of the stall, then backed off. The second day she put one foot in. The third day most of her body went in but when the side of her belly touched the side of the stall she backed out like a greased bullet and wouldn't go near the place for days. But her oats and her curiosity finally overcame her fear. The day came when we actually had her standing in the stall, bolted in, with her head hanging over the front of the stall, contentedly munching her grain.

It was time to call Dock. "Leave that there mare right where she is," he whispered. "I'll be over in twelve, fifteen minutes. When you see my car coming down the road, tie her head down with the ropes. If you wait until I turn in the lane, it'll be too late, you know she'll smell me."

As soon as we heard Dock's car, Dutch and I snapped a rope to either side of Widowbird's halter and tied the ropes with slipknots taut to the rings that Normal had staked in the ground. When Widowbird saw Dock, she tried to pitch and rear, but the stall held her tight on all sides. Dock stripped naked to the waist, washed his arm in the pail of warm water we had ready for him, and soon his wet soapy arm began to disappear into Widowbird's body. Soon there was so much grunting, groaning, and panting that Dutch and I couldn't tell whether it was coming from Widowbird or Dock. Muddy rivulets of perspiration were running down Widowbird's flanks and Dock's flabby stomach. His arm went in deeper and deeper, inch by inch, exploring, until it was in over the elbow, and then it began coming out again, covered with what looked like stale brown blood. Then his hand came out filled with a viscous mush which he threw on the ground. He reached in repeatedly and brought out more of the same, muttering, "She-e-e-t!" as he threw it on the ground.

Dock happened to look at Dutch and me standing by and saw we were turning an ashen green. "That there is no account," he said. "Nothing but 'tisha. Pay it no mind."

And then Widowbird could stand it no longer. Her rear end came up like a torpedo and she did a back somersault over her head. She landed on the soft grass in front of her stall and lay there stunned, her head still tied to the ropes at the ground. Dutch and I stood paralyzed as Dock came running around from the back of the stall shouting, "Jerk them ropes loose, get her up before she knows what hit her and lead her right back into that there stall. I know what's wrong with her and I want to give her a shot!"

Dutch and I pulled the dazed Widowbird up on her feet and walked her back into the stall and bolted the door, which was unnecessary, because when Dock gave her the shot, she didn't even feel it. Dock splashed his arm in the bucket, wiped it off with his shirt, and headed for his car. "It'll be some easier for you if I take my scent out of here before she gets at herself," he said. "Give that there mare two, three weeks, and you should see some action. She starts to jumping fences, I could quit doctoring."

Exactly twenty-one days later, Widowbird came into

normal heat. It took her several days to convince Stalwyrt Beau that her intentions were serious. She didn't conceive during that period, but eighteen days later she came into heat again, and this time she "took," as they say in the trade.

During a severe rainstorm in late September of the following year, Widowbird marooned herself on the other side of the creek high up in a corner of the front meadow, and gave birth to a foal as the water raged below her. We were afraid she might try to take her foal across the high waters. We were prepared to sit with her that night up on her island; but just at dusk the water receded enough so that Witt could carry her foal through the creek and up to the barn.

I went to town the next day and purchased two neckties monogrammed with the initials D and N. I gift wrapped and delivered them to Dock and to Normal Hayes. I told them that they had become joint fathers—along with Beau—of a beautiful bay roan Welsh filly.

Dock and Normal didn't know it then, and neither did I, but their efforts counted for a lot.

Widowbird had nine foals in nine successive years.

6
At Last!
Ponies for Sale

*W*ith Widowbird unstoppered and producing, we soon had ponies for sale. In fact, it seemed that one day we had a dearth of ponies and the next we had the barn and pastures bursting with them. It takes only a few years of living on a farm to realize how thin a line there is between feast and famine. In the pony business, we learned that it is not surplus that will kill you as much as *categories*. They come upon you insidiously, like creeping paralysis, if the market isn't strong enough so that you can sell all of your foal crop every year.

The Welsh pony market had been just lying in wait, it seemed, for us to have ponies for sale before it began to plunge. Witt had accurately predicted, back there in 1957, that Shetlands were bottoming out and that a larger pony would be coming up into popularity. What he had not foreseen was that in the five years it would take us to build up our herd, the "bigger" craze—the one that had people clamoring for bigger cars and bigger houses—would also have hit the pony buyer.

By the time we had ponies to sell, the Welsh pony was already too small for the Middle American family's taste. Although the Welsh market never did fall as low as that of the Shetland, the year of the thousand-dollar Welsh pony

51

was over, too. It was very difficult to get more than several hundred dollars for weanlings and yearlings. Even at that, it was impossible to end every year with a clean slate. So by the time Widowbird had dropped her second foal, we were beginning to feel the pressure of *categories*.

This is how categories will get you: When the foals are six months old they must be weaned from their dams. The foals must have a separate enclosure far removed from their mothers for another six months, or the weaning process will not go forward. Before the weanlings become yearlings, the fillies must be separated from the colts, or they will mate with each other. Aha, you say! Now the yearling fillies can go back with the mares. Wrong. It is now breeding season and Stalwyrt Beau is running with his mares. If you throw in the yearling fillies, they will get bred, too. (The Welsh Pony Society will not register a foal out of a mare who is less than three years old.)

As for the yearling stud colts, they are the hardest category of all to sell. Chances are that by the time they are two-year-olds, you will have at least one left. This loner now has all the instincts of a full-fledged stallion and becomes a category by himself. What is more, he can't be put in a field contiguous to mares, fillies, colts, or other stallions, because if he can smell them or touch them he will tear down the fences.

Five years after we began raising ponies, our herd had swelled to fifteen ponies, which doesn't sound like very many until you realize that these fifteen ponies represented *six* different categories. Only a half-dozen mares were of breeding age: Egrett, Widowbird, Mourning Dove and Hummingbird (Egrett's two fillies), plus Pandora and her filly, Poinsettia. But we couldn't throw Beau in with this mare herd, because Pandora and Poinsettia were Shetlands. So Beau and his mares must have a field; and Pandora and Poinsettia, with a Shetland stallion leased for the breeding season, must have another field. We had one two-year-old colt we had been unable to sell, now a full-blown category by himself. We still had Hector, now a three-year-old stallion, for sale but unsold, another category. Plus three yearling fillies, and three yearling colts, two more categories. All of which meant six different pastures or enclosures, none of which could be adjacent to another without an electric fence or lane in between. And what frightened pure hell out of me was that if we didn't sell the three yearling colts, in another year they could be three more categories which would need three more enclosures, none of which could be next to the other.

Putting up wire fences became a never-ending job, a Sisyphean task if there ever was one. At first we had a large department store in South Metropolis put up fences, but the cost was wanton, and worse than that, the fences collapsed almost before the truck returned to the city limits. Then we were lucky enough to latch onto a fantastic old fencemaker named Ferbie, who had the reputation of stretching the tightest wire fence this side of Alcatraz. With Ferbie's help, we soon had an impressive wire network.

We ran a fence down from the barn to the bridge—a mighty long stretch, even in Ferbie's book—because the limestone under the ground made post-setting rough going; this created twenty acres of woods pasture for one herd of ponies and a three-acre pasture in the rolling meadow below the house for a smaller herd. We ran another wire fence parallel to the first one, making a lane down from the barn to the woods. We fenced in a side pasture off the lane. We fenced in the orchard for a stallion run. We divided, and subdivided, and sub-subdivided our barnyards. Finally, when we had used up all of our front space, we cut three acres off the twenty-five-acre back hayfield, and fenced that in for more stallion pasture. On top of our regular fences, we had more electric wire than the first Berlin Wall.

Fences must have gates. Our need for gates was insatiable. We had sixteen-foot gates to let farm machinery through, fourteen-foot gates to let four ponies abreast through, twelve-foot gates to let two ponies and two people abreast through, and every dimension on down. One day a neighbor, a Church of God pastor whose parsonage was just down the road, stopped in to pass the time of day and to watch me chase ponies in and out of gates.

"You seem to have more gates on this farm," he said, "than there were doors in the Valhalla."

Coming from a fundamentalist preacher, this remark rather set me back on my gum boots, and I replied cautiously that we might not have quite that many, but I knew one thing for sure, if all our gates were tilted skyward and stacked up, end on end, an eager soul could get a good leg up to heaven.

We learned that the only things that would fasten gates securely enough to let us sleep at night were long heavy dog chains, which I bought by the dozens. One of the biggest fights I ever had with Witt was when I dropped and lost the last dog chain on the place; there was nothing to hold the gate shut until someone went to town for reinforcements.

Oddly, the depressed pony market depressed Witt scarcely at all. Despite the fact that in five years we hadn't turned a dime of profit after having sunk thousands of dollars into breeding stock and fences, he simply refused to believe that the business of raising ponies was not the halcyon enterprise portrayed in the now notorious (to me) issue of *Business Week*. To hear him tell it, the year coming up was always the year we were going to get out of the red. Witt had what is known in the horse trade as a chronic case of "filly fever." The victims of this malady (which sweeps virulently through the entire horse and pony industry during breeding season in early spring and summer) tell themselves that next year there won't be a stud colt dropped on the place—a happy incidence that will bring relief from the dread *category* syndrome.

With this attitude to buoy him, Witt cheerfully got up every winter morning at six o'clock, went out into the murky barn to feed the ponies before driving twenty miles to his public relations office in South Metropolis. While there he had to work twice as hard as in prefarm days to support his family and the burgeoning population of ponies, cats, dogs, and divers strays. Arriving home after dark, he went back out to the barn for his evening stint of chores. He never indicated for a minute that it wasn't worth it. It didn't seem to bother him that we were having a difficult time selling our ponies. I think he believed that by a sort of equine osmosis our surplus of ponies would seep into the barn woodwork in time for new ones to come along.

At any rate, when the barn and pastures were ultimately bulging with ponies and we had so many unsold stallions that we were exercising them in hour shifts in the barnyards and I mentioned that in the upcoming breeding season we were going to have to take some of our mares out of production, he said with absolute sincerity, "But you can't do that. We'll have nothing to sell!"

Or perhaps he thought that anyone who tried as hard to sell ponies as I did would eventually succeed. During the summers we had small ads running almost continuously in one newspaper or another within a hundred-mile radius, and in the horse and pony magazines. We managed to lure quite a few people up the lane to look at our ponies; and that's what most of them were: just looking. So "pony-lookers" became our catchword for anything driving up the lane that was not immediately identifiable.

If they weren't pony-lookers, they were Jehovah's Witnes-ses, and one was about as hard to figure out as the other. The Witness ladies were lovely, all of them, and they always promised sweetly as they pressed *The Watchtower* into our hands that the present wicked world was coming to an end, to be replaced by a paradise on earth—we could count on that, and soon. But never soon enough, it turned out, that we didn't have to deal with more pony-lookers, the barometers by which our tides rose and fell.

Pony-lookers come in all sizes and varieties—young and old, rich and poor, dumb and smart, likable and hateful—but one overriding trait covers them all: their staying power. No pony-looker ever comes on this farm unless he has at least three hours to spend—mine and his. And, like a child at the county fair with five dollars in his pocket, he isn't going to go home until he's spent them.

He must look at and evaluate every yearling filly in the front meadow, every yearling colt in the east pasture, the two-year-old colts in the back field, the stallion in the orchard, and miscellaneous stallions in the barnyards. Then, fresh out of ponies, with his thirst still unquenched, he looks eagerly around and his eyes catch the movement of ponies far away in the woods. My heart sinks. Up until this moment I had been entertaining the absurd notion that maybe, just this once, we might be able to skip the woods tour—which we privately termed "the grand tour." Resigned, I point the way. Slowly, because he has plenty of time, our pony-looker heads down the lane to the bridge, flanked by his wife on one side and by me on the other. Trailing behind him are his children, my children, and any self-styled pony experts he may have brought along for advice; bringing up the rear, far behind, are two cats who love this sort of expedition.

Our pony-looker crosses the bridge, climbs over the board fence and heads into the woods, entourage in tow, where he ferrets out and makes judgments on every pony under every hillside, under every tree, hopping from stone to stone back and forth across the creek several times to be sure he hasn't missed one. Then he reverses himself, climbs back over the board fence, crosses the bridge, and starts trudging back up the lane.

And now a strange thing happens: our pony-looker speeds

up and manages to lose the rest of us, who have been slowed down by having to help his fat wife over the fence and having to fish his children out of the creek and rescue sneakers floating downstream. When we catch up with him at the driveway, we find he has ducked into the barn and is furiously peering in all the box stalls.

Just as the sun is sinking into the western woods, and our pony-looker actually has his hand on the car door, ready—oh sweet miracle—to leave; just at this very moment, his eyes will ineluctably, as if drawn by a magnet, focus on the closed door of the nearby corncrib, and he will say accusingly, his eyes full of hurt, "There is something in *there* we haven't seen, isn't there!"

Most of the people who drove up our lane and asked to see our ponies were just looking; they didn't know what they wanted—but they sometimes bought on impulse. We learned it was never wise to shortchange them on the grand tour, because if we did we might very well hear, a few days later, that they had gone right down the road and impulsively purchased a pony from the competition. But some of those who came were not just lookers; they were serious about buying. If we could have captured a share of these, we might have done all right in the pony business.

Unfortunately for us, most of the serious buyers didn't actually want a pony. They wanted a horse. Only they swore up and down they wanted a pony. They just wanted it to look like a horse. You see, they were buying it for their children, so of course it had to be a pony. Only it wasn't *really* for their children, it was really for themselves (who had never had a pony as children). And because it was for themselves it had to be bigger, like a horse. And because "bigger" everything was coming into fashion, this fell fortuitously into their line of thinking, but boded ill for everyone in the pony business.

I wish I had kept a head count over the years of the number of young married couples driving up to our farm in a station wagon, three or more children between the ages of eight and diapers peering out of the tailgate, who said they were looking for a "fifty-two-inch mare." (As the years went by it became a "fifty-four-inch mare," and then a "fifty-six-inch mare.") They preferred to have her trained to ride and drive, and if she were in foal "it wouldn't hurt," and it turned out they usually thought a fair price for such a package was seventy-five dollars. But most of all she had to be "fifty-two inches."

Always I express astonishment. "You want a fifty-two-inch mare for *these* children?"

"Of course. We want something the children can't grow out of!"

"Would you buy an automobile for these children and store it in the garage for five or six years until the oldest can drive it?"

"What's that got to do with anything?"

"Perhaps nothing. Anyway, our ponies go only to twelve hands, or fifty inches at the most, so you'll have to look elsewhere."

Comes the inevitable answer: "Now that we're here, we may as well see your ponies—see what you've got. Could be we'll see something that takes our eye."

So the grand tour begins, and somewhere along the way, the children spot one of our Shetlands: either Pandora or one of her three daughters—Poinsettia, Mimosa, or Cassandra; or Ganymede, Pandora's only son, who is the color of red Christmas candy and who is usually cavorting in the barnyard. The children stop dead in their tracks, pointing: "We want *that* one!"

I'm on their side, instantly. "The children are right, you know," I say. "What they really should have is one of these lovely small Shetland mares they can enjoy right now, and in a few years you can get a Welsh pony, and then when your oldest is a teenager, you can work up to your fifty-two-inch mare."

"Wouldn't have a Shetland on the place. They're *mean*."

This always gets my blood up and I tell them how we had purchased Pandora as a two-year-old; how we had set our children on her back, although she had never been trained for a riding pony; how she had carried them carefully and safely through their childhood years; how her three daughters are every bit as sweet as she is.

By now pandemonium has more than likely broken loose, because the children, having seen the red-and-white pony of their dreams, have decided to stand their ground and fight for it. The parents drag them away with the soothing words, "You wouldn't want one of those mean Shetlands if you knew what was good for you," and they stuff their children back into the station wagon, which is soon rolling back down the lane, shaking and shuddering from mutiny in the ranks.

A scene like this always made me sad, because we had learned from our experiences with Pandora and her off-spring that there are no other four-legged animals in the world more suited to carrying small children than Shetland ponies. They are almost built-in trained. They accept halters, bridles, saddles, and children—your own and those of strangers—with such sweet placidity the first time around that you'd swear they'd been through it all before. They take only the fraction of work that Welsh ponies require to arrive at the same level of training. As for their being "mean," a popular notion that has persisted for years and that we heard hundreds of times from visitors, I could never see an iota of innate meanness in any Shetland pony we ever raised. And I would have raised them in quantity with joy—if there had been a market for them.

One of the most curious things to come out of our years in the pony business is that we had three enchanting Shetland mares and an exquisite Shetland stallion for sale for over ten years, and not a soul who came ever wanted one. After that we stopped offering them for sale; they had become a part of the farm, like the buildings and the fences.

7

Our Gentle Stream, Our Babbling Brook

On the early morning of January 21, 1959, I slipped out of bed and went out to the darkened living room to peer through the north windows where I could see the front meadow, the creek, and diagonally across into the woods. I wanted to see what kind of a day was brewing. It had rained hard all night, and a sound that I took to be thunder had awakened me. I pulled the draperies apart a few inches, quickly jerked them shut again, and went back into the bedroom.

"You'd better get up," I whispered to Witt. "There's something coming at us out there."

There was indeed. It was water. At first glance it looked as if it had already engulfed us and taken us down stream. There was nothing familiar in sight. A raging ocean covered everything. The bridge was gone, the lane and front meadow were gone. Great waves were charging up the hill, just a few yards from the white fence that surrounds the house and farm buildings. Looking eastward into the woods, we could see the water come roaring through the trees, carrying with it wooden gates, fence posts, logs, and small debris it had picked up along the way. It made a low thundering sound as it pounded across the front meadow and into the neighbor's woods.

"What happened to our sweet, gentle stream, our babbling brook?" I babbled, walking around in shock while Witt turned on the radio and heard that three inches of rain had fallen in the night on top of several inches of snow already on the ground; that another inch was expected before the day was out.

As I kept looking out of the windows and shuddering at the sight, I suddenly thought of something that cheered me mightily. "With this house sitting so high on the hill, at least I'll never have to worry about water in the basement, come hell or high water," I said.

To reassure myself, I went down to the basement. It was inundated with water. Seven pairs of boots were swimming around on their sides.

But when I rushed back upstairs and announced tragically that everything down there was afloat, Witt replied that he didn't give a hoot about water in the basement, wasn't even going down to look at it. He said he had enough on his mind trying to decide what to do about all the world's water passing across the front of our property.

Was Witt actually stewing about something? I couldn't believe it. I had always thought of him as the original "no problem" guy. In fact, that is one of his favorite expressions: "No problem." The reason there is no problem is that none is important enough to exist. He operates on the assumption that we'll all be dead in a hundred years anyway—God, maybe even fifty—so what's to worry? Since nothing is all that important, he can usually cope superbly with any situation. He isn't hampered by anxieties or hang-ups because he doesn't have any. It is quite comforting when you are the kind of hand-wringer I am to be married to *unflappable incarnate.*

But now it occurred to me that Witt might possibly be showing an Achilles heel, because he just wasn't taking this water-over-the-bridge business at all well. In the forty-eight hours he was a captive prisoner bound to the farm, he began to pace the floor and fume and fuss at the raging waters passing endlessly in front of our windows. How often did this happen out here, anyway? It was damned restrictive, that's what it was. How was he going to get to his office? Should have known better than to buy a place with a damned drink in the front yard. He began to talk darkly of "selling this place for what we can get for it."

And then the flood waters left as suddenly as they had come, as if someone had turned off a giant spigot and pulled a gargantuan drain plug. Now we could see the damage. The bridge, as we had feared, was not there. Nothing remained but a few pieces of twisted pipe on the bottom of the creek bed. Our long graveled lane had become an uneven gully of mudholes, the gravel scattered across the front meadow. The levee between the pond and the creek was all but washed out. Mud and debris were scattered up one side of the creek bank and down the other.

Ours was not the only damage. Roads, levees, and dams had been destroyed all over the county and state. The President declared Ohio a disaster area. Water and ice had boiled down rivers and streams into the Ohio River, causing a hundred-million dollars' worth of damage and leaving thousands homeless. It was the worst flood in the state since the infamous one of 1913, which had wiped out Dayton.

Our most pressing problem was that our automobiles were marooned with us on the hill. There was no way to get in or out without fording the creek. Witt tossed about for a way to get back and forth to his public relations office. If anything was going to pay for repairing the wreckage, he said somewhat bitterly, it was probably public relations. He had checked our farm insurance policy and found it didn't cover floods. Yes, I agreed, plunging in the shaft even farther, if he were to maintain his family in this idyllic life to which we had become accustomed, he had better get cracking.

A neighbor who lived on a farm a half mile down on the

other side of the road said he had a nephew living with him temporarily who worked the early morning shift in a South Metropolis factory and who would be glad to give Witt a ride to work. For the next month, Witt left the house at five in the morning, flashlight and briefcase in hand, walked down the dark lane that was now a gully, forded the creek on a teetering two-by-four plank, walked down the road to rendezvous with the nephew who, it turned out, must also pick up his mother-in-law somewhere along the way and drop her off at her hospital job before letting Witt off downtown. Even then, Witt arrived at his office before six. He had to leave in the middle of the afternoon and take a city bus to the hospital where the nephew picked up both Witt and the mother-in-law for the home trip.

Witt complained the hours were not favorable for plying his trade of public relations.

The children and I were having our own troubles. Stoyer had to give up kindergarten for the rest of the winter, because the school bus would only take him one way. A neighbor who did her grocery shopping at night offered me a lift and dropped me off at the road with my bags. Witt came with his omniscient flashlight and helped me carry the groceries over the plank. After several loaves of bread landed in the creek, I started making my own bread. That, and the fact that the children didn't have a cold all winter because we were isolated, were two nice things that came out of the flood. When Stoyer finally got back to kindergarten in the spring, I heard that he was making himself obnoxious, bragging that *his* mother made her own bread. I didn't mind too much. I thought he owed me some favorable publicity. He was also the one responsible for the story going around school that cats sat up to our dinner table right along with the people.

It was also my job, Witt said, since he was principally absorbed in fording the creek at ungodly hours, to check around locally and try to get a line on someone who could build us a new bridge at a price we could afford. The only one I knew to call for advice was Hervey Hake, the old carpenter who had done several jobs for me in the house a few months after we'd moved to the farm. Hervey Hake had been the only listing in the yellow pages of the Peatville directory under "carpenters" that year. It turned out that he was the man who had built the house after the original one burned down in 1942.

When I had shown Hervey Hake where I wanted a door cut in from the kitchen to the center hall, we had shared a good laugh, because he had initially put a door in the spot where I wanted one. The lady before me had had it plastered up, unmindful that this cut off her direct access to the bathroom, bedrooms, and basement and forced her to make a lengthy circuit through the dining and living rooms. Aha, I thought, now I knew why she wanted to move after two years. She couldn't take the running anymore.

Anyway, I was taken with Hervey because he had done such a neat job of cutting in the door for me, and because he was such a pussycat. I loved the way he said, "Y-e-e-e-s-s," in the most soothing, singsong voice, when I was explaining something I wanted done: a tone probably cultivated through years of listening to fussy housewives saying they wanted their spice cupboards moved one inch more to the right and two inches less to the left. After he had finished the door, I had asked him if he would make a bar for the rathskeller in the basement. The previous owners had taken theirs with them. This was rather a ticklish business, because Hervey was a strict old-order Brethren and didn't believe in strong drink. But he had gone to his drafting board and designed a handsome curved bar made of choice knotty pine and, getting into the spirit of the thing, even went to a sheet-metal shop and had a tremendous piece of iron pipe curved for a footrail. All the time he was building it, he and I had called it a "snack" bar between us, and even when I requested a lock on one compartment, he didn't bat an eye.

When he was finished, he was really taken with the looks of that bar. He said he had never done anything like it before. He asked me if he could bring his wife, Araminta, over to see it.

More than anything, even to his church, Hervey was totally devoted to Araminta. When he had brought her over that day, he had handed her out of the car like a queen. She weighed two hundred pounds, and she was beautiful. Her salt-and-pepper hair, tightly parted in the middle under her snowy lace cap, was coiled and gleaming, and her movements were stately under the black fringed shawl. As Hervey had helped her down the stairs and led her to his "snack" bar, I had my qualms about her tolerance of its intent. Araminta had run an exquisite plump little hand expertly around the curved knotty pine, then put a tiny plump foot in its high black shoe tentatively on the iron rail. She had sucked in her breath, and Hervey and I had held ours. Then her eyes had suddenly twinkled behind her steel-rimmed glasses, and she murmured huskily through the whitest of teeth, "Hervey is always one to do fine work, no matter what it is!"

Hervey Hake came over and looked at all of the damage the flood had done us, and at first he said he couldn't rebuild the bridge, because he didn't know how to build bridges. He said he'd built four hundred houses, a baker's dozen churches, and beautiful ones at that, and several schools, but never a bridge. But several days later he came back and his cheeks had a high color, like that of a teenager antici-pating his first set of wheels. He said that he was seventy-one years old and it wouldn't be too long before he'd be hanging up his hammer for good, but before he did, and if the Lord was willing, he was thinking he'd like to build a bridge. He had an idea for a stronger and higher bridge, reinforced at one side by a giant culvert, which would let more water pass through during high waters and lessen the chances of a washout. He already knew where he could get some good used steel girders at a reasonable price from a county bridge that was being torn down. He said he couldn't actually start construction until the weather warmed up enough to pour cement, but there was plenty to do to get ready. We told him to go ahead.

Hervey ordered a giant culvert three feet wide and twenty feet long delivered and placed in position at one side of the creek. He also had seven truckloads of sand delivered and poured in a pyramid beside the culvert, in preparation for mixing cement.

On the night of February 10, 1959, another three inches of rain came down, accompanied by high winds. We woke up to find that the creek had gone on another rampage, taking the culvert and all seven truckloads of sand with it! Again we were marooned on the hill for forty-eight hours as the water raged across what was left of our front meadow. Again the basement was flooded, and Witt wouldn't go down to look at it. He was too busy pacing the floor and talking murkily about "selling the place for what we can get for it."

Just when it seemed that the winter would never end, especially for Witt and his flashlight, the weather warmed up enough the first week in March for Hervey Hake to pour cement. He found the runaway culvert a hundred yards downstream in the neighbor's woods and used a bulldozer to pull it back with a long cable. To sweeten Witt up for the dead loss of the seven truckloads of sand, he also pulled Witt's car over the creek, so Witt could park it in the field near the road and drive to and from work. Then Hervey ordered another seven truckloads of sand.

Hervey and his "boys," as he called his perennial crew of four, worked most of that spring building the new bridge. They set the steel girders in tremendous cement abutments, one of which encased the culvert. They laid the floor of the bridge with sixty-three two-by-six creosoted planks, laid on edge against each other. On the side of the floor that lay in the direction of the farm, they placed iron pipes several inches apart, with the creek visible below, to keep the ponies in the front meadow from crossing the bridge. They hung a gargantuan floodgate under the bridge to prevent the ponies from going under the bridge and getting into the woods; before that we had made do with an electric wire.

Hervey brought in another bulldozer to build up the levee between the creek and the pond, and he reshaped and put new gravel on the lane. When he was finished we were better than ever. What's more, we had the seaworthiest farm bridge in the entire county. Hervey Hake could scarcely stop admiring it.

The next Sunday, which was Easter Sunday, a somber black station wagon stopped at the road and half a dozen men in long beards and broad-brimmed black hats walked down the lane to our new bridge. They stayed a long time, gazing at the bridge from every direction. We guessed who they were. They were an after-church delegation of deacons from the Brethren-in-Christ, come to admire Brother Hervey's handiwork.

I was as happy as anyone to be mobile again, but bitter, too, because no one had taken the slightest interest in helping me solve the riddle of my flooded basement. Why in the world did the water come up the drains during a heavy rain, when the drain tiles supposedly ran straight downhill? It didn't make sense. One day, when Hervey was working on the bridge, I thought, well, of course: Hervey would know, because Hervey had built the house. But when I asked him about it, he suddenly became very bland and didn't say "Y-e-e-e-s-s" at all in his soothing singsong, but instead said how could he be expected to remember how the tiles lay after seventeen years?

We had many heavy rains that spring, and after every one I called a different plumber from a different town—thinking that each would bring with him a different theory to deal with my problem. But all they brought with them was the ubiquitous motor-driven eel. They spent hours hanging onto the eel and shuddering and shaking their hearts out in the nether regions, and they all came up and pronounced my tiles clear as rain, vowing the water would never back up on me again—if indeed it ever had. (Implying that it may have been a mirage on my part, after all.) I mentioned my problem years later to a neighbor across the road, an amateur plumber in love with his avocation, who came over and poked around for a day just for the sheer joy of it, using a small manual plumber's snake. He said he could prove conclusively that the exterior drain tile located just outside the basement door was connected dead center under the house with the interior drain tiles in such a manner that whenever a long, hard rain fell, all the water that dropped from the heavens into the exterior drain took the line of least resistance and backed up into the basement. According to him, it was a diabolical subterranean network, which only tearing down the house would remedy.

Before this wicked blow had been dealt me, I also had thought I could do something about several huge cracks in the concrete-block basement walls, through which the water frequently poured after heavy rains. These cracks gave me fits, because they were located in the rathskeller, and they were prone to spring a leak just when we were having guests. I hired a professional crack-fixer out of South Metropolis, who was a frequent visitor over the next three or four years, the reason being that he guaranteed his work to the end of time. I still have his guarantee, dated April 1, 1963, written in a precise, schoolteacherish hand, which may have been his wife's. "I, Orval Cramm, do guarantee this job against any defects pertaining to my work also against leakage, time no limit, and if any occur *within that limit* will return and repair free of charge."

I remember Mr. Cramm as a sad-faced man in hip boots, with a luxuriant head of hair. He was always most willing to make the trip out here when I telephoned him that yet another of his crack repairs had sprung. But the last time he was here I noticed a peculiar twitching in his jaw. When I called him after that I learned he had moved, with no forwarding address. I had a sudden twinge of guilt, which soon passed, that I may have pushed him to the brink. If so, I can only hope he was wearing his hip boots. On the other hand, he may be happily plying his trade right over here in the next county, or in Puno, Peru, ministering to waterlogged Punovians and offering them his guarantee to the end of the world. Whatever, I have long since lost interest in repairing the cracks. The water will just back up in the drains anyway. I am resigned to mopping up. If I suspect a flash flood coming on in the night, I go to the basement, turn all the chairs upside down on top of the tables, and put everything not seaworthy on top of the chairs. I am always careful to put the rubber boots up.

Our new bridge, over the years, proved impervious to flash floods, and the row of pipes, with the water visible beneath, which Hervey Hake had built into the bridge floor to keep the ponies from crossing, was quite effective. The ponies would come to the edge of the bridge, look down between the pipes, see the water beneath, and turn away. We often left a herd of ponies in the front meadow at night, confident that they wouldn't get out on the road. One summer night, however, around three A.M., a thunderous pounding on our door awakened us, and we leaped out of bed. As Witt went to the door, I looked out of the front windows and saw red flashing lights all over the front meadow. Witt opened the door to a burly sheriff's deputy, whose voice boomed excitedly through the house.

"I happened to be cruising past here and seen your ponies had broke out! But don't you worry, sir, we got everything under control! I radioed for reinforcements and we got the whole herd in a corner up here at the top of the hill so's they won't get over the bridge and out on the road! Just tell us where you want 'em and we'll run 'em in for you!"

Witt said afterward that his first impulse was to go out, put the ponies in the barnyard, and express his thanks to the sheriff's department for saving us from disaster; they were being so doggone nice about it and making such heroes of themselves. But then he realized they'd probably be back the next night, so he broke the news to the deputy as gently as possible that the ponies wouldn't step over the pipes in the bridge. The deputies climbed rather sheepishly back into their cruisers, turned off their flashing lights, and drove away into the night.

The giant floodgate that Hervey Hake had hung from the bottom of the bridge did its job, too, in keeping the ponies in the front meadow from going under the bridge and crossing into the woods—except for one pony. Our tiny, geranium-pink Shetland mare, Cassandra, Pandora's third daughter, was rather a spooky pony, with great popping eyes that gave the impression she was clairvoyant or had strange transcendental powers unknown to other ponies, or even to people. One day, quite by accident, I suppose, as she was playing under the bridge, she learned that she could slip her nose under the gate and then push, push, push until she was able to slide the gate, which was sixteen feet wide and weighed at least three hundred and fifty pounds, over her back and reach the other side. After that, there was no stopping her. Some days she slid that heavy gate on her back half a dozen times, going in and out. But she was sneaky. She never did it when she thought the other ponies were watching. As a matter of fact, before we had even discovered her secret, she was already pregnant by Beau, having broken into the Welsh breeding herd in the woods for many a night without our knowledge.

Once, during a flash flood, when the waters were raging almost up to the top of the bridge, and we were confident that not even an elephant, much less the ponies, would attempt to cross the torrent, we watched, horrified, as Cassandra suddenly plunged into the water. We never expected to see her alive again, but just as we were running, screaming, down the hill to see what had happened to her, she emerged, shaking herself, on the other side! The only way she could have made it was to lift the gate over her head while swimming. She walked around like a drowned rat for days afterward, however, and for months after that she stayed away from the bridge. But one day the grass was so much greener on the other side that she could no longer resist it and I saw her walk, as though hypnotized, under the bridge and emerge, a moment later, on the other side.

The 1959 flood receded in our memories after a few years, to the extent that we could look back and laugh about it, thinking that nothing worse could ever happen to us. If we had known that we were soon to embark on a classic water-rights fight, reminiscent of the Old West, Witt might well have carried out his threat to "sell the place for what we can get for it."

One summer, we had about twenty ponies grazing in the woods and depending for their drinking water on the creek. It had been an exceptionally hot and dry season; the water in the stream was not running at its usual brisk pace. One day in early August we walked down to the bridge and were alarmed to see that the creek was no longer running. Stoyer and Liz and I walked along the creek bed to the far end of our woods, finding only two stagnant pools of water from which the ponies could still drink. When we came to the line fence that marked the end of our land, we looked over and beyond the fence and saw that a big glob of cement had been poured into a narrow place in the creek bed. Walking up and down the line fence and craning our necks across for a better look, we noticed that the creek bed on the other side of the little concrete dam had been dug out and deepened, so that one of our neighbors had himself a reservoir of water, while we had none.

That night Witt telephoned and asked him for an explanation for the concrete in the creek. Our neighbor replied that we didn't have a thing in the world to worry about. He had only poured cement so that he could ford the creek with his farm vehicles, and he had put a twelve-inch culvert in the concrete to let the water through.

"A twelve-inch overflow pipe," Witt answered. "That's quite generous of you. When you have all you need, we can have the runoff."

Witt suggested I visit the county engineer the next day to see whether there was a law against obstructing or diverting public waterways for private use. Yes, indeed, the engineer said, there was a state law to this effect, but we would have to institute a private suit against the neighbor if we wanted redress.

"If he has broken the law," I asked, "isn't it up to the county to bring him to rights?"

The county engineer, sitting back in his desk chair, shrugged. County officials are the best shruggers in the business. "My hands are tied," he said.

I couldn't see that his hands were tied at all. They were clasped together indolently and elegantly on his desk. His only occupation seemed to be shooting his cuffs. I thanked him for his efforts on my behalf and left, but it goes without saying that he didn't get my vote in the next election.

We worried our ponies along for the rest of the summer, letting them drink from the small farm pond, which hadn't been designed for watering a large amount of stock. The sides were steep and soft, and as the ponies descended down into it to drink, they gradually cut down the sides into a muddy morass; as the drought continued, the pond water became stagnant and murky, and we began to think it was unsafe for drinking. But just when we had decided that we must take the whole herd up to the barn and water them from the well at the house, the hot weather broke, we had a hard rain, and the surface water replenished the crevices in the creek. All the next winter Witt and I sat around and tossed our water problem back and forth, worrying it around like a dog worries a bone. One thing we agreed on, we didn't want to get into a messy and costly lawsuit, if it could be avoided.

And then as spring came on, the creek itself began to solve the problem. After several hard spring rains, the water began to gouge around the neighbor's little dam, cutting new channels for itself, and soon much of the water was bypassing the dam and returning to the creek bed. We congratulated ourselves that time and patience had solved the problem, until one day we again looked across the line fence, to see that our neighbor had not only filled in the new channels with sand and gravel, but had poured new cement on top of and around the old, making the dam higher and wider. And it looked as though he really meant business this time, because he had fancied it up with rails on the side!

Now we knew our problem was not going to be swept cleanly downstream with the current. Witt consulted a lawyer, who went to court and obtained a temporary restraining order, which prevented the neighbor from making any more repairs or additions to his dam.

Now, said Witt, we just sit around and do nothing and wait. And wait. And let nature take its course.

We went through another summer of drought; every day Stoyer and Liz and I walked the creek bed to make certain there was at least one slough of water from which the ponies could drink. The following autumn, however, was exceptionally wet, and the water began to rush down into the creek with such force that it began to chisel around the new dam, making more fresh channels for itself. The next spring, several flash floods continued the erosion, cutting more new channels, now directing the water into our neighbor's barnyard, washing around his barn, and generally making a mess of things. Because of the restraining order, he couldn't turn a shovel of gravel to help his situation. He could have pressed for a court hearing, but this he didn't seem eager to do.

Finally, one late summer evening, almost two years to the

day from the time that our "water-rights fight" had begun,
Witt received a telephone call. It was the first time they had
spoken to each other in all of that time.

"Aw hell, Witt," our frustrated neighbor said. "I never had
any quarrel with you. I'm going to blow the damn thing up."

And blow it up he did. The blasts of dynamite could be
heard for miles around, and the funniest thing was that the
rumor started we were excavating for a swimming pool.
Everyone I met in town that week said, "Say, I hear you folks
are building a swimming pool out there on your farm."

When I relayed this interesting piece of gossip to Witt, he
didn't even look up from his newspaper, but his fingers
crackled the paper convulsively and he got a deadly tone in
his voice. "Anyone who tries to wish a swimming pool on
me," he said, "even if it's platinum lined and comes with a
dozen mermaids thrown in, had better start running."

Witt has never really made his peace with the creek. Even
after all these years, when we have an especially violent
flash flood that hurls the water over the creek bank, sends it
running into the front meadow, and washes the gravel out of
the lane, we can always count on Witt's threatening to "sell
this place for what we can get for it."

These outbursts used to worry me, and I began having a
dream that I must have dreamed a hundred times over the
years. I dreamed that Witt, in the nebulous way that dreams
have, had sold the farm without my knowledge and we were
back in our split-level in the suburbs, and I was in the
backyard clipping the wilted roses off those hundred
rosebushes. No matter how long I clipped, I could never get
all the dead roses. I would waken in a cold sweat and when I
realized we were still on the farm, the relief would be
tremendous. The dream taught me two things. One, that I
was becoming fonder of the farm than I would admit; two,
that I had secretly hated those rosebushes. I dreamed
endless variations of this dream. Sometimes Witt had sold
the farm and bought another farm, but it wasn't nearly so

nice as our first farm, and we would drive past our first farm and see our old ponies there, and the remorse would be terrible, and then I'd wake up.

But something happened one summer evening a few years back that, even though it didn't keep me from dreaming this same dream again, somehow took the sting out of it. A real estate salesman drove in, as they often do, and asked us if we'd like to sell our farm. They always just happen to be driving past, and they always have a hot customer, cash in hand, who is waiting somewhere out there, always for the privilege of paying "more than a fair price" for a farm like ours. Witt had always gone out to talk to these men. I often wondered what he told them.

But on this particular hot summer's night one of them sneaked up on us and rang the back doorbell as I was washing dishes at the sink. Witt stepped outside the door to talk to him, and I overheard most of their conversation through the open window.

"Now why in God's name would anyone think, just driving past, that we would want to sell this farm?" Witt was asking. The salesman started to sputter, but Witt went on. "I imagine you saw that beautiful stream running down there. That isn't your average muddy creek. Do you know that stream has a *solid limestone* bottom?"

The salesman was impressed. "No, I didn't know. Actually, in that case, we could maybe—"

Witt interrupted him. "Don't you know that any farmer in the county, in the country, for that matter, would give his eyeteeth for a fresh-water stream running through a farm like this—why every fluid ounce is worth its weight in gold!"

As the salesman was slinking back down the lane, probably slowing down as he crossed the bridge to gaze with new-found admiration at the creek with the "solid limestone" bottom, Witt came back in the house.

I said, "I heard most of that. That was quite a line you handed him."

"What do you mean, line?" Witt answered. "Every word

was true." And then, wounded to the quick, "I can't imagine your saying a thing like that."

I knew then that, between floods, amnesia set in. But what about *during* the floods? That's when he was really vulnerable. Suddenly I laughed to myself. I was safe. During a flood, a land salesman would have to ride a canoe to get up here. And besides, at a time like that he wouldn't touch this place with a ten-foot pole.

8
Pushing Toward Green Broke

*I*f we could have gentled several ponies at a time and then offered only these for sale, life on a pony farm would have been much less hectic. But, unlike a department store, we couldn't hide new merchandise under the counter until the old display was sold. All of our merchandise was on display in the pastures from sunup to sundown for all the world to see. Yet it was impossible to get all the ponies we wanted to sell halter trained at once. And when a pony-looker drove up the lane, it seemed never to fail: if he was in a rare buying mood, the wild ones that had never had the touch of a human hand were always the ponies that took his eye; he looked through and beyond the ones that were haltered, groomed, and ready to go.

The children soon were old enough to help with farm chores. By the time he was ten, Stoyer was cleaning stables, spraying weeds in the pastures, picking apples, and stoning cherries for canning; planting and weeding the garden. He was a born woodsman; our twenty acres of woods was a utopia that never ran out of trees to be chopped down, or transplanted, or trimmed. He wore out an ax a year. Over the years the ax grew from a toy to one so heavy I couldn't lift it over my head. Stoyer could identify fifty varieties of trees and bushes on our farm by bark or leaf alone. But when it came to the ponies, he was a chip off the old block. Like his father, he could never get the hang of, or really see the need for, a lot of training and handling.

But I was growing an ace in the hole. It was Liz, who had perched in the haymow and in the mangers those summers, watching Dutch and me train. It turned out she had absorbed most of that and more. When Dutch departed down the matrimonial route, seven-year-old Liz was ready to jump into the breach. She had the one thing it takes to be successful around ponies: the ability to inspire trust.

This happy fact came to light when I discovered Liz had been sneaking into the barn and working with Puma, Widowbird's tawny two-year-old colt, who was not his mother's son for nothing. Puma was not only as skittish as a dry leaf in the wind, he had altogether intimidated me by laying his ears back and giving me the impression that he would take my arm off at the elbow if I approached anywhere within grabbing distance. I had been reduced to Witt's favorite form of handling: chasing. Humiliating as it was, I was forced to chase Puma in and out of his box stall, and I had all but given up on him. I already knew the truth of the old horseman's axiom: "If you can't halter 'em, you can't load 'em. And if you can't load 'em, you can't sell 'em."

The day I came into the barn and found Liz sitting in Puma's manger and letting him nibble oats out of her hand, I couldn't have been more alarmed if I'd have found her in the tiger's cage at the zoo. Knowing the jig was up, Liz protested that Puma was "sweet" and showed me how she could lead that supposedly dangerous stallion around by the mane. I decided on the spot not to look a subdued gift horse in the mouth. I knew I had me a partner.

By the time she was ten, Liz could wrestle down and halter many of the weanlings, saving us hours of time that we otherwise would have had to spend "sitting" with them, using Dutch's method. With Liz's help, even *sitzfleisch* took less time, because the two of us devised a crafty procedure for getting the initial halter on a pony: I crouched in the manger of the stall, feed pan gripped between my knees, the nosepiece of the halter spread cunningly under the oats in the pan; Liz stood leaning against the manger, clucking and cooing and sweet-talking the pony to come up beside her to eat. When the pony was munching contentedly in the pan, unaware of the dastardly trick that was about to be perpetrated upon him, I edged the nosepiece of the halter an inch or two up his nose with my right hand, while my left hand stealthily flipped the end piece of the halter over his head. Liz had her hand up waiting to catch it on the other side and slip it into the buckle before the pony knew what was up. It didn't always work the first time, or the second time, or even the second day. But we could usually get a halter on even the spookiest pony in a week by working with him just a few minutes a day.

Liz became so adept at cutting a pony out of the herd that I called her my "cutting horse." She could go into a herd of twenty ponies with a long whip and in a few minutes, with much coaxing, shouting, snapping, cracking, wheeling and dealing, she could cut out the pony or ponies we wanted. Before she learned how to do this, we had been forced to have "roundups" whenever we wanted to separate ponies; the entire family was needed in a roundup, and it often ended in such a brouhaha that ill will hung over the farm like a stale cloud for hours afterwards.

A roundup was necessary in May, for instance, when we must cut the yearling fillies out of the woods herd so that we could put Beau in with his mares for the breeding season. We all convened in the barn, armed ourselves with whips, and Stoyer was commissioned to ride his bicycle into the woods and chase the whole thundering herd up the lane and into the outer barnyard. Already the operation had taken on the nature of a stampede, with enough whickering and neighing to give credit to a national rodeo.

Witt's job was to stand at one gate to let only the fillies that were wanted into the inner barnyard; Stoyer's job was to stand at the other gate to let the mares that weren't wanted back into the lane. Liz and I were supposed to weave through the herd and attempt to shove the mares toward Stoyer's gate and the fillies toward Witt's gate. If some poor devil fumbled his job, there was hell to pay. If Stoyer let a filly slip back through into the woods, or if Witt let a mare into the inner barnyard, or if, God forbid, Liz or I chased the fillies toward Stoyer's gate or the mares toward Witt's gate, the entire operation was snafued, and the most heinous imprecations would be hurled into the air at the culprit who had blundered.

Someone always ended up mad. It's a hard thing to be called "dumb," "stupid," and "witless" by three members of your family at once, uttered in vile tones loud enough to be heard over the neighing and stamping of twenty ponies. So, after Liz had turned herself into a human cutting horse, she and I decided, in the interests of family harmony, that never again would we have a family-sponsored roundup. Whenever we wanted ponies out of the herd, we called them all up to the gate, and while I manned the gate, Liz cut out whomever we wanted, one at a time.

The day after school was out in June, Liz and I would embark on an ambitious training program. Every year we vowed that this was the summer we were going to get every pony on the place halter trained. But we never made it. There were always a few yearlings, even two- and three-year-olds, who had never been touched. One summer Liz and I worked up for sale three handsome two-year-old stallions named Dasher, Prancer, and Blitzen, that we had passed over in previous years. They were now in the desperate category; although they were still running amiably in the same field together, we lived in fear that any day they would turn on each other and have to be separated. If this happened, we had no place to put them; our box stalls and stallion runs were already filled with unsold remnants from other years.

Blitzen and Prancer had been foaled on the same rainy April morning out of Widowbird and her first daughter, Mynah. I always remember that wet spring morning when we found the two mares and their foals far up in the corner of the back pasture, together with a dozen other mares, because something strange had happened when we chased the entire herd up into the barnyard and out of the cold driving rain. During the chase, the foals had momentarily become separated from their dams and when we caught up with the ponies at the barnyard we saw that the foals had traded mothers. Widowbird was standing with Mynah's foal, and a few yards away, Mynah was standing with Widowbird's foal. The mares had stared at each other, sniffed the foals at their sides, then looked away, utter confusion in their eyes; the hard rain had washed away the scents. We held our breaths; mares who have just foaled have exquisitely delicate temperaments that are not to be tampered with. Finally, Widowbird bent her head, sniffed the foal at her side all over, from front to back and from back to front, and made her decision. She walked over to Mynah, cut her own foal away from the other mare, and nudged it away. Mynah, seemingly relieved that the older mare had made her decision for her, quickly claimed the other foal.

Dasher was born a few days later out of Egrett's daughter, Blue Mist, and from that day on the three colts had never been separated. By the time they were two years old they were as comely a triad as any Welsh pony enthusiast would ever want to see. I became increasingly critical of the conformation of my own ponies as the years went by, and there was scarcely a one I couldn't fault, but it was hard for me to nitpick at these three. Blitzen was a brilliant bay with a blaze, Prancer was red roan, Dasher was grey roan, and they all had the huge bold eyes, the strong jaws, and the dense short bones of the classic Welsh.

Liz loved those colts. They were fat, sassy, and frisky; almost full-grown stallions but yet more coltish than stud. After we had halter trained them, Liz spent much of her time brushing them and combing out their thick manes and tails.

She got the idea of braiding their manes into tiny braids and securing the braids with multicolored rubber bands, the effect of which, she insisted, would attract a better class of pony-looker. She talked me into spending money for fine leather halters that complemented their coats. She had the threesome groomed, glistening, and ready for display from sunup to sundown all that summer—and we couldn't get a licking soul to take a second look at them.

Which points up one of the most maddening traits of a pony-looker: if you are willing to sell him a pony, he assumes there is something wrong with it; on the other hand, if it is not for sale, it becomes instantly perfect and desirable. If he is looking at a pony for sale and the pony is so beautiful he can't fault it anywhere, he will, in all probability, say suspiciously, "Why are you getting rid of him?" But if he comes upon a pony with three crossed eyes and an extra leg, and you tell him it's not for sale, he'll say snidely and enviously, "You're keeping the best for yourself, aren't you?"

And so when our pony-lookers that summer saw Dasher, Prancer, and Blitzen plumped, polished, and ripe for sale, they figured, priding themselves as they do on not being born yesterday, that under those gleaming coats there was something wrong; and when we injudiciously threw the expensive halters into the bargain, they knew they were right. Their eyes cast about for better things and they saw in the east pasture the yearling colts: a scraggly group, because yearlings are hard to fatten up, and, like awkward teenagers, they stick out in all the wrong places. These colts were not only scruffy but wild as Apaches, because Liz and I had let them go; they were not yet in the desperate category, since they could run together for at least another year.

We understandably tried to play down the little savages when the pony-lookers descended on them. We even went so far as to make little deprecating remarks. ("Oh, you might not want this one. His mother has been known to bite.") But comments like this only whet a customer's appetite; just another indication that you may be thinking of keeping this gem for yourself. And if there is anything a pony-looker loves it is being able to discover, all on his own, on your property, a diamond in the rough: "I could load a few groceries into this one," he'll say, "give him a good brushing, and have a prize winner on my hands. You'd be amazed."

The upshot of it was that, instead of selling Dasher and Prancer and Blitzen that summer, Liz and I ended up selling, one right after the other, three of the spookiest yearling colts we'd ever raised. And when the buyers asked to what extent their ponies had been trained, we replied blandly, not wishing to lose a sale of any kind, "Just green broke." Then we offered to keep their colts on the farm for several weeks to "settle them down" for their new owners—an offer which was never refused; the unspoken dividend of two weeks of free room and board that went with the "settling" didn't go unnoticed.

So, in three successive fortnights, Liz and I sat in the barn with one wild Indian after another, frantically pushing him somewhere into the neighborhood of "green broke." And all the while our slicked-up two-year-olds pranced in the back pasture, all dressed up and nowhere to go. The day before school started that fall, I found Liz in with them, taking off their fine halters and snipping out with her manicure scissors the multicolored rubber bands from their braided manes. I heard her crooning to them softly, and a little sadly, as she worked. "Don't you worry, my pretties. Next summer we'll ugly you up a little, and then watch out!"

But we didn't ugly them up enough, because we didn't sell them the next summer, either. At that, we were lucky, in a way: we were able to keep Dasher and Prancer and Blitzen together without fighting until they were five years old, when we finally broke up the combination by selling Dasher.

Selling ponies when there is not much of a market for them is a hard job. Yet it isn't the hardest part of the pony business by any means. The hardest part is seeing your ponies leave after you have used all your wits to sell them. It doesn't make sense, but it's true. Starting two days before a sold pony is scheduled to be picked up by his new owner, Stoyer and Liz accuse me of stuttering and dropping dishes.

I begin to think about all the imponderables. What kind of a conveyance will they bring to haul the pony in? Most people bring a horse trailer of one kind or another, but many have brought farm trucks, pickups with hayracks on them, windowless U-haul trailers meant to haul furniture, and once someone even brought a luggage trailer. Will the pony walk up into the conveyance with a minimum of fuss? Or will he spook and have to be pulled and forced in, an operation that might take two or three hours and leave us so limp and quivering we can't make it over the barn stoop afterwards. And, most anguishing of all, is the pony really getting a good home? Will his new owners be satisfied with him, be good to him, or will they telephone in a week or a month or a year complaining about him?

Liz has had the heartbreaking job of loading most of the ponies we have sold. Most of them have trusted her enough to follow her, oats in hand, up a swaying, creaking ramp and into a dark, unknown enclosure. After the deed is done, Liz doesn't hang around. She disappears fast. She goes behind the barn and cries.

I know exactly how she feels. As I stand at the edge of the driveway and watch the trailer roll slowly down the lane, the pony lifts his head high and nickers shrilly to the ponies he is leaving behind; and they answer him, from every corner of the woods, from the front meadow, from the east pasture, the back field, and the orchard—they all lift their heads and nicker back to him.

To me he seems to be saying, "Why must *I* be the one to go? Do you love me any less than the rest of them who are allowed to stay?" I have seen him born and I have sold him.

The two or three hours after a pony has left the farm are remorseful, guilt-ridden ones, and Liz and I do not like to meet each other's eyes. We wander aimlessly around, watching the clock. Mealtime comes and goes unnoticed. When we think the new owners have reached home, we telephone. If we hear that the pony is at that very moment contentedly munching hay in his new stall, has, in fact, stood the trip very well, then for the first time we look at each other and smile. We go in the kitchen and start preparing supper. We can eat again.

9

The Burshmen

*K*eeping a farm painted can become an obsession; *demands* an obsession if even a modicum of paint is going to be kept on the four to eight buildings that comprise the average farmstead. After we had lived here a few years, Witt remarked once, as he looked over the bills, "It just doesn't seem right, or even sensible, to spend more money for paint than we do for groceries."

It wasn't that the farm needed painting when we bought it, either. On that sunny August day when we moved to the farm, every building had been gleaming with such bright white paint that it almost hurt our eyes to look: house, barn, corncrib, two sheds, and a seven-board, crisscross fence. The former owner had probably thrown up his hands, withered from years of soaking in turpentine, and cried in utter frustration, "I'll paint one last time and *sell!*"

We were surprised, that very next spring, when we took our first appraising look at how the farm buildings had weathered the winter, to see that they no longer gleamed; they all showed a touch of gray.

But the real shocker was the house: it was not only weathering, it was moulting.

The paint on the second story was peeling off in great sheets, the bare wood showing underneath. The sheets were sprinkled over the lawn and curled up in crisp white cornucopias. In some spots where the paint had not already come off, it was ballooning out in huge bubbles, giving the uneasy feeling that if you pricked it with a pin the whole house would collapse.

We lost no time in calling out a professional painter from South Metropolis whom some friends had recommended to us as "expensive but worth it." He diagnosed our second-story problem in a minute as *moisture*. He said a new dramatic cure had just been invented, which was simply to pound little round plastic louvres about one-half inch in diameter all over into the wood to let the moisture out. Relieved that there *was* a cure, we hired him on the spot to do the job. He executed it with great dispatch. He also primed and repainted the entire second story, summarily presenting us with a sizable bill, which we gladly paid. Our friends were right. It was worth it to have our paint troubles solved so quickly and so easily.

We were understandably depressed to find, the very next spring, crisp white cornucopias on our lawn. The second story of our house was again bubbling yeastily, shrugging off its outer layer in great sheets. The dear little plastic louvres had not, apparently, let the moisture out, but they had found another use. The wasps had taken them over for nesting places, buzzing busily in and out of them, making weird, droning noises in the children's upstairs bedrooms.

We decided to adopt a wait-and-see policy. Wait and see what the house does. Wait and see how long it takes before the whole place actually starts to look like Ruin Gulch. At the end of three years we knew exactly how long it had taken.

The house looked as if it had come through the kind of once-in-a-lifetime hailstorm that very old men love to tell about—when the hailstones were "as big as hens' eggs." The other four buildings were showing more gray than white. The seven-board crisscross fence was bare bones.

We called in three of the largest painting contractors in

South Metropolis and asked for estimates on painting the entire farm: five buildings and all that fence. When the estimates came in, Witt said, to heck with it, let's treat the family to a trip around the world instead. But he gave the job to the contractor who swore on a can of the best paint money could buy that he had a permanent solution to our paint-peeling problem.

The answer, the man said, was *latex paint,* which at that time was just gaining recognition. He said the oil-base paint with which the house had previously been painted didn't allow the wood to "breathe." It therefore retained behind it the moisture picked up from all of our trees, and soon peeled. Latex paint would be the ticket.

He pointed out that converting to latex paint would mean a two-coat job overall. He said that latex paint would not adhere to a surface that had not been primed with an oil-base coat made especially to go under latex paint. This didn't make sense to me and I asked him why, if latex paint were so great, it still would work only on top of oil-base paint. He said that there were some things in this world one had to take on faith, two of them being the Bible and latex paint, and one was as reliable as the other.

The next week so many painters moved in it looked as if martial law had been invoked. They were a pretty decent lot, except that they *would* pilfer tomatoes, onions, carrots, and radishes out of the garden. When they took to carrying saltshakers in their overall pockets and munching openly on the job, the children and I decided to play a trick on them. Stoyer's garden specialty that summer was cucumbers, and his crop had been so bumper that supply had exceeded demand. I had already culled the crop, choosing the small tender ones from which to make dill pickles, and had told Stoyer he must throw away the big tough ones. But, having raised them himself, he loved every one of those cucumbers like a brother, and he had squirreled the castoffs in the basement in the fond hope that somehow they could be rehabilitated. Now he was quick to see that a bad home would be better for them than none at all. He eagerly went along with our scheme. We took the several dozen toughies back out to the garden and arranged them in conspicuous spots among the old cucumber vines. Then we all got in the car and went away for the afternoon. When we returned, every single old cucumber was gone. Some rather green faces headed down the lane for home that evening.

At any rate, with all of those painters on the job, it was no time at all until they had polished off every building on the farm, and the fence as well. The whole place looked as spanking as a small girl going to church on Easter Sunday. We paid the ransom and decided it may have been worth it, after all, when friends and strangers alike drove in and exclaimed, "What a beautiful place you have here! If only we could find one like it."

When the familiar crisp white curls appeared on the lawn the next spring, we didn't have to look up to know what had happened. Like Chicken Little, we knew the sky had fallen.

Hope springs eternal in the human breast—not of seasoned farm dwellers—only of city people who have moved to a farm and refuse to relinquish, for a few years at least, the silly notion that a farm can be kept looking bandbox fresh. I give this as the reason that we had the fortitude to call in yet another painter—this time a pair of brothers who advertised that they had been painting, satisfaction guaranteed, for twenty-seven years, no job too large or too small.

The spokesman for the two surveyed our second-story disaster with a practiced eye. The difficulty was obvious, he said: the old oil-base coats still on the house from many previous paint jobs were still lifting up from the wood and pushing off the new latex coat. He said we would keep having this problem until every inch of old oil-base paint had come off and had been replaced by the special oil-base primer, together with a coat of latex. Only then could the wood *breathe,* and let the moisture out.

When I commented that this peeling process could very well go on until the year two thousand, paint being the perverse creature it is, he shrugged dramatically and said, "Could very well be, unless you want to blast it off!" Oh, yes, he said, he and his brother could take it off with one of those enormous electric sanders, but the time and expense would be so great we might just as well burn the house down and rebuild it again, and really *have* something this time.

After I had appropriately shuddered at this possibility, he grew quite cheerful and said that he and his brother could hand scrape a *lot* of it off, maybe even most of it, and he would put a good coat of oil-base primer on the bare spots and put another coat of latex paint on the entire house. He said he couldn't guarantee anything, the kind of problem *we* had. I understood that, didn't I? I did.

For neatness, paint economy, and especially speed, the brothers had no peer. They scraped and painted the entire two-story house, with its forty windows, including all the screens and storm windows, in two nine-hour days, plus three hours on the third day. They used only nine gallons of paint, and when I cleaned the windows afterwards my razor blade went begging. They eschewed all time-wasters, such as eating lunch, quaffing liquids, or going to the bathroom. They ran on candy bars and cigarettes—concurrently. Ambidextrousness was the secret of their speed. The right and left hands worked completely independent of each other, marching to a different drummer, mute to the other tune. Stoyer would watch, transfixed, as one of the brothers, while painting swiftly with his right hand, took a candy bar out of a breast pocket with his left hand, peeled the paper off with the same hand, stuffed the candy bar in his mouth, and before it was half swallowed, took a loose cigarette and a kitchen match from the same pocket, struck the match on his thumbnail, lit the cigarette, and pitched candy wrapper and match to the ground in one throw.

The left hand could also expertly caulk a window while the right hand kept up the rhythm of painting. A soft wad of putty was kept in a low front pocket of the coveralls. When needed, a piece of putty was pinched off in the pocket, pressed to the window, and the putty knife removed from a back pocket to smooth the seam—all in one swift motion. When it came to scraping paint, the competitive spirit took over. The left hand and the right hand engaged in such fierce combat as to which could scrape old paint off faster than the other could put new paint back on, that I never could decide which was winning.

When the brothers were finished, the house looked just terrific. It had never looked better, not even the day we moved in, and that was going some. The other buildings still looked fairly good from the year before, and we began to feel that we might actually be pulling ahead.

When yet another spring rolled around, however, and our infamous second story again started to shed its skin like a snake that knows its season, we were not really surprised. The fact that the barn had suddenly taken a turn for the worse and looked almost as bad as the house rather helped to equalize the pain, like carrying water on both shoulders.

"We ought to credit ourselves with having a little sense," said Witt, "and stop this expensive nonsense. We are never going to win the battle of the paint. Never as long as we live here. If we fight it at all, it has got to be by guerrilla warfare, and it will never stop. Our only hope is to get a nonunion, self-employed handyman who will keep chipping away every summer at all the buildings, whenever they need it."

It seemed almost too good to be true when, that same summer, a man turned up who seemed to be tailor-made for the job. A neighbor, an elderly widow who lived alone on her small farm and managed to make ends meet on a modest budget, telephoned me one day and said she had found the most marvelous man to paint things, and he charged only three dollars an hour! As a matter of fact, she said, he had just finished painting her house, and he was looking around for another job.

"For heaven's sake," I said, "send him over. He sounds like the answer to our prayers."

"Just so you've got a lot of paint, and plenty of hours in the day," she answered, laughing a little, "he'll do all right for you."

I had no more than time to check my paint supply before a very well-preserved black Edsel rolled into the driveway and a natty, stocky, red-haired man, dressed in black from head to toe, hopped out. He was what my father would have called a "smiley" man.

"Ol' lady over there says you needs a man to paint. I paint three dollar a hour. Ain't that cheap?" He burst out laughing and blushed pink up to his red-hair roots.

He reached into the Edsel and took out a cigar box, placed it on the hood of the car, and flipped it open. "I show you some my jobs, you see how good I paint," he said, rolling his eyes at me.

He took out a piece of cardboard on which two small snapshots were attached with safety pins. They were "before-and-after" photos. "See this yere little old house here? Shabby, ain't it. See this house yere? Same house, would yer believe it? Arter I burshed nineteen ganners paint onter it!"

He pulled out another cardboard. "And looker this'n. A hunnert foot of dotiest ol' fence yer ever seen. Burshed thirty-nine ganners paint onter this'n 'fore I was done."

He pulled out still another one and his chest heaved and puffed out of his black shirt. This must be the *pièce de résistance,* I thought, as his lips quivered and he shouted, "And will yer look at this yere big ol' barn, mebbe a hunnert year old, the biggest barn I ever did see, ain't had a drap paint on her mebbe twenty year. I burshed *ninety* ganners paint on her 'fore I was done and looker her now!"

I stared at the "before-and-after" snapshots of the ninety-gallon job. The first photo looked like a hundred-year-old barn in need of paint. The second photo looked like a hundred-year-old barn holding up gamely under a very heavy load of paint.

"That's very impressive, sir," I said. "But I'm sure you won't have anything quite that extensive around here."

"Jes' call me Pearl," he said, blushing up to his red-hair roots again.

Thinking prudently that it might be well to try him on an outbuilding until we knew him better, I asked him if he would like to start painting the barn the next day. I already had the paint. I had purchased twenty-four gallons on sale earlier in the summer at the Montgomery Ward store in Peatville for just a little over half price. Their best guaranteed one-coat latex exterior paint, regularly $9.99 a gallon, for only $5.39. The last painters had used thirty gallons on the barn, but that included a prime coat to convert to latex, which would not be needed again.

Pearl laid down three stipulations before taking the job. First, he would paint only with his own "burshes." Second, I must never, never try to pressure him into using a paint roller. Rollers gave him fits, he said, at the same time rotating his eyes up into his head and quivering so alarmingly that I promised then and there that I would never approach him, even from a distance, with a paint roller. Third, he must have payment in cash, because he never had anything to do with banks. I agreed to give him cash on the condition that he would sign a receipt. This he was willing to do.

In what seemed the dead of the night, a loud banging and scraping brought the entire family out of bed to huddle in terror in the kitchen. Stoyer, the practical one, had the presence of mind to look out the window. He said someone was up on a ladder painting the side of the barn. Witt and Liz and I peered out in disbelief. The exterior light under the eaves of the barn had been turned on, and in its dim illumination there *was* a man up on a ladder slap-slapping a brush against the barn wall. I looked at the kitchen clock. It was four-thirty in the morning.

"We've had everything else. It figures we'd come up with a moonlighting painter," said Witt, as we all staggered back to bed, leaving Pearl to fend for himself until daylight.

I couldn't go back to sleep. Every time Pearl moved his
ladder the metallic scrape on the driveway and the thump on
the barn wall brought me bolt upright. As dawn lit up the
windows, I pulled on jeans and shirt and went out to
confront my nocturnal handyman.

"You didn't tell me you are such an early starter," I yelled
up at him.

The ladder shuddered as convulsive gales of laughter
streamed down on me.

"Scared the daylights out'n you, din't I?"

"Isn't it a little damp to start painting so early? I mean,
even with rubber-base paint, most painters think eight or
nine is early enough."

"Heylissen." The voice floating down was a little bellige-
rent now. "Most them fellers don't drive thirty, forty mile to
work neither. I don't make no trip lessen I put in a full day."

I ducked into the barn. Pearl had been busier in the early
hours than I'd dreamed. For one thing, he'd taken over the
empty box stall and made it into a dressing room. Draped
neatly over the hay manger was his black outfit: shoes,
trousers, T-shirt (a black T-shirt? Must have shopped a long
time for that one), black sports shirt to go over the T-shirt,
and black porkpie hat with a green feather in it. A mirror was
pounded to the wall, and in the empty manger were towel,
washcloth, soap, and the biggest jar of Vaseline I'd ever
seen. In the feedbox was an outsized lunchbox molded in
the form of a Dutch Colonial house. Pearl must have
shopping outlets the rest of us had never heard of, I
marveled.

My eyes fell on the twelve-gallon carton of paint that I had
put out the night before, and it sort of hit me between the
eyes that Pearl was already on his third gallon of paint, and
the roosters were just starting to crow on the farm across the
road.

"Look at the bright side," I told myself. "You haven't *ever*
heard those roosters crow before, and it's very refreshing.

Besides, since he came so early he'll be worn out by midafternoon and we can have a peaceful late day to ourselves."

Midafternoon? At nine P.M., when the ponies had been fed, the dog locked up, dinner long since eaten and digested, and the sun had dipped out of sight behind the neighbor's woods, Pearl was still slap-slapping that "bursh" of his against the barn wall. At five o'clock I had gone out and asked him if he didn't knock off at five o'clock. He had given me a disdainful look, his face a brilliant pink from twelve hours in the sun and heavy applications of Vaseline every hour on the hour.

"Mizzer, I don't work lessen I put in a full day—and that's sixteen, seventeen hour. When I drive thirty, forty mile, you don't see me putting in no puny eight-hour day, no sirree, mebbe them other fellers, but not Pearly here."

Just to show me he meant business, he didn't roll his car down the lane until Witt was turning on the eleven o'clock news. Actually, he had ceased painting an hour before that; but, as a curious Stoyer observed when he went out to the barn to check the ponies for the night, Pearl had spent much time with noisy ablutions at the barn faucet, slicking up his red hair in front of the mirror, and donning his black outfit.

The next morning it was four-thirty again, and there was really no sleeping after he got here. Pearl saw to that. I could always count on the doorbell ringing, for one thing or another. One morning, a pony didn't look right to him. I staggered out into the front meadow to check. Like all sensible creatures at that hour, the pony was sleeping. One morning the cats were killing each other. One morning he smelled smoke. I stumbled out to sniff, but all I could smell was paint. Pearl said the reason he could smell smoke was that he had long since lost his smell for paint. One morning he craved an ice cube. One morning he saw a "flying sorcer." This really got the whole family up in a hurry. At that, we missed it coming and going.

On top of everything, there was the nagging threat of Hummer.

The third day, just about the time I had brought him out his third glass of lemonade, or "lemerade," as he called it, which was the only libation he would touch, he had broached the subject of Hummer.

"Say, mizzer," he began, "my boy, Hummer, he the doggondest painter you ever seen. You ain't never seen a body can go through a bucker paint fast as Hummer. Sometime Hummer like to make a little money on his day off, I bring him, okay? Don't cost you no more for sich a whiz-bang painter. He paint three dollar a hour like me. Okay?"

When he saw me hesitate, he added craftily, "You get rid us faster, too."

He had, indeed, touched a weak spot. "I guess it would be all right," I said, and then could have bitten my tongue off as the horror of riding herd on not one, but two seventeen-hour, paint-guzzling painters washed down on me.

That night at the dinner table, I said, "Pearl has this son with the queer name of Hummer."

"It's not really Hummer," Stoyer said, not missing a bite. "It's Herman."

"And just how did you figure that out?"

"Easy," Stoyer answered. "You have to figure Pearl's way of talking. You see, he says 'ganner' for gallon, and 'bucker' for bucket, and 'lemer' for lemon. He was telling me today when things got slow last winter he built 'cabbers in his kitcher.' See? Cabinets in his kitchen. He also cut a 'pitcher winder in his liver room.' So, you take the *er* off Hummer and put *en* on it, and you've got Hummen. You've never heard of anyone named Hummen, have you? So it's got to be Herman."

"A wild deduction," his father said.

"I tested it out," Stoyer persisted. "I asked him, 'Where does Herman work?' Pearl said without even looking up, 'Swing shift at the Rim Works.'"

"If you're so smart," I said, "I wish you'd try to find out from Pearl the exact day he plans to bring Hummer, or Herman as the case may be, and we'll pull up the bridge the night before. There isn't enough paint left in the county to pull the two of them through a seventeen-hour day."

As a matter of fact, the twenty-four gallons of paint I had placed in the barn were rapidly evaporating toward the end of Pearl's fourth day of working single-handed, and he came panting up to me, worried about it. "Saylissen, mizzer," he said, "them ganners is about gone, and you'd best git you to town."

He blushed up to his hair roots and burst into an embarrassed giggle. "You can do it tomorrer, cuz I ain't comin' tomorrer. I got a date tomorrer night, and I can't never work the day I has a date. It jes' makes me too nervous."

He rolled his eyes up into his head and I thought for a moment he was going to have one of those fits he went into when someone tried to make him use a paint roller, but he came out of it.

"Why, Pearl," I said, "I thought, since you talked of a son, that you were married."

"Not no more I'm not," he answered bitterly. "This womar I married, she had a flea in her bonner. She couldn't hardly wait 'fore Hummer was dry in his dideys 'fore she took off on me. But Hummer and me, we done fine all these year. Jes' las' winter we laid in new kitcher cabbers, cut us a nice pitcher winder in the liver room, got us a nice cozy little house. Hummer and me, we loves to dance, we go to dances ever' whip stick. But not neither of us don't trust no womar too far, I can tcll ycr that, 'ccptin to squeeze on the dance floor."

Pearl was as good as his word and more. He didn't show up for work the next day, nor did he come the following day. This really vexed me, because both days were lovely painting days, dry, not too cool and not too hot. I had gone to Peatville as per Pearl's request and had purchased another six gallons of paint. The paint sales were over for the summer, and I had to pay a full $9.99 a gallon, so I was determined to buy no more than I had to. Besides, I thought if Pearl should see a dearth of paint, he would be more sparing with it.

"I'm surprised you didn't come yesterday, Pearl," I said, when he finally showed up on the third day. "It was a lovely painting day."

"Din't I tell yer, mizzer?" He turned crimson and swallowed a giggle. "I don't never paint the day *arter* I had a date neither. Jes' makes me too nervous."

He spotted the six new gallons of paint in the barn. "I tell yer one thing, mizzer. Them puny ganners is hardly gone ter give me a start. If I'd knowed that was all yer was gone ter buy, I wouldn't have showed today neither."

He said that he was already nervous from his date, and it just made him "fitty nervous" whenever he saw he was down to his last half-dozen cans. This frightened me into going back to Peatville and buying another twelve gallons of paint at full price, and laying out over a hundred dollars for it. When the store manager carried the paint out to the car for me, he remarked, "For all the paint you've been buying the last couple days, you must have a big crew of painters out to that farm of yours."

"Would you believe one nervous redhead?" I asked. He just laughed.

The mystery of where the paint was going became a hotly debated issue at our dinner table. We knew the last painters had used thirty gallons on the barn—but that was for two coats. Pearl (the children had renamed him *the burshman*) had now passed the thirty-gallon mark and was still on his first coat. We agreed he certainly wasn't stealing the paint because, whatever his other faults, he looked as honest as the day was long—and taking the length of his own day as a criterion, that was being mighty honest. Besides, the car he used to come to work in was not the Edsel, which, he said, was his "date and dancin' car," but an ancient wreck of a Plymouth with three doors missing and the lid of the trunk tied down with twine. He couldn't have hidden a thimble of paint in that.

We all had our pet theories as to where the paint went. Except Witt, that is, who had other things to think about than where the paint went, for God's sake. Liz thought he ate it for breakfast. I told her she obviously hadn't seen the size of his lunchbox, which poured forth wondrous things. I was about to offer him a sandwich for lunch that first day—when I saw him munching on fat, crispy chicken legs, flaky cornbread, and something that looked very much like shoofly pie. I knew I couldn't compete with that—not at lunch. He and Hummer must have tried to outdo each other in the "kitcher," as well as on the dance floor, I thought.

Stoyer, the straight thinker, had based *his* theory of where the paint was going on diligent observation. "I think half of it just drops off his brush. When you are around, he is so careful. He dips his brush in the paint, then wipes some of it off on the side of the can before he puts his brush to the wall. But when he thinks there's no one around watching, he just dips his brush deep down in the can and brings the whole mess up to the wall. And have you seen that "bursh" of his? It's as old as his Plymouth. It has a hollow handle with a big crack in it, and after the Burshman's painted a couple of hours, the handle is heavy as lead with paint that's seeped through the crack. You can hear it gurgling around in there. When it gets too bad, he has to stop and soak it in water until the paint inside the handle is thin enough to shake out of the crack again. That's where the rest of it goes."

My theory, which I could not prove because I didn't want to get up at four-thirty and stand at his elbow until sunup, was that the first three hours Pearl painted, the atmosphere was so humid that the paint simply dissolved on the barn wall and ran off; so Pearl just kept painting the same area over and over again, until the sun came up and the paint would finally begin to "set up." The best argument for my theory was that he had always used up two gallons of paint before I got out to the barn in the morning; whereas three or four gallons would last him the rest of the day.

Late in the afternoon of Pearl's eighth day on the job, he came panting to the door and yelled accusingly, "Mizzer, I got two, three square yard of barn left ter bursh, and I'm fresh outer ganners. *Now* what you gone ter do?"

I hurriedly rummaged in the tool shed and came up with a half gallon of old oil-base paint left over from the first house painter. Pearl finished with this, grumbling all the way, because it didn't mix with the water-base paint on his "bursh" and messed it up.

He spent another two hours gathering up all his supplies, cleaning out his box stall dressing room, loading his ladders on top of his car, and taking an "after" snapshot of the barn with his box camera. He appeared at the door, resplendent in his black outfit, with the jaunty feather sticking out of his hat.

"I figgered I burshed forty-two ganners on that yere barn, wouldn't yer say, mizzer, not countin' that doty ol' can of earl base you give me?"

"I certainly think you would be safe in saying that," I answered, and he looked relieved. He said I owed him $393 in cash money. I had the bills ready and a receipt typed out for him to sign. He looked at the receipt for a moment, remarked that he had never learned to read typewriting, and signed his name in a huge childish scrawl.

Now I could ask him the question I had not dared to ask in recent days.

"Why didn't you ever bring your son Herman?"

"Hummer? That bum went and got married on me t'other day. Come up agin some widder womar with three chillers. Turned his head so bad he's looked sideways ever since. Them chillers is wild ones. I wouldn't have 'em in the house. Hummer he moved out lock, stick, and burrel.

"Leastways I still got the kitcher cabbers and the pitcher winder," he said, and on that philosophic note he took his leave.

The barn looked good, and I boasted to the family that the Burshman had been a find, after all, despite the seventeen-hour days. I pointed out that he had charged me only $393 for labor, whereas a union painter at $8 an hour would have cost $1,048 for the same number of hours. But Stoyer, always eager to set the facts straight, came up with a different set of figures. According to his calculations, Pearl had used twenty-six gallons of paint more than the average painter, and if I added the cost of those gallons, eight at the sale price, and eighteen I had purchased later at the regular price, and added this total of $222.94 to the $393 charge, Pearl's hourly wage would average out to $4.70, instead of $3 an hour. And this, Stoyer concluded triumphantly, didn't include sales tax on the extra paint.

I answered defiantly that it was still a savings of over $3 an hour in anyone's book, and the next spring I announced that I was calling the Burshman back to paint the house.

It was, in a way, a retaliatory action. Because by this time I had proof that my theory of where the paint went was correct. The barn still looked good—*except* for about a foot of wall directly under the eaves. This area was peeling off in crusty crinkles. This was the part Pearl had painted in the darkness before dawn, before the sun came up to get in his eyes.

"See?" I pointed accusingly, "I'll bet he painted under the eaves a hundred times over before the sun came up in the morning. And the paint never did set up, ever. Because the eaves protected the sun from ever hitting the area and letting it dry. I'm getting him back to do the job over if it's the last thing I do. I know he won't come back if I tell him I just want him to repaint under the eaves. Oh, I can just hear him. 'Drive thirty, forty mile for a three, four hour job? No sirree, not this feller,' he'll say. So I'll tell him I want him to paint the house, and when he's a captive prisoner, I'll confront him with the eaves."

"Forget the eaves! Forget Pearl! Forget everything but the horror of those seventeen-hour days!" said Witt. "Are you a masochist or something?"

"Not at all," I answered. "There aren't any eaves on the house. So that won't be a problem. And he'll be up here where we can watch him like a hawk. I'll be watching from every window, so he'll have to be dainty with his brush, and wipe it off on the side of the can."

I added, "Besides, I'll make it a condition of his coming this time that he not start so early."

"If you think you can make *that* leopard change his spots," Witt said ominously, "I think you and Pearl deserve each other!"

It was a more coquettish and brilliantly blushing Pearl than I had ever seen who leaped nimbly out of his black Edsel to look over the house job.

He fairly reeked of orange blossoms.

"Don't tell me," I said. "You got married over the winter."

He burst out laughing, then doubled over with the pain of it. "Now how did yer find out about that? Yes, sirree. I gone and done it. It was Hummer's fault. I figgered he done it, I could, too. This un's a widder womar, just like Hummer's. "Course *her* chillers all growed, and she works, and takes in good money. Oh, I hung back, first off. But she was crazy 'bout me. Jes' kep' eggin' me on. When she seen she couldn't get me no other way, she said she'd go halfsies on ever'thin'. Food, 'lectric, 'surance on the house—ever'thin'. That done it. I let her hogtie me."

He rolled his eyes into his head and gave such a huge sigh that I was certain this time that he was going to have one of those fits that paint rollers induced, but he recovered and began to shake his head back and forth at the wonder of it all.

"She sounds like a lovely person, Pearl," I said, "and I wish you much happiness—and now that you have a new wife, I'm sure you will not want to work such long hours, which will be perfectly all right with me."

He conceded, blushing, that he might want to put in just a short twelve-hour day now that he was a bridegroom. We discussed the house job.

"By the way," I said. "After you've finished the house, I'd like you to touch up the barn a little. See that space under the eaves that is crusting off? I'm afraid you painted it too early in the morning when it was wet, and it just never dried."

His eyes began to blaze and his lower lip shot out, so I went on hurriedly. "I'll pay you your regular wage to do it, you understand that, don't you, that I'm not expecting you to do it for nothing? The only thing I'm asking you to do is to paint there when the sun is hot, *never* before nine o'clock in the morning. Okay?

"Okay," he said shortly. Then he added, "I never took the bad habit of gor'nteeing my bursh job. It don't pay."

Although I was planning to ride herd on Pearl very closely this time, I took the precaution of stocking up on thirty gallons of paint when the Montgomery Ward store had its big spring sale. I was not going to be caught in the expensive squeeze of Pearl's running out of paint in the middle of the job, and my having to go to Peatville and pay the regular price for paint. I had to hook up the utility trailer to the Jeep to bring it all home. "I guess you're going to paint the town," the clerk said in an awed tone as he helped me line the trailer wall to wall with cans.

Idyllic is the only way I can describe those first five days the Burshman spent painting the house. He didn't come until eight o'clock. By then I had breakfast out of the way and was outside trimming bushes, spraying weeds, cuddling cats, or just reading under a tree; but always in sight of Pearl's "bursh." It worked like a charm. How he loved an audience, and how daintily his brush was dipped into the can, how judiciously some of the paint was wiped off against the rim of the can before it was applied to the wall.

Once, when it was necessary for me to go into the house for a short while, I stationed Stoyer as a lookout down at the bridge to see if he could determine whether Pearl's brushing technique changed if he thought I wasn't looking.

"First he looks one way, then the other," Stoyer reported, "and then he dips his brush deep down into the can and splashes the whole mess up to the wall. He does this three or four times, and then his head shakes back and forth like he's giggling, and then he goes back to being neat again."

Despite these short lapses, Pearl had used only a dozen gallons of paint and the house was well on the way to being finished—except for the gabled front porch with its two big white columns. I was congratulating myself all over the place that I had engineered a smooth job this time.

On the sixth day, Pearl showed up late. Very late for him. It was almost nine o'clock. I was hoping he wouldn't come at all, because it was a gloomy, overcast day, threatening rain. Pearl was not his usual ebullient self. He said he and the Plymouth had been caught in the random inspection line of the state highway patrol and he had been given a list of nineteen items to get fixed on the Plymouth by a certain date or get off the highways.

"What them lazy, high-binding slickers was doin' on the road 'fore eight o'clock in the morning I'll never know," he said.

He lost no time in putting his ladder up against the porch and starting to paint, even though by now a fine mist was coming down rather steadily. After an hour, I approached him and remarked tactfully that it didn't look much like painting weather, did it, at which he barked, "I tell yer one thing, mizzer, it ain't gone ter rain today!"

He painted steadily for three hours, never stopping—

except now and then taking a black handkerchief out and mopping the mist from his face. He painted the gabled front, the two side beams, and finally the two large columns that rested on the concrete floor. At the very moment he was through and was stepping off his ladder, the heavens opened and let out a torrent of rain that washed off every lick of paint from the porch, sending much of it onto the floor in a bubbling, milky foam. The cloudburst didn't last more than a minute, just long enough to do the job.

I rushed to the basement to get several brooms with which to sweep the paint from the floor. I pushed one of them at Pearl, but he threw it away, yelling, "Paint in my hair!" and ran for the barn. I called for Stoyer and we frantically swept paint.

"I haven't seen so much milk since the day you dropped a half gallon on the dining room carpet," I said.

"You were plenty mad that day, too," said Stoyer.

Diluted paint was flowing down the hill in a great white waterfall when Pearl finally emerged from the barn. He was slicking back his red hair, which had obviously been shampooed. "That looks better, don't it?" he said.

"The porch, you mean?" I asked blankly.

"Naw, my hair."

"Your hair! What about the porch?"

"Why, that just ain't no-account," Pearl said, flicking the back of his hand as if sloughing off a teaspoonful of paint. "I hadn't burshed more'n a ganner or two. Now yer want to see *paint* washed off, you should 'er seen the time I was burshing that big ol' barn jes' 'fore you get to the Catwalk Bend. Been burshin' for seventeen hour straight, when a sudden thunderstorm come up, and whoosh—"

"Don't tell me!" I shuddered.

He gave a giant shrug. "Tell you the truth, I'm too nervous to paint today anyways. That woman she's drivin' me crazy. Know what she had in her head last night when I come home? She said she warn't going to go halfsies on the house 'surance, 'cuz she don't own half the house. You know what that means, don't yer? Next thing she'll want half the house. Next thing she'll want half the Edsel!"

The thought of sharing the Edsel was too much for him and he sank down on the wet concrete, shaking with helpless rage. "I got to have me a nerve pill," he muttered. He dug a single white tablet from his breast pocket, threw his head back and gulped it down.

"What kind of nerve pills are they?" I asked, forgetting my annoyance for a moment, in my fascination for other people's medication.

"It's somethin' dreadful strong the doc give me name of Asper," he said, hissing the word out and rolling his eyes impressively. "It sure settles me."

When I was relating the day's debacle at the dinner table that night to a very unsympathetic Witt, who thought I was getting my just rewards, I said, "By the way, the poor man is really in bad shape because he's taking a potent nerve medicine called Asper. Isn't that the wickedest drug you ever heard of? It sounds like an antitoxin for a deadly snake bite. Pearl says it really settles him."

"Boy!" Stoyer hooted. "You let your imagination run away with you that time. That's just plain aspirin. I saw the bottle in the box stall, sitting next to the Vaseline. You wouldn't think you could make such a mistake, after I cracked his code for you last summer."

Stoyer was right. I should have had that one.

But I wasn't too discouraged about the painting situation at that moment. After all, the house was almost finished. I felt that if I could coddle Pearl through another day or two things would be in good shape. All he had left to do was to repaint the front porch, and scrape and repaint under the barn eaves. I vowed I would be gentle, kind, and considerate.

When Pearl stepped from his car the next morning, I thought it was going to be one of his better days. He was grinning broadly, and when he saw me come out of the house he burst right out laughing.

"I'm certainly glad to see you're feeling so good today, Pearl," I said.

"Yer want ter hear somethin' that will make you bust out laughin'?" he whispered conspiratorially, and pulled me under the privacy of a tree, although there was not another person in sight.

"The womar and me we had a bad fight las' night. It was turrible, I tell you. I wanted to go ter the dance, see, and she didn't want ter. Sez she's tired workin' all day. Tired, mind you! Puttin' in a puny little ol' eight hours in that lorndry. Me, I c'n put in a seventeen, eighteen hour day and dance all night and never know it.

"Anyways, I jes' got dressed up fit to shoot to go ter the dance without her, and this makes her mad, see, and she puts on her coat and sashays out the door and sez she's spendin' the night at her datter's house.

"Now here's the part'll bust you. I don't go ter the dance, see. I stays ter home, and I takes the locks off both the doors—both the front 'un and the back 'un, and I puts new ones on, and when she tries to git in this mornin' to change her clothes to go ter work, her key won't work in them new locks!"

Pearl was laughing so hard I thought I would have to pound him on the back to keep him from choking. "Wisht I was a bird up in that yere willer tree front o' my house right now so's I could see her huffin' and puffin' tryin' ter git in."

He staggered weakly toward the barn to get his ladder. "Best part of it was, them locks needed changin' anyways. Them new ones was bought three, four year ago on sale at the Western Auto. Jes' my own laziness kep' me from changin' 'em."

While Pearl laughed, I shivered. Hell hath no fury, I thought, like a woman who has to go halfsies and is locked out of the house to boot.

Pearl did an enormous amount of work that day. His little secret seemed to buoy him along. Whenever he caught sight of me, he burst out in a fresh fit of uncontrollable laughter. It disgusted me, and I finally just stayed out of sight.

By the time he knocked off work in the evening, he had not only finished painting the house, but had scraped and repainted under the eaves on three sides of the barn. All he had left was the eastern broadside of the barn, the one facing away from the house.

"Now remember, Pearl," I warned him. "I don't want you coming tomorrow before the middle of the morning. I don't want you painting under those eaves before it's good and dry."

He was still laughing when he drove down the lane.

Witt had an early meeting at his office the next morning, and I had gotten up early to make his breakfast; was just crawling back into bed for an extra forty winks when I heard a car come over the bridge.

It was Pearl, and it was not even seven o'clock.

Something snapped in me. I think it was my last shred of patience. I had put up with his nocturnal arrivals, his seventeen-hour days, wasting God only knows how many gallons of paint, deliberate painting in the rain, but if he thought he was going to get away with painting under those eaves one more time in the wet of the morning—well, just let him try!

I pulled on jeans and shirt and stormed out, my conciliatory intentions evaporated.

Pearl was already headed around the corner to the other side of the barn with his ladder.

"Just a darned minute there, Pearl," I shouted. "You're not painting under those eaves at this hour of the morning. I told you and I told you."

"Don't care what yer tol' me, mizzer," he shouted back. "I'm finishin' this job in the next hour or two, 'fore it gits so damn hot up there. I jes' can't stand it no more!"

"Why can't you stand it any more?"

"I'll tell yer why!" He turned suddenly and threw the

aluminum ladder flat on the driveway with a terrible clang. "Do yer know what happent to me las' night when I come home? I was turnin' the key in one them new locks ter git in my house, and that yere damn womar o' mine lept out from behind a tree and whomped me a good one on the head with her fry-pan."

He bent down, parted his red hair with both hands, and showed me a tiny laceration on his scalp. "Never seen anything like *that*, have yer?"

"It's just a little scratch, really."

"Scratch, my foot! She opened up my head, that's what she done. And you know what else is drivin' me crazy? I can't figger out how she got in my house to git her fry-pan to whomp me with!"

"Maybe when she realized you'd changed the locks on her it made her so angry that she went out and bought a new frying pan for the express purpose of hitting you with it."

"No, sirree, no ma'am! That yere fry-pan was the same old greasy one she fried my chops in the night 'fore. The grease was still in 'ere and ran down on my nice black shirt when she hit me."

"Well, after all that I'm sure she took her things and moved out for good, and perhaps it's just as well."

"Not on your life she din't! I had to make up with the damn womar 'til I figger out how she gits in my house. Do you think I'm gone ter have her slippin' in and out of that yere house when I'm gone and her *mad* at me? She c'd take ever'thin', even tear the cabbers off'n the kitcher walls, she's so damn smart! No, sirree, I'm havin' her on *my* side, leastways 'til I figger out how she got in that yere house with all them locked doors and winders."

"I'm sorry, Pearl, sorry about it all, but you can't let your personal life interfere with your work. Now I will not have you painting under those eaves for at least another hour. Not until nine o'clock. But I'm willing to compromise, so I'll let you paint a few storm windows until the sun gets warm."

"Storm winders!" Pearl went livid with rage. "I ain't never had no truck with burshing storm winders. That's womar's work. I'm packin' up and leavin' this ver' minute. Jes' pay me my cash money and I'll git out o' here!"

I stood my ground. "I'm sorry, Pearl, but my agreement with you was that you were to paint the house and repaint the area under the barn eaves at a decent hour. I am not going to pay you until the entire job is completed."

Pearl was jumping up and down on one foot. "You're just a damn womar like all the rest 'em. I work by the hour and not by the job. I'll git me a lawyer. He'll sue you up one side t'creek and down t'other."

"Tell him to go ahead. And while he's at it, tell him to see my lawyer at the same time."

I walked hurriedly over to the back porch and grabbed up as many storm windows as I could carry. I hadn't been planning to have Pearl paint them, because he was too sloppy. I was going to paint them myself. But the situation called for desperate measures. I walked back and put the storm windows down in front of Pearl, and quickly returned to the house.

As I came into the kitchen I heard Stoyer talking excitedly on the telephone. "Mother has locked horns in battle with the Burshman!"

When he hung up, I said, "So you called your father. I thought you were asleep."

"Who can sleep with all that yelling going on out there?"

"I don't suppose your father's going to do anything rash like rushing home to protect my honor?"

"Not the way he talked. He said he'd pit you against the Burshman any day, and lay a fiver on you to win."

"It's nice to have a vote of confidence at a time of crisis," I said. "Stoyer, peek out the window and see if he's packing up to leave."

"No. He seems to be painting storm windows, and the paint is really flying."

"Imagine that."

"Say, will you really hold up his money for the house like you said, if he doesn't finish painting under the barn eaves?"

"Probably not. He tried to bluff me into giving him his money before the job was finished. I called his bluff, and I'm now in the act of trying to pull off one of my own."

"It sounds like what they call in the Westerns a standoff," said Stoyer.

Keeping a watch from the window, Stoyer reported, just as the kitchen clock struck nine, that Pearl suddenly dropped a storm window, grabbed up his ladder and headed around the corner to the far side of the barn.

After a half hour of not knowing what was going on behind the barn, I could stand it no longer and told Stoyer to take his bicycle and ride down the road about a mile east. "When you ride back," I said, "You'll be able to see the east end of the barn and what he's doing."

Stoyer duly reported that from the road he could see Pearl up on his ladder painting under the eaves "so fast his brush is just a steady stream in and out of the bucket. He's painting so fast that every few minutes he has to rush down from the ladder and move it into a different position."

I knew then that it would not be long. I sat down at my desk, figured up his hours, counted out his cash in tens and twenties, and typed out his receipt. Soon I heard scraping and banging, and Stoyer said that Pearl was tying his ladders up on his car.

The doorbell rang. Pearl was standing at the door, tears running down his face and making great splotches on his black shirt that was already splattered with grease from the night before.

"The job's all done jes' like yer wanted it, mizzer. I swear I don't know what come over me, and yer being so nice to me totin' me lemerade ever' whip stick."

"All right," I said. "If the job's done I'm ready to settle with you." I took the roll of cash out of my jeans pocket.

At the sight of the cash, his face lit up and a wide grin began to spread under the tears. "I see yer got my cash money for me."

I gave him the bills, which he counted expertly and neatly, facing the twenties all in the same direction, and shoring them up with the tens.

After he had signed the receipt with a great deal of tongue work, he stepped back and announced, "Well, mizzer, this gone ter be my last bursh job."

"You mean you're retiring?"

"Leastways 'til I figger out how that yere womar gits in my house. Could take me long as two, three year." His eyes narrowed into cunning slits. "If I ain't takin' in good money, she can't hardly make me go halfsies, can she?"

I had an irresistible urge. "What about Herman?" I asked. "Is Herman still happy with *his* wife?"

"Hummer?" His eyes rotated up into his head and came around full circle. "Still lookin' sideways," he said gloomily, and headed for his car.

That's the last I ever saw of Pearl. In the next year, Stoyer grew four inches, reaching a height of almost six feet. As he himself pointed out, we now had our own live-in "Burshman," nonunion, and willing to work cheap.

Our paint troubles, at least for a few years, were over.

10

Dressing for the Grand Tour

When people want to see ponies, they want to see ponies. The hour or condition of the day is immaterial. The runaway favorite time is just when we are sitting down to Sunday dinner, but many have come at night or in a pouring rain, and these are always the ones who aren't wearing their gum boots. Why frantic young men drive in at eleven o'clock on a Saturday night, so desperate for an untrained harness pony prospect that they will go out in the woods with a flashlight to look for him has always been a mystery to me. But then if I had been able to read pony-lookers, I would have been tempted not to give everyone the grand tour—and I might have given short shrift to the man who came to see ponies one August afternoon when the thermometer registered ninety-nine in the shade.

I was beating the heat by soaking in a tub of cool water when Liz rushed into the house, screaming that a station wagon was coming up the lane. The children became frantic when they thought they might have to greet a pony-looker by themselves; sometimes if I failed to make my appearance promptly, they were asked leading questions, such as, "What's the most you people ever get for a pony around here?" Or, even trickier, "What's the least you people ever take for a pony around here?" Stoyer and Liz had learned that there was no way they could answer these questions with impunity.

I hastily pulled myself out of the bathtub and told Liz to fetch me a pair of pants and a shirt from my dresser. "Hurry, hurry," Liz was whispering, "you know they'll go in the barn and start looking in the box stalls." She reminded me that Stoyer wasn't out there to ride interference either, having just taken off with his ax for the woods.

It wasn't until I was headed out the door and down the walk toward the car that I noticed what Liz had chosen for me to wear: a red-and-white zebra-striped shirt and a pair of neon-violet kneeknocker pants that had enormous purple apples running around on them. The shirt and pants had, at different times, been carefully chosen gifts from my children, and I had worn them before, separately, but had never made so bold as to combine the two. It was too late to turn back.

A towering man, at least six and a half feet tall, with the heft to go with it, was coming toward me. He said his name was Windmiller, and he and his wife and four children were on vacation, happened to be driving past, saw the ponies, and would like to have a better look at them. He had a gravelly voice, with a slight German accent that reverberated down from the heights like rocks falling in a landslide. When he spoke he tried to look directly into my eyes but had to stoop a little to do it; even then his eyes, one of which had a list, missed mine and skimmed the top of my head. It occurred to me that those eyes might never fall as low as the purple-apple kneeknockers.

Not that it mattered, I thought to myself, because I knew I had spotted a genuine, dyed-in-the-wool, nonbuying pony-looker if I'd ever seen one. On vacation, that's the giveaway: he and his family are just cruising around in the station wagon, looking for a diversion for the kids; they drive past our place, spot our ponies, and decide they'll give the kids a couple of hours of enjoyment on my time instead of taking them to the zoo.

It was a torpid day, in which the heat bore down from a cloudless sky like an unrelenting interrogation. As I stood there with the formidable Mr. Windmiller looming over me, I could feel my bizarre costume soaking through with moisture—whether from residual bathwater or perspiration I couldn't tell. I thought wildly of excuses why I couldn't show ponies. *We just sold the farm with the ponies thrown in. . . .* No, he'd never buy that, not at today's pony market. *I'm on my way to the doctor. . . .* In *this* getup?

"I'd be most happy," I said, "to show you the ponies."

Mr. Windmiller turned around and introduced me to a tiny, doll-faced wife, whose short dark hair clung in damp tendrils to her forehead, and to four children between the ages of four and twelve. They were stocky children, broad-faced and fat-legged; towheaded, all of them; smiling, happy-looking children, but silent. Liz and I subsequently showed the Windmillers the yearling fillies in the front field; the two-year-old colts in the back field; the three yearling colts in the east pasture; and Hector, now a perennially unsold stallion, in the orchard. This took an hour. I could very well see that the same kind of heat that was pouring down on Liz and me was also attacking the Windmillers. Suddenly a wave of cold cunning swept through me like a refreshing April breeze.

"Now if it were a cooler day, Mr. Windmiller," I said in my most gracious manner, "we would take you into the woods to see the rest of the ponies, but we wouldn't think of subjecting you to that on a sweltering day like this."

"Not at all," said Mr. Windmiller, his eyes missing the top of my head and hitting the barn wall. His short, guttural laugh poured down on me. "Now that you mention it, we wouldn't think of going home without seeing the ponies in the woods."

Having tidily clamped me into my own trap, Mr.

Windmiller, rather smugly, it seemed to me, in great long strides led the procession down the lane, across the bridge, over the board fence, and into the woods, Liz and I flanking him on the right, his Dresden-doll wife and the four children following respectfully behind. I looked back up the lane and noted enviously that the two cats who love to follow this sort of excursion had elected to stay behind on the shaded driveway. As we plunged into the woods we dispersed ranks somewhat. Liz grabbed my arm and whispered, "Mr. Windmiller is turning out to be one of those *No-Commenters*, isn't he?"

"Yes," I whispered back. "And they are the worst kind." We smiled knowingly at each other and continued on.

What Liz meant was that Mr. Windmiller had turned out to be the kind of pony-looker who will gaze at pony after pony after pony and not say one word—either of praise or criticism. This silent treatment can, by the end of a grand tour of between twenty and thirty ponies, be totally devastating. A *No-Commenter* is ten times worse than a *Nitpicker* or a *Raver*, the other two most common types, both of whom have some redeeming qualities.

A Nitpicker, for instance, walking round and around your ponies in a field, will make comments like these:

"Is this a mare or a stud?"

"Don't they make ponies with small ears anymore?"

"What *causes* swayback, anyway?"

"If this one wasn't standing uphill, wouldn't you say he was a mite steep in the croup?"

But the saving grace of the Nitpicker is that he is often a serious buyer in disguise. His comments are designed to make you so despondent over the low quality of your stock that you will knock your prices down. The Nitpicker seldom tips his hand on the first trip to the farm, or even the second trip. But if he comes a second time, you can probably count on getting a telephone call from him a few days later:

"You still got that blaze-faced stud?"

"You mean the one you said was steep in the croup?"

"Aw, hell, he ain't all that steep I couldn't live with it if you'd come down on your price."

"The price is firm."

"Best you can do, huh?" . . . Be all right if I pick him up Saturday a week?"

No, the Nitpicker is not all bad. Neither is the Raver, who seldom buys anything but who has such bubbling enthusiasm and is so disarmingly ignorant about anything equine that you love him for himself alone. Take the woman in chiffon, for instance, who was given the grand tour and called every pony on the place, from start to finish, a "gilding." We had, at that time, twenty-eight ponies, not one of them a gelding. As she came panting up the lane from the woods on her high heels, she trilled, "You have just the loveliest gildings I have ever seen!" And sweeping her arms ecstatically toward Beau, who was running in the orchard during off-breeding season, she rhapsodized, "And you, you beautiful creature, you are the most beautiful gilding of them all!"

Or take the Raver whose child asked, "What is the difference between a pony and a horse?" and she replied, "My sweet darling, a pony is just a young horse." (This child will grow up thinking it's only a matter of time until his pony—if he ever gets one—will look like the Budweiser horses.)

Or take the dozens and dozens of Ravers as they looked at Egrett, who has a sagging belly like most fat females with many offspring, and said knowingly, "That mare is about to have a colt, isn't she?" even though at that very moment Egrett was giving suckle to a fresh foal. My children developed poker faces in time, but this remark would always bring a giggle, no matter how stern I looked. . . . The Ravers, come to think of it, were sometimes the only reason it all seemed worthwhile. And they gave us something to talk about on long winter evenings.

But the No-Commenter—a pox on him! Three-quarters of the way through a grand tour you are ready to shake him until his teeth rattle. You show him what you think is your best pony, expecting, at the very least, a small word of praise, and he stares. Just stares. You show him your worst pony and he stares—just stares—in exactly the same way he stared at your best pony. What is this supposed to mean? That the best is no better than the worst? The only time he speaks is when he prices something. And he prices *every-thing*. Soon it becomes a rote. How much are you asking for this one. . .how much are you asking for that one? Even the prices don't bring a comment out of him. It could be a hundred or a thousand or a zillion (toward the end of an especially exasperating grand tour, it sometimes is), but his eyes never flicker as he goes on to the next one. The only good thing about a No-Commenter is that he never comes back. He takes your prices, and whatever he thinks about your ponies, and he gets in his car, revs up his motor, hesitates a moment, and then says mysteriously, "I may be back." Always he says, "I may be back." Your reward is the delicious expectation of his return.

So as Liz and I now hurried into the woods after the no-commenting Mr. Windmiller we were resigned to spending another hour in the broiling heat for nothing. "At least," Liz whispered again, sweetly, "you've got a cute outfit on."

We had in the woods that summer just under thirty head of ponies, including eight mares with suckling foals. Liz and I tried hard every summer to sell the foals while they were still running with their dams, so that the foals could leave the farm at weaning time in November. This not only got us out of the emotional turmoil of the weaning process, but saved us from having to winter the foals and having to separate the colts from the fillies after the first of the year, creating the ever-nagging category problems. Strangely, even though the foals were much more appealing than the awkward yearlings, we seldom were able to sell one. Buyers just didn't trust their judgment in anticipating what a foal would look like in a year or two.

But Mr. Windmiller, true to his type, was pricing everything—including foals. It was hard to keep up with him because his legs were twice as long as anyone else's, and he was loping over the hills and down into the dales, going up to every pony, staring at it, walking around it, then asking the inevitable question in his gargled voice. I noticed that his German accent was becoming more pronounced as we went along.

"How much is this von . . . how much is this von?" he demanded, time and again.

His wife and children trotted along behind him, not curious, but then again, not disinterested either, bearing up remarkably well under the heat, not saying a word. When one of the Shetland mares trotted up to the children and began nuzzling them, they touched, and they petted, but they didn't say a word, didn't lie down on the ground and scream, "I want that one!"

"Wow!" I thought. "Have those children been trained."

Finally, Mr. Windmiller could find no more ponies to look at and he was perspiring worse than anyone, because he was closer to the sun than the rest of us. The sweat was falling from his chin onto his great belly, making a puddle on his shirt. I was glad there were no more ponies to price, because several times when he had asked me the price of a pony, his eyes had tried to meet mine, and they had missed, and skimmed over my head; the eye with the list had landed on a pony slightly to the side and back of me, and I had turned and said, "Oh, that one?" and Mr. Windmiller had answered rather impatiently, as if he had been through this sort of thing before, "No, no! The von I am looking at right now!" It had been embarrassing for both of us.

"Haf I seen them all?" Mr. Windmiller now asked. I nodded emphatically.

At that he spread his legs wide apart, hitched up his trousers, and threw out a long arm. "All right," he boomed, "I'll take that von . . . and that von . . . and that von!"

He had pointed to three of the suckling foals.

It seemed that every living thing in the woods froze for a moment under the blazing sun. There wasn't a sound, except for Stoyer's ax ringing out on his wedge from a distant corner of the woods.

Mr. Windmiller pivoted on a great foot, turning his body toward the farm buildings, and pointed again. "And that von!" he shouted. "That black yearling colt up in the pasture."

Then he dropped his arm, relaxed, and said softly, "I vant a pony for each of my children."

I looked at the Windmiller children. They didn't yell, "Whoopee!" or start screaming, "Which one is mine?" or "I want that one," or "You can't have the red one, I saw him first," like most children would have done. They just stood in a row and smiled, as if it were the most natural thing in the world that their father should buy a pony for each of them without giving them any choice in the matter. The only one who broke rank at all was the four-year-old, who grabbed his older brother's leg, hid behind it, and giggled joyously.

As I suspected earlier, those children had really been trained. But then again, I thought, as we all straggled back up the lane, not any more than my own daughter, who was walking just ahead of me, matching steps with the Windmiller daughter. They had become suddenly chummy, those two, having discovered they were both eleven years old. I heard Mr. Windmiller's daughter ask Liz, "Do you often sell four ponies at once?"

And Liz replied, throwing her long hair nonchalantly over her shoulder as girls of that age do, "Well, not *every* day!"

Mr. Windmiller said he would pick up the yearling colt in a week, and his three foals at weaning time, and he was as good as his word. The first of November he came in a big truck covered with a tarpaulin for the weanlings. Liz and I had them halter trained, eating grain and hay on their own, and ready to leave their dams. It had been a lot of work, but we were rewarded the next spring by having no yearling colt category, for the first time in years.

It would seem that Mr. Windmiller had disproved my theory on the No-Commenter—had, in fact, shot it to pieces. I thought so myself for a long, long time. Not only that, but I thought my red-and-white zebra-striped shirt and my purple-apple kneeknockers were my good-luck charms; for years after that each time a pony-looker drove up the lane I hurriedly changed into them before showing my ponies. I think I finally gained a reputation of sorts as the peculiar woman in the purple pants. It always gets back to you. Another pony-breeder told me once that a pony-looker had come directly from my place to hers and said of me, "She must be weird to wear the kind of clothes she does. Strange, because her husband looks like your normal type. Came home when I was there and he was wearing a respectable suit and tie."

But my lucky getup finally went to rags, and still we had never had another four-pony sale—or even a three-pony sale. Several times we had sold two ponies at once, but even that was Before Windmiller. I stand pat on my description of a No-Commenter, because we never again sold one a pony. And time eventually proved that Mr. Windmiller was a bounteous windfall I would never see again.

11

Will and the Hearing-Ear Dog

My best friend in the country is Will Suttle, who lives down at the crook of the road on the twenty-acre farm that he had from his father, and his grandfather before him. Will is eighty-four, a wiry little man with pink skin and hair white and fragile as an angel's wing, wet-slicked to one side. His bib overalls always look so neat that I suspect, although I have no hard proof of this, that he irons them after he gets them home from the Peatville laundromat. When you ask Will how he's feeling, he invariably replies, "Not doin' too bad for a boy."

Many of our other neighbors don't have time to be friendly. On most of the nearby farms, both husband and wife work at outside jobs. In the evening the wife wearily catches up on her ironing, and in the summer she tends a huge garden, a backbreaking job. The husband moonlights in his fields at night, seeding corn and soybeans into the small hours of the morning, following the furrows by the lights of his tractor. But Will has plenty of time to be friendly. He has nothing to do but watch out for himself and his dog and a host of itinerant cats that come like clockwork every morning at eleven for Will's free soup-line breakfast of cornmeal mush, served in a dishpan to all comers. No cat or dog is ever turned away. But promptness counts. After half an hour the pan is taken away and no more gratuitous sustenance is available until the next morning.

Until Will's wife Eula died a few years ago, she and I had been good friends, because Eula always had plenty of time, too. She didn't give a hoot-'n-holler for keeping house; she considered it much more productive to sit on her porch and read the latest issue of *Ladies' Home Journal,* which had arrived in the morning mail, than to be forever cleaning and sweeping. Eula had a good, roomy set of wood cabinets over her kitchen counters, but there was nothing in them. A ponderous woman, she found it much more convenient to have her dishes, canned goods, and all of her staples—the cornstarch, cocoa, tapioca, and cereals—sitting out on the counters and overflowing onto the kitchen table. When mealtime came, she cleared off a tiny place on the kitchen table, just big enough for two plates and some cutlery for herself and Will. I thought it rather a sensible arrangement myself. Some women spend half their lives taking dishes out of their cupboards, putting them in the dishwasher, taking them out of the dishwasher, and putting them back in the cupboards.

Eula spent as little time as possible at housekeeping, but she did have two special neighborhood projects. She always took it as her own personal responsibility to report the electrical failures along our road after a storm; and she always called on the neighbors to collect money for flowers when someone on our road died. This was rather a delicate job that required a good deal of diplomacy, considering one or two long-standing neighborhood feuds, on which moratoriums were not always declared in the event of a death. Eula didn't have an enemy in the world, and her utmost discretion usually paid off, but occasionally she asked me to go with her for moral support. The last time we collected for flowers together, she asked me in for lunch, and she made a special trip to the cellar to bring up a jar of her pear preserves for me to sample. As she cleared off a tiny place for us to eat at the kitchen table, she suddenly looked at me, smiled, and said, "Maybe you'll be going the rounds for *me* next time." I stared at her, startled, and then laughed and said that was the most ridiculous thing I'd ever heard, and then she laughed a little, too.

Several weeks later, Eula died in her sleep.

A few days after the funeral, I knocked on the screen door of the cottage with a pumpkin pie in hand, and when Will let me into the kitchen, I looked around, and I knew he was going to be all right. He had swept the kitchen table clean and he had shined up the oilcloth, and he had put everything on the counters back into the cupboards, except the bug spray and the mug that held his teeth. And he was walking around the kitchen with somewhat of an air of authority.

I had known Will for ten years by now, and I had never heard his voice. Always before, when I had dropped in for a visit, he had nodded to me ever so courteously, then gone straight for his hat and out the door. It came as a surprise to me now to hear his voice—not the high monotone of the deaf that I had expected—but a soft, low voice with the words slightly slurred and jumbled together. His problem was, he told me once, that even with a hearing aid he had ninety percent hearing loss. And it had become easier through the years to let Eula do the talking, instead of struggling with it himself. But now that she was gone, he found he must make the effort again, and I think he discovered that he had missed talking, and the more he talked, the more he could not get enough of talking.

He purchased a new hearing aid, and he fiddled with it constantly, tuning it up and down. It made whining little noises as he talked, like a spoiled child who wants attention. Will and I hit it off immediately because I had a voice he seemed to be able to hear, one reason being that I was not afraid to shout. I had learned to make myself heard as a child in North Dakota, being the youngest of six children. More than that, a deaf aunt had lived across the road from us, and my mother was always sending me over to her house with things, like a choice piece of calf liver because we'd butchered, or to borrow a dozen cups because an unexpected batch of company had dropped in. I not only had to shout to make myself heard, but I had to shout in Norwegian, which wasn't easy and took a great deal of rehearsing beforehand.

The one thing that worried me about Will's "batching it" was that he never used his telephone. Couldn't hear a dad-blamed thing at the other end, he said. I said I bet he could hear me. Unfortunately, we were on the same party line, so it was necessary to go through a complicated procedure of dialing two digits plus the regular phone number, then hanging up, then waiting for a few seconds so that the phone could ring at the other end, then picking up the receiver again. The secret of success in this operation is that the dial*er* and the dial*ee* must both pick up the receiver and say hello at the same time or neither will hear anything but an ear-splitting clicking noise. Will and I spent all one afternoon with the phone—he at his end and I at my end—until we finally had the timing down perfect. He would dial, hang up, count to fifteen, then pick up the receiver. As soon as the telephone rang at my house, I would start counting to fifteen as I went for the telephone. I talked good and loud, and Will was surprised to learn that he could hear me better than in face-to-face conversation.

After that, Will telephoned me every few days, and we had long, interesting talks. One day he called and said ominously, "Something's in the wind. Them two old bullfrogs in my garden is headed north. That's something I never seen in my life before."

"Headed north?" I asked stupidly.

"You know good and well as I do that the creek's south," he answered reprovingly.

"Of course, I see what you mean," I said, not wishing to push my ignorance further.

At other times he merely called to find out how things

stood on the other side of the creek today, and after he had
relayed to me the more pertinent tidings from the *Peatville
Daily News,* to which I did not subscribe, he often embarked
on a few reminiscences of the old days. He had ranged far
and wide in his youth, going out West as a very young man,
taking on odd jobs on the big ranches, working his way
through Montana, Oklahoma, Texas, Louisiana, and back to
Ohio again.

One of his stories I never tire of hearing is the one about
the time he hired on as a hand at one of the big Texas
ranches. He was only sixteen years old, and soon he had
picked up a severe case of homesickness, and nothing would
do but he must hit for home. But the ranch foreman, a kindly
soul, knew just what to do for the disease. He got him drunk
and kept him drunk for three days and three nights, and
when Will finally sobered up his homesickness was cured,
and what's more it never came back. He remembers that
foreman as one of the most understanding men he has ever
had the good fortune to come across.

Another one of his favorites, which I don't care so much to
hear, is about the old mule driver he knew while he was
working in a lumber camp; the man mistreated his pair of
mules day after day, until one dark dawn the mules cornered
their master in the barn and kicked him to death, the mules,
in the true code of the West, having taken justice into their
own hands—or hooves, as it were.

When Will tells the story of how in 'Forty-nine the chiropractor in Peatville cured up his bum back—which had
stumped the medical brains in South Metropolis—I can just
hear my vertebrae crunching. While he was on his job as a
lathe operator at a furniture factory, Will's back had gone out
of whack, and he was laid up for months, sitting at home in
his rocking chair, racked with pain. All the doctors that the
factory recommended had given up on him. But the Peatville
chiropractor had other ideas. He strapped Will to a table so
tight he couldn't move, and for days he stretched his bones,

each day a little more, by rocking the table back and forth with a motorized gadget underneath. On the final day, the chiropractor decided to go for broke, to let go with everything he had, and he reached under the table and flipped the switch all the way; the table gyrated violently on full power for the first time. There was first a bone-crushing pain and then a loud pop as Will's back snapped back into place. The next day he went back to work. The factory doctors, confounded, pronounced him fit as a fiddle.

A story I hear often is the one in which he sees himself as a steely man of the Old West, forced by circumstance into taking the law into his own hands. It was a period in his life when he was riding a motorcycle back and forth to a factory job in Peatville. For weeks a neighbor's dog, a fierce German shepherd, had been leaping onto the road to harass him, coming at him and snarling and trying to grab the motorcycle tires. One day the dog succeeded in running him into the ditch. Will walked over to the farmhouse and confronted his neighbor. "Thurlow," he said, "that durn dog of yours run me into the ditch. You know what's good for you, you better keep him off the road."

But Thurlow had merely spat tobacco juice out of the side of his mouth and allowed as how any man out on the road had the responsibility to take care of his own self. Will climbed back on his motorcycle and took off. That night he went to town and bought himself a secondhand 38-caliber revolver and put it under his belt. He bided his time, waiting until the next time the dog confronted him on the road with bared teeth and tried to grab him, and then Will took the revolver out of his belt and shot him. He took the dead dog and heaved him up on Thurlow's porch, got back on his motorcycle and rode off. End of story.

When Eula died, her small black poodle soon followed her, and Will looked around for another dog. He soon came up with what he wanted—a half-grown puppy he named Fer-

gus. He said he had always liked the name; he had known
several men by that name out West in his youth. "They was
sociable," he said.

Part collie, part German shepherd, Fergus grew to be a
big, gangly red-and-white dog with a skinny turned-down
nose, freckled around the muzzle. He had beady eyes and
skimpy laid-back ears. He would win no beauty contest even
with the uglies, but as Will knew the minute he laid eyes on
him, Fergus was not behind the door when the brains were
passed out.

In fact, it was no time at all before Fergus seemed to be
running the whole show down at the corner. So much so
that we started to call him Will's hearing-ear dog. It was
Fergus who greeted me at the car to frisk me before he let me
in the gate; Fergus who set up a horrendous howl so his
master would open the door and let me in. If the master
happened to be in the outhouse, Fergus was very discreet
about it, running a few steps back and forth from privy to
house as if to say, "Don't rush him now, he'll be out shortly."
If the master was taking his afternoon nap, Fergus would be
patrolling inside the screen door, very pussy-footy. A few
quick little steps back and forth to the bedroom, and Fergus
had warned me the master was not to be disturbed. This was
the sign for me to put the pie on the table and leave.

Whenever Will invites me into the living room to sit down
for a chat, Fergus frisks me, then takes up his seat on the
only upholstered armchair in the room. After a few minutes,
things are getting dull, so he leaps down and barks loudly in
Will's ear. Will lets him out the door. Before you can say
ring-around-the-rosy he is making a terrific racket and
pushing the house over to get in. Having gained reentry, he
frisks me all over again to make sure I haven't come up with
anything suspicious in his absence, after which he makes a
new security check on the entire house, going from room to
room, sniffing up and down all the walls, even checking
things out under Will's bed before he settles down on his

chair again. If I stay as long as a half hour, Fergus has gone through this routine at least three times.

Will said once that the only real disappointment he has had with Fergus is that he has never learned to tell him when the telephone is ringing. I had often wondered about this, too. I thought that was something a smart dog like Fergus would have picked up in no time. One day, in a flash of insight, I knew the reason. Will and I were sitting in the living room, and Fergus was snoozing on his chair. The telephone rang, an ear-shattering noise, because Will had had the telephone company turn the bell up as high as it would go. Will didn't hear it. Fergus heard it, all right. He looked up with his beady little eyes, his head still on the cushion. I could see his body grow taut, but he didn't move a hair, except to edge his paws up around his head until the racket was over. I knew the answer. Many times before, Fergus had probably barked fiercely in Will's ear when the telephone rang, and each time, Will, not hearing it, had thought that Fergus must want to go outside, so he had put him out the door. After a few times like that, Fergus undoubtedly was smart enough to figure out he mustn't bark when the telephone rang—if he didn't happen to want to leave his cozy nest and go out.

One summer it was necessary for Will to go to the hospital for surgery. Fergus stayed to look after the house and farm, lying for hours at a time in front of the door, pricking up his ears expectantly every time a car passed, moving only when someone came to feed him.

But when Will's closest neighbors, the Hardustys, learned that Will would have to spend six weeks convalescing at a nursing home, they came and got Fergus and kept him at their farm. They had no other dog, and soon I was hearing reports around the neighborhood that Fergus had developed quite a crush on Mrs. Hardusty; that it was hard to budge him from under her kitchen table, day or night; that he liked her husband, Fruitcake, almost as well.

Will finally gained enough strength to come home, and the next day I drove down to the corner to see him, and found him sitting on the porch. As I took the chair next to his I said, "I suppose Fergus will be coming home now."

"Fruitcake brought him home yesterday," Will answered. "Fergus, he only stayed around a couple of hours, then he took off. Reckon he's back at the Hardustys."

"He'll come back," I said. "You're going to have to give him some time, you know. He might go back and forth between you for awhile." Will didn't answer.

I dropped in the next day, and there was still no sign of Fergus. When I asked about him, Will replied, "He ain't back," so brusquely that I knew I wasn't going to mention it again.

Every afternoon that week I dropped in for a few minutes, and as we sat rocking and talking, Fergus's absence hung heavy in the air. His mat—an old, washed-out, pink throw rug—had been folded neatly and wedged into a corner where the porch joined the house. Then the weekend came up, and I didn't get over for a few days, and when I did get back I was surprised to see Fergus lying on his old mat, dozing with his front legs stretched out in front of him and his head down on his paws. Will was rocking and reading his newspaper, and the whole scene looked to me as if time had moved back a summer.

"I see you got him back," I said, "and he really looks good." I meant it. I had never seen Fergus's coat looking so smooth and glossy.

"You mean ol' Fergus over there?" Will asked carelessly, folding up the *Peatville Daily News* and giving it to me, as he always did, to take home. "Fruitcake brought him back again day 'fore yesterday. I went and got his old brush down from the high shelf over there and spent an hour or so workin' him over. We like to got acquainted again. Wouldn't surprise me none if it come back to him that him and me been together for more'n seven year. That's some longer than he's been over down the road.

"Howsomever, he takes a notion to go off again," and here Will looked over his glasses at Fergus and raised his voice. "I'm not goin' to fuss with him no more. I know a party over town has sheep dog pups for sale, and I'm goin' in and get me one."

Fergus looked straight into Will's eyes without lifting his head from his paws, and he didn't twitch a muscle. He was the one with the sharp ears in the family; the one, as Will often said, who had not been behind the door when the brains were passed out. I think he got the message. He stuck around.

Every time I bring Will a pie, usually pumpkin because this is his favorite, Will thinks he has to give me something in return. He thinks it is up to him to see that I don't run out of "readin' material." He is a voracious reader himself, and the first good day of the week will find him driving to Peatville in his '65 Ford Fairlane to pick up the week's reading at his favorite newsstand. He buys most of the western horse magazines, then loads up on paperback novels. He is partial to the Harlequin Romances, and he is always scrounging around for a western novel he hasn't already read. He has bushelbaskets of books sitting around in his spare bedroom, including most of the novels of Zane Grey, Ernest Haycox, Max Brand, Luke Short, and Louis L'Amour. He hauls these out and tells me to take my pick, and if I don't remember to bring them back, well, I shouldn't worry about it. One day I was shocked down to my toes to see a brand-new paperback copy of *Fear of Flying* among the lot. I hurriedly borrowed it and never brought it back. I hope he hadn't read it. It wasn't thumbed through at all. He probably thought it was about airplanes, which fascinate him, although he has never ridden in one.

Reading is Will's winter delight, but in the summer his garden occupies him. This is mostly a labor of love, because he has a very delicate stomach. He doesn't eat more than you can put in a thimble. His tomatoes are always earlier and bigger than anyone else's. He gives most of them away to his sisters-in-law in Peatville and other friends who don't have gardens. He grows a special pumpkin with seeds he's kept going from years back. After you've eaten a pie from one of his pumpkins, it spoils you forever for ordinary pumpkin pie. Some years, when fall comes, Will has too many pumpkins, so he puts them out at the road and sells a few. After he's sold all he thinks he's going to sell, he leaves them out on the stand at night to be stolen. In just a night or two, they are all gone. This really tickles him. "Someone sure needs 'em worse than I do!" he says.

There's just one thing I don't like about Will—as a matter of fact, drives me wild. He won't gossip. I drop in for a short visit with some interesting news of a divorce or litigation of some sort concerning someone we both know, hoping that he will have something of his own to contribute to the story. But he usually silences me with, "Well, I guess there isn't anything you or me can do about that, is there?"

The only derogatory remark I've ever heard him make about anyone was about a former neighbor who was forever borrowing Will's tools. Once he borrowed Will's brand new Rototiller and brought it back, weeks later; both neighbor and Rototiller smashed. This moved Will to say, "He's a right decent human bein' when he's sober, which I'm sorry to say ain't often enough."

According to Will, there is scarcely anyone who isn't a decent human being, or at the very least, has got it in him to be one if he'd straighten up just a lick. This benign attitude toward his fellowman seems to be reciprocal. When Will sits on his porch of a summer evening, he is almost within touching distance of the automobiles that must slow down to make the right-angle turn in the road. A car comes along every few minutes, because a golf course is contiguous to Will's acreage, and the golfers are going home to dinner. The sports cars and the hatchbacks and the Cadillacs come racing down the road because the men driving them have chased the ball too long; the roast and the spouse are shriveling at home. But the men are forced to brake as they take the sharp curve, and when they do they see Will rocking on his porch, and they wave jauntily to him. Will raises his arm slowly and waves back, his great gnarled fingers curled in a majestic salute.

Sitting with him one evening, I asked him if he knew all these men. "Don't know a lickin' one of 'em," he answered. "But they all know me."

12
Wagon and Six

*T*he perennial joke in the family is this: that we could have made it big in the pony business if we could have stocked just two types of ponies: (1) A pregnant fifty-two-inch mare, trained to ride and drive, priced at seventy-five dollars, and (2) A wide selection—in the manner of used auto parts—of the missing half of a matched pair that make up the pony hitches for the fancy antique farm wagons shown at county fairs, none priced over fifty dollars.

The first time a "wagon-hitch" man came looking for the missing half of a matched pair, and said he had to have a forty-seven-and-three-quarter-inch sorrel pony with a blaze face, silver mane, two white fore ankles and one rear sock—this pony to be matched up with a similar one he had at home—I thought he was kidding.

"Would a pink dimple in the right cheek spoil it for you?" I asked.

When he answered guardedly, "Well, I'd have to see him first," then I knew he was dead serious.

Wagon-hitch men are a breed unto themselves. They are generally middle-aged, well set in life, own a small farm or a house in the country with a few acres on which they have erected a prefabricated pole barn or shed; they often work in a factory, very likely on the eleven-to-seven night shift, and they spend their days dreaming and scheming how just once in their lives they can win the blue ribbon in the Draft Pony Hitch Four-Wheel Wagon class at a county fair. (Their county or a contiguous county.) And if they finally manage to snag the coveted first prize, do they rest on it? Not on your blue rosette they don't! This only serves to whet their whistles. Their next goal is to win it more times at more fairs than any of their damn friends in the game. And then—on to the big time—the state fair!

Wagon-hitch men all know each other. They know each other's ponies, each other's wagons, but most of all they know each other's Achilles heels. Friendship is what gets them into each other's barns to take inventory. When they get into the show-ring, it is each man for himself. Let the poor devil whose wagon wheel comes off take the hindmost.

Money—and the way they spend it—is what puts wagon-hitch men in a class by themselves. Up to a point, they are the last of the big spenders. It is not unusual for them to have twenty thousand dollars tied up in all the accoutrements of a fancy rig—even more if they are driving two or three span. It is nothing at all for them to spend several thousand dollars for a wagon custom made to their design by the Amish, with ten coats of paint, twenty coats of varnish, intricate wood-spoked wheels, and ornate decals. They don't blink twice about spending another five to ten thousand dollars for a four- or six-horse trailer in which to haul their ponies, and a flat-bed truck or trailer to transport their wagons from show to show. They plunk down anywhere from five hundred to fifteen hundred dollars cash for a fine leather brass-studded harness for each pony, again often custom made by the Amish—and if they have a six-pony hitch this can add up. But when it comes to the ponies themselves—the *sine qua non* of the whole outfit— right here is where the wagon-hitch men veer off from the last of the big spenders and enter cheap city. Fifty dollars a head is their speed. For the missing half of a matched pair, yet.

The thing about a wagon-hitch man is that his macho stems from being a horse trader *par excellence*. If he doesn't have the moxie to pick up good ponies for chicken feed, he doesn't deserve to be in the club. All you have to do is to walk through their camping grounds at the county fair and you will hear wagon-hitch men telling each other how they had purchased their ponies with pocket money, and the conversation always ends with, "I got more in the harness than in the horse, you can bet on that!"

The reason I know so much about wagon-hitch men is that they are wild for Welsh ponies. The Welsh is the only pony around that can be tacked up to look like a miniature draft horse—which is, of course, what the draft-pony classes are all about. First come the Belgians, the Percherons, and the Clydesdales, and then come the minihorses. Shetland ponies are too small for this purpose, and Hackneys would be ridiculous; the Welsh pony is the nearest thing to an old-fashioned carriage pony—short in the back, short in the leg, with a naturally high tail set. He has the balanced movement necessary to pull weight. His action extends from the shoulder, and he has his hocks well under him. And because our own particular Welsh ponies had denser bone and shorter coupling than any other Welsh ponies in the vicinity, the wagon-hitch men were attracted to our farm like sailors to the Sirens.

At least once a week during the summer I could count on one of them driving in. The one who came most often was Helmet Tearson. Helmet came twice a year for maybe ten or twelve years. When I first knew him he was just starting out at the fairs showing two ponies to a wagon, but in coming years he worked himself up to a four-pony hitch, and then to a wagon-and-six, the class that pretty well separated the men from the boys. There were as many as a dozen entries in the two-pony class, but by the time the wagon-and-six came up, the entries had whittled down to three or four. Still, Helmet was somewhat of a fringe man, on the outside looking in, because the blue ribbon had always eluded him. He was not a very good driver. He was heavy handed on the reins, and his ponies were known to have the hardest mouths on the wagon circuit. His wagon friends called him, ironically, "Hackamore." Far from being offended, Helmet found it amusing, and had emblazoned on his pony trailer:

CAUTION! SHOW PONIES
Helmet "Hackamore" Tearson

But Helmet never stopped trying to improve himself— with my ponies. Around the middle of April, and then again in late fall, whenever I saw a yellow pickup coming up the lane, I knew it was Helmet. He was always wearing bib overalls and a Benjamin Moore paint cap, and he unfailingly gave the impression that *this time, this time around*— unlike the other times he'd been here, when he'd acted serious but ended up not being serious at all—this time he was really serious about paying a fair price for a pony. And such was the nature of his sincerity that I believed him.

When Helmet stepped out of his pickup onto the driveway, his dark face with the day-old beard creased ingratiatingly in a wide smile, he was invariably on the acute lookout for the missing half of a matched pair. "You got a strawberry roan mare just a smidgeon under forty-nine inches, with maybe a little age on her? I don't want no spring chicken to outdistance what I got to hitch her with. 'Course now she has got to have four white stockings, you understand. 'Course now you know I don't want her roachy neither."

When I answered that I had no strawberry-roan mares at all—let alone roachy ones—Helmet expressed wonder that I would let myself get into such a down-and-out condition. He had come, he said, prepared to pay a good price for the right animal.

"I knowed I should of come sooner," he clucked. "But now I'm here, I might as well see what else you got."

What else I had, this particular time, was a stunning pair of perfectly matched dappled-gray mares grazing in the front meadow. I had named them, enticingly, Rio and Flamenco, and I had them out front to lure pony-lookers off the road. They were granddaughters of Egrett and born in consecutive years out of her daughter Hummingbird, who had been bred back to Beau, her sire, to produce these beautiful fillies. Our policy was to keep all of Egrett and Widowbird's daughters for breeding stock and to put up for sale all of the granddaughters.

Helmet turned now toward the front meadow as if he had just that very moment noticed Rio and Flamenco. "I see you got a couple grays out there. They wouldn't be for sale, would they?" I nodded. "What kind of price you got on 'em?"

"Six hundred and fifty dollars for the pair," I answered, not batting an eye.

Helmet didn't bat an eye, either. He just allowed as how he'd have to look at them. He hitched up his overalls, walked down into the meadow, and walked round and around the mares, jerking up a stem of bluegrass to ruminate on as he walked. He didn't say anything for a long time, and then he started to talk in a low reflective voice, making judgments. In his opinion, they wouldn't make what you would call a first-class harness pair because one was at least a quarter-of-an-inch taller than the other. What's more, one was long in the face and the other was not, I could certainly see that, couldn't I? And the one had maybe the least little bit of a tendency to be cow-hocked, while the other one, if he was to be purely truthful about it, leaned just a mite toward the calf-kneed.

Finally, Helmet went up to Rio, broadside, walked backward ten paces, squatted on his haunches, sited his eyes under her belly, and squinted long and hard. He went through the same procedure with Flamenco. Then he stood up, sighed, and delivered the *coup de grâce.*

"I kind of hate to be the one to tell you this," he said, "but you know I suspicioned it all along? Both of them mares has got too much daylight under them!"

Could you beat his rotten luck, Helmet said. Here he had come prepared to pay a good price for a pony, and what's more he was always on the sharp lookout for a good matched pair, and now this had to happen to him. He'd have to think about it a little while longer but he might, he said, he just might be willing to take the grays off my hands and do his best to whip them into some kind of shape, but he couldn't in all good conscience pay more than a hundred dollars for the pair.

That's when I escorted him rather precipitously back to his pickup.

My visits from Helmet Tearson were like childbirth pains—after a certain length of time you forget about them. Helmet seemed to know the exact amount of time it took for me to forget about the more painful parts of his visits, and that is when he showed up again. He tried to talk me out of Rio and Flamenco at least a half-dozen times in the next few years, until I finally sold them to a nice young couple from Indiana, who thought six hundred and fifty dollars was a fair price for such a beautiful pair of mares. For another long period of time he had his eyes on Dasher and Prancer, who would have made a handsome harness pair, but at various times he found them to be not only bench-legged and coon-footed, but goose-rumped, and he suspected they might have a tendency to cross fire; but worst of all, they had too much daylight under them, and he couldn't find it in his heart to offer me more than a hundred dollars for the pair.

The truth is that all of the visits I had from wagon-hitch men over a period of about fifteen years resulted in the sale of not a single pony. And finally they stopped coming, because Helmet Tearson stopped coming, and the word always gets around.

Here is the way it happened:

I had been telling Witt for years about my experiences with Helmet Tearson, but Witt had never met him—had never been at home when Helmet came—because Helmet always came in the middle of the week, when Witt was at his office. But one balmy October Wednesday, Witt decided to stay home and mulch some bushes around the house with the leaves that were piling up on the driveway; and I decided to take a day off from the farm and go into South Metropolis on a shopping spree. When I came home late in the afternoon, Witt beckoned me to a stop as I pulled onto the driveway. He obviously had something amusing to tell me, because he was grinning.

"You know that fellow, Tearsome or Fearsome or whatever his name is, who has been bothering you about ponies for years?"

"Tearson."

"That's the one," Witt said. "I don't think he'll be bothering you any more."

This is how Witt told it: He said it was around midday and he was about ready to knock off the mulching and go into the house to fix himself some lunch, when a yellow pickup drove in and a man in bib overalls got out, said he was looking for the missing half of a matched pair, and described the pony he wanted in detail. Witt had told him we had no such animal, and then the man, who had at first impressed Witt as a likable sort, asked to see the rest of our ponies. Witt was about to tell him to wander around, help himself, have a look at anything he wanted to see.

"But then," Witt said, "something kind of snapped in my

brain. Maybe it was the yellow pickup, or then again maybe it was the Benjamin Moore paint cap. Anyway, I said, 'Your name wouldn't be Pearson, would it?"

"Tearson," Helmet had answered with a wide smile, pleased that his fame had spread through the family.

"That's close enough," Witt had said. "Aren't you the fellow who has been coming around here for years, always letting my wife think you are going to buy a pony for a fair price, and then offering her fifty dollars for it?"

At this point, Helmet had apparently got on the defensive and answered that things were tough all over, that the hitch business was not a money-making proposition, was in fact only a hobby, that there was no way he or any of his wagon friends could spend more money than that on their ponies—no way.

"So," said Witt, winding up his story, "I told old Tearsome to get going, and I don't think you'll see him again."

"You mean you *ran him off the place?*" I asked, rather horrified now.

"Let's just say I invited him not to come back."

"Poor Mr. Tearson!"

"What do you mean, poor Mr. Tearsome?" Witt said. "I don't understand you at all. I did you a favor getting rid of this tightwad who thinks he's some horsetrader, and now all I get is poor Mr. Pearson."

"Tearson."

I knew in my heart that what Witt said was true. Helmet had conned his way onto this farm for years and years, taking up hours of my time and running down my ponies and getting away with it. The rat deserved exactly what he got.

What I wouldn't admit to anyone was this: when things got a little dull on the farm, I could always look forward to the time when Helmet would be coming around to stir things up a bit—even if it was just my ire. And for that one exquisite

moment that always came—when he would finally pace
himself backward, hunker down, squint and take aim, and
then make his pronouncement that yet another of my ponies
had flunked the daylight test—for that one moment I could
put up with almost anything.

13

The Dogs:
The Versatile Litter

*T*he morning after Holbein died, a fine snow sifted over the farm and blanketed the old German shepherd's grave at the end of the garden. A strange stillness lay in the air. None of us mentioned that the stillness was all the more strange because in his last years Holbein had seldom barked. Two years went by, and no one mentioned getting another dog, either.

Witt came in from the barn one sultry Sunday morning in late June and said there was a stray dog in the barn. "She's carrying cargo," he said, "and it looks to me like she's about ready to unload it."

The children and I went out to find the little hound lying just inside the barn door. When she saw us she bobbed her nose up and down and pounded her tail furiously on the barn floor. She was speckled blue all over, except for a huge black patch on the side of her belly and another draped over her rump. She had floppy brown ears, the set of which defied any breed, enormous brown eyes, and she was pregnant, all right. When we lured her out on the driveway, she was so weak she couldn't get the load she was carrying over the barn stoop, and she fell on her nose. She was so skinny her backbone was pulled away from the rest of her and stuck straight up in the air. One back leg had all but given up, and knuckled over when she walked.

We gave her a bowl of cat food, and she wolfed it down. She ravaged a quart of milk and rattled the bowl furiously around the driveway to get another drop. She polished off half a dozen stale doughnuts, each at a gulp.

Meanwhile I was working myself up into a fine rage. "You *know* someone ditched her. The lowest form of life is someone who ditches a pet, but these rats who drop their *pregnant* pets should be parboiled in purgatory."

I said I was going in to call the dog warden.

"You know what's going to happen to her at the pound, don't you?" Stoyer said. "Whoosh, in the gas chamber, just like that. Strays are supposed to be held for three days to give people time to come in and claim them, but I've heard if they don't think an animal can hold up that long to litter they'll destroy it before then, rather than have the litter on their hands. Remember that story in the *Peatville Daily News* about somebody's dog named Major? He wasn't even—you know, he was a male, and even he got it on the first or second day—"

"Spare me the gory details," I snapped. Instead of calling the dog warden, I telephoned an ad in to the *Peatville Daily News*—"Found: Very Pregnant Bluetick Hound."

That, apparently, was the signal for all owners of very pregnant bluetick hounds to go underground. The telephone sat and sulked for four days, while the hound was cleaning out my refrigerator like there was no tomorrow. In twenty-four hours there was nothing left but the pickles and the mayonnaise. I had to dip into my cache of a dozen cans of evaporated milk, which I had stored on our emergency shelf in the basement in case of sneak attack. I moaned that on a farm one never knows in what form a sneak attack will come.

The little hound was not going to give up an inch of her entrenchment. She very quickly established a position on the lawn, from which she could watch every movement in and out of the back door. All we had to do was wiggle the doorknob from the inside and her tail started thumping wildly. Let a face appear in the kitchen window and her head would go up and those enormous brown eyes would light up expectantly, the tail going into motion again. Stoyer and Liz began to call her Patches, because, like the girl in the song, she was always "watching the door." This, despite the fact that I had warned them, no names; names could only lead to a personal relationship.

When it became obvious that the lost-and-found ad was not going to produce a grateful owner who would rush out to be tearfully reunited with his pregnant hound, we entertained the notion that perhaps she was not as far along in her pregnancy as we thought, and she could still be spayed.

I telephoned Dock, and he said he could still spay her if her mammary glands weren't yet enlarged. I rushed out to look at her mammary glands. They were out to here. "You might as well take her to the pound as bring her here," Dock said. "In the condition you describe her, she'd die on me."

I hung up the phone. "Dock says take her to the pound," I told the children, cagily shifting the responsibility.

Two pairs of eyes looked hard and unblinking at me. I said we might as well get it over with, and told Stoyer to go into the barn and get a chain while I revved up the Jeep. When we came out the door, the hound set up her wild tail thumping as she lay in her sentinel post on the lawn. Liz ran to her and sat down beside her. "Say, do you know this dog just loves to sit in laps?" she asked.

The moment Liz flopped down, the hound climbed into her lap, dragging the huge bag of puppies in with her, and just curled up.

I knew when I was licked.

"We've never had puppies before," I said. "It might be kind of fun."

Instead of going to the pound, we went to the grocery. We bought three cases of evaporated milk and all the pork liver in all the groceries in Peatville. Although pork liver sells for half of what beef liver does, it is difficult to find. I guess the strong taste turns people off. But it is simply loaded with vitamins A and C and niacin.

I boiled the precious four pounds of liver I had collected and put it in the refrigerator, feeding the little hound half a pound a day, along with dry dog chow, three quarts of milk, and all the meat and vegetable scraps from the table. She soon became so spoiled she wouldn't eat the dog chow. But what a sweet tooth she had! She must have been brought up on stale doughnuts, for those were her favorites. To my amateur-midwife's eye, it looked as though I had about two weeks to fatten her up for the whelping. In the shape she was in, it was a risky business at best.

One thing was certain, with all of her liabilities, the hound was not feeling sorry for herself. She had most certainly come a dreary hungry trail, but you could tell in her eyes she knew she had reached the end of it. I told the kids to stop calling her Patches. Patches in the song was a tragic figure, and this dog was living it up. She was flying so high she didn't even feel the baggage underneath. We named her Dewbug, because she was always crawling around in the high dewy grass in the early morning to cool herself off. Besides that, she was mighty fresh.

The guessing game began as to how many puppies Dewbug would have. She was nothing but puppies. A skeleton and a hank of hair dragging around a bag of puppies. Dock hazarded over the telephone that she'd have four to six. One elegant lady in high heels and a floppy hat, who came to look at ponies and who described herself as "knowledgeable about dogs," proclaimed that Dewbug had already *had* her puppies. "It's obvious that parturition has already occurred," she sniffed. "Look at her mammary glands." When I pointed out that our mares often dripped milk like that for a few days before foaling, she said rather loudly, "Dogs are not mares," and stepped down hard on the accelerator.

The United Parcel man said, "That bitch is carrying twelve or I miss my guess." This struck such terror in my soul that I took Dewbug down to Will Suttle's and asked him to repeat his declaration that to those old eyes of his she was carrying two, one on either side.

"You can expect a pair of *big* ones off of her and that's it," he saged. "See how balanced she is?"

Considering the fact that one back leg had all but collapsed under its burden, while the other one was holding up rather well, I couldn't help but feel his opinion lacked some credence.

On the Fourth of July, Dewbug had her puppies. That is the day, as well as the three succeeding days, which I have down in my diary as one word: harrowing.

Independence Day did not augur well early on. The day broke hot, with nary a breeze to stir the air. Witt left early to spend the holiday weekend with his mother. Liz woke up with an unbelievably hideous case of poison ivy on both hands, meat-red and swollen from having scratched them in her sleep. I covered her hands with calomime lotion and bandages, and she lay back helpless as an heiress on her bed.

I suspected that Dewbug's time had run out when I went to the barn to feed her and found she had burrowed herself at least a foot deep under the partition in the middle of the barn. As I pulled her up I reflected on the fact that animals, most of the time with such good instincts in difficult situations, often have rotten judgment when it comes to choosing a place for giving birth. Widowbird, of course, marooned herself in a corner above flood waters when she had her first foal. Mourning Dove always foaled in a high spot right next to the road fence, where curious motorists would stop and gawk at the entire operation. And one of our cats littered in the corner of the box stall already occupied by our Shetland stallion, Ganymede. The only thing that saved her and the kittens was that she was wedged in a corner so tightly that the stallion couldn't get his foot in to strike her.

I put a chain on Dewbug and had to drag her to the doghouse, which Stoyer had prepared nicely for the whelping. It wasn't really a doghouse, but an old shed with a concrete floor about eight feet square. I don't know the original purpose for which it was built, but the former owner had used it to store the oil and gasoline for his farm machinery. It had been Holbein's house for twelve years. Now Stoyer had scrubbed it out and had put a good thick bed of straw over the concrete. Dewbug flatly rejected this private and sanitary maternity room and twice broke away from me to burrow back down in her dirty hole in the barn. I had to call Stoyer for help and we managed to get the door shut on her. She set up a nasty whine.

An hour later we came back and she was still whining and scratching at the door. We decided this wasn't her day after all and we let her out. She went right back to the barn and burrowed back down in her dirt hole, gave me a defiant look and started labor contractions. That did it. Back she went into the shed. The howl she set up this time would have impressed the coyotes I used to hear in the night back in North Dakota. Stoyer and I ran buckets of water in the barn to muffle the noise while we watered the stallions in the box stalls.

The howling stopped as if it had been sliced off in midair. I winked at Stoyer. We leisurely finished watering the ponies, then went back to the shed and listened at the door.

The slurpiest, slimiest, suckingest sound imaginable came from inside. We opened the door a crack and peered into the dim shed, which has only one tiny north window. Dewbug was lying in a far corner with a shiny wet ball of black puppy between her paws. She was really working him over with her tongue, pulling off membranes, nosing him from side to side, every few moments biting into the puppy's throat so hard that Stoyer winced and grabbed his own throat. So absorbed was she in her task that she neither heard nor saw us. We closed the door and crept away.

I told Stoyer I was giving him the maternity watch. I had

things to do in the house, with Liz languishing away on her hot bed of pain in her room upstairs. All through the simmering afternoon he came to the door with his periodic reports.

First report: "Now she's got four."

"If she stops at that, I'll forgive her."

Second report: "Now she's got six."

"Good grief. Are you sure you didn't count one twice?"

"No way. They're all different patterns and colors."

Third report: "She just had number seven. I think it must be the last. She's so worn out she didn't bother to clean him up. I think she wants out."

Now it was hot dusk, and when I opened the door of the shed Dewbug wearily shook herself free of puppies and stumbled stiffly out to the back alfalfa field where she walked round and around, having a difficult time. I waited patiently and understood. I had experienced parturition a couple of times myself. When she returned, she hungrily snapped up a bowl of dog chow and warm milk, then sank down again with her puppies, utterly limp and damp as a dishrag.

I stroked her head. "Poor Dewbug. Don't worry. Seven is bad. But it could have been worse."

If she could have talked, she would have said, "You don't know the half of it, sister!"

When I went back at dawn to check on her, all hell seemed to have broken loose. There were puppies everywhere. To my horrified eyes, there seemed to be dozens of puppies, mewling and squirming and crawling over a very confused and almost terrified dog. One black-and-white puppy lay dead in the middle of the floor. I started to count. I counted thirteen puppies, and then Dewbug suddenly shook herself free of puppies, stood up, and there was another one lying dead underneath her which she had crushed and didn't even know it. I touched the dead puppy and something just curled up inside me and I rushed out.

The day was already blistering. The weatherman had said

the night before that we could expect temperatures near the hundred-degree mark for the next few days. I leaned against the shed and broke out into a cold sweat. *How was I going to keep a dozen puppies alive in this kind of heat with Dewbug in the shape she was in?* I swore a horrible hex on all those faceless humans out there who drop their pregnant pets, and then I went into the house and told the children that Dewbug had given birth to seven more puppies in the night.

I gave Stoyer an empty cat-chow bag and told him to go into the shed, put the two dead puppies into it, and bury them. I was ashamed of myself, but I couldn't touch those dead puppies again. Stoyer was my rock. He didn't flinch from doing things that had to be done, such as picking up dead things and burying them.

It became an hour-to-hour battle for survival in the deadly heat. I was seized with the phobia that all the puppies were going to die. This was intensified when, in the middle of the searing afternoon, another puppy expired. Stoyer buried him.

Every two hours all day and through the night, I brought Dewbug a pint of cold milk, which she lapped while nursing the puppies. Afterwards I rubbed her with a cloth rung out in cool water. I kept the door of the shed tightly closed because the coolness coming up from the cement was the only coolness anywhere. I boiled a large brisket and gave her the succulent beef stew mixed with liver. The next morning another puppy was dead. Now I was sure they were all going to die. Again I gave Stoyer an empty cat-chow bag and asked him to bury the puppy.

There were ten puppies left, and for the first time I took a good look at them. A black, who looked like he'd had a jump on the rest—probably the firstborn; two blueticks that looked like Dewbug; four spotted puppies and three solid-colored ones—burgundy, brown, and yellow.

Brown and yellow were tiny and rather weak, but squawky as heck.

Next I took stock of the larder. I carefully counted teats. Dewbug had ten, but the two nearest her forelegs seemed to be token goods at best, and the next two were not much better. The four in the middle were active producers, but not exactly fountains. The real gushers were the two nearest her hind legs.

I devised a survival plan for the brown and the yellow puppy. Whenever Dewbug had been out on a break and came in with a full supply of milk, I snuggled the two weak puppies up to the lush teats between her back legs, and kept the other puppies away for a few minutes while the tiny ones gorged themselves.

I was terrified that Dewbug either was going to become ill and die or get sick of the whole business, run away, and leave me with ten orphaned puppies. I didn't let her out of my sight for a minute. Every four hours I took her out on a leash and walked the fields with her so I wouldn't have to let her go.

With daylight on the third morning, I was certain there were going to be more dead puppies. Again I pressed the cat-chow bag into Stoyer's hands and asked him to go into the shed, pick them up, and bury them. He came back and said they were all alive.

The near-hundred-degree heat continued and I was like a zombie, going back and forth from the house to the shed with a pitcher of milk every two hours, sponging Dewbug, walking her, making stews. I didn't go to bed until after the eleven P.M. feeding. I set my alarm for three A.M., staggered out to the shed with pitcher and flashlight, tried not to step on puppies while I held the bowl for Dewbug. She wouldn't drink unless the puppies were actually suckling. She seemed to think she was passing the milk directly on to them in this way. Then I took her out on a leash into the night. The two of us seemed to be walking utterly alone on top of the world, with the sky so close I could reach out and pluck the stars from the handle of the Big Dipper and stroke the

Northern Lights, and still Dewbug had not found a spot that suited her.

Flying saucer sightings were running rampant at this time, and I thought, good enough for the little green men if they are frightened back into outer space by a crazy-looking blue dog with black patches, backbone sticking up in the air, stomach dragging on the ground, running around in circles in a stubbled field of alfalfa, wildly searching for something, even as she dragged along on a chain an even crazier-looking wild-haired woman in a yellow nightgown and barefoot.

Again on the fourth morning I gave Stoyer the cat-chow bag and asked him to go and look for dead puppies. He came back a few minutes later, tossed the bag in my direction and said, "I'm not going along with this silly routine any longer. There aren't any more of those puppies going to croak. They're getting to look like fat little things to me."

I didn't believe a word of it, until Will Suttle came over later in the day and we took him in to see the puppies. I graciously did not mention his "big pair" prognostication, nor did he. He took a long, long look. Then he sighed.

"That is a larruping litter if I ever seen one," he said solemnly.

"Do you suppose that's good or bad?" I whispered anxiously to Stoyer.

"Has a pretty good sound to me," Stoyer whispered back.

Only then did I admit to myself that the puppies were, in fact, getting plump and vigorous. All that liver and Vitamin D milk passing through Dewbug was starting to pay off. My system for giving the brown puppy and the yellow one first lick was doing the job for them. They were still tiny, but feisty. And then Dewbug herself devised a system which I would never have believed if I hadn't seen it. One day I came out and there were puppies in two distinct nests on opposite sides of the shed. Dewbug would nurse one set of puppies for awhile until she had put them to sleep, and then she'd get up, walk across the room to the second set of puppies, and feed *them*. I wish I could say she had divided them up evenly, five and five. But she wasn't quite that smart. She had them four and six.

The author of a puppy-care book I pored over said he had never been able to get a puppy to lapping milk under fourteen days. I felt we must try to beat that record. Dewbug was getting to look more like a doppelgänger every day, with ten lusty mouths draining her like a sieve. Liz's poison-ivied hands had now healed enough so that she could help me, and when the puppies were nine days old we took small stools out into the shed, along with two saucers and some warm milk. The puppies were starting to open their eyes a crack and crawl around on rubbery legs. We each sat down on a stool, took a puppy on our laps, along with a saucer and a teaspoon of milk on it. We put the saucer up to his nose and let him sniff the milk. The first day there was mostly sneezing and messing, but by the twelfth day all of the puppies were lapping milk nicely out of saucers while sitting on our laps. For the next week, until the puppies were able to stand up and drink by themselves, we spent hours and hours just sitting out in the shed lap-feeding puppies. It was fun, and a legitimate excuse for endless cuddling. (The house rules were still in effect that none of us must form a personal attachment.) With all the giggling and the squealing, we always lost track of which puppies had been fed and which hadn't, so the lapping sessions always ended with a test run: picking each puppy up and feeling for the hard round belly.

The day I thought the puppies could survive on their own without their mother's help, I don't know which of us felt giddier—Dewbug or I. I threw off her chain and let her run. She spent hours out in the back meadow, first on the trail of one rabbit, then another, loping and whirling and doing figure eights. I was delighted to see that she was actually a young fast hound with a fine scent.

The puppies were picking up steam, too, and could no longer be confined to their shed. With old warped boards he found in the corncrib, Stoyer built out from the shed a tight pen four feet high and about twelve feet square so that the puppies could run in and out through a small dog door. Dewbug could come and go at will by jumping over the pen. Every day, while Stoyer scrubbed out the shed and put fresh straw in the pen, Liz and I rode herd on ten puppies loose on the driveway. This ended up in a stampede and roundup that left us limp the rest of the day. Along with speed, the puppies' appetites picked up. They ingested mountains of cooked Cream of Wheat, oatmeal, canned soups by the case. One historic week at the grocery I bought sixty cans of evaporated milk—and in another week it was gone.

The day came when Dewbug jumped in the pen with her puppies and they attacked her like a school of piranhas. She yelped and ran for her life. They would soon be bursting the bastions of Stoyer's makeshift pen. They had literally become, in Will's words, "a larruping litter." It was time to wean the puppies; time to find new homes for them. And it wasn't going to be easy.

The children and I carefully analyzed the classified dog ads in the South Metropolis newspapers. Dogs did not seem to be selling hot off the presses. The dog ads went on ad infinitum, up one column and down the other. There were three types of ads: first, the registered dogs: the AKC's; second, the dogs advertised as a specific breed but with no mention of registration papers; and last, the "darling puppies free to good homes."

On one thing I was adamant. We were dispensing no "darling puppies free to good homes"—except to friends of impeccable character. Anything free is most often expendable. Even a ten-dollar price tag might be the kind of investment that would prevent one of our puppies from suffering the same fate that had befallen Dewbug.

We decided that our best bet was to advertise the puppies as a specific breed—with no mention of pedigree or papers. But what breed? At the moment, few looked as if they belonged in the same family!

There were six males: the firstborn, the big black puppy we first saw Dewbug cleaning up, looked like a bloodhound; two were bluetick hounds like Dewbug; two resembled black-and-tan coonhounds; one was a beagle type, but had the glossy burgundy color of an Irish setter.

Among the four females, there were twins that resembled tricolored beagles; the third, also a beagle type, was colored an exotic pale blond; the fourth female was a rich chocolate, with the handsome head of a Weimaraner.

The children and I finally came up with what we considered an ingenious plan: we would advertise a specific breed—one at a time—until we had sold the puppies who resembled this breed; then we would go on to the next breed.

On the weekend the puppies were five weeks old we ran our first classified in the *Peatville Daily News:*

BLUETICK HOUND PUPPIES
out of A-1 hunting dog
$10

The telephone rang. We had rustled up a customer. We just had time to lock the other puppies up in the shed and put the two bluetick puppies on display outside in the pen before the customer drove in. He was a burly man in a red hunting cap who said he trained and sold hunting dogs. He instantly scooped up one of the puppies and ignored the other. "Damn!" he said. "Here's a little sucker should be worth a sawbuck!"

As he was putting the puppy in his car, he tilted his head toward the puppy shed, which was shuddering with eight puppies trying to break the door down, and he shouted over the heinous yipping and yapping. "You must buy and sell dogs, huh? Sounds like a hundred of 'em in there!"

We were jubilant that we had sold our first puppy, but the ad ran continuously for a week, and we received no more calls. Then Dutch brought her two small children out one day and they fell in love with one of the two black-and-tan coonhound puppies and took him home with them. We decided it was time to change the ad and try to sell the other one. A new ad went out:

HANDSOME COONHOUND PUP
Black and tan, smart, fast,
A-1 hunting prospect. $10

This ad unearthed three unshaven men in bib-overalls, all listing slightly to the wind as they climbed out of a battered pickup. They passed the black-and-tan puppy roughly among them, starting him quivering as they blew on him with great malty breaths. "We'll take him," the one bellowed who could still talk. "I'll write you a check."

I was up a tree. I surely wasn't going to let this tippled threesome have the puppy, but if I said, "You can't have the pup because I don't like your looks," I would have a brouhaha on my hands. So I fell back on the classic delaying tactic most farm women use when their husbands are away. It's called "my husband says." Witt hopes in hell, or wherever he goes, he won't have to listen to a playback of all the dastardly things he has said in absentia on this farm. "My husband says it's too wet for you to make the hay today. . . .My husband says I can't let anyone take a pony off the place until it's paid for. . . . My husband says if he finds you hunting on this place one more time he'll turn you in and he means business. . . ."

To the bowsers who were now having a great time

manhandling the puppy, I said, "My husband says he'll skin me alive if I accept any checks for these puppies."

My words had the effect of waving a red flag in front of three sotted bulls. "Whassa matter, you don't trust us?" the spokesman yelled belligerently while the others leered at me.

I thought they were going to take the puppy and bolt, when Dewbug, who had been standing unnoticed behind them, gave a low, nasty snarl. The bruisers jumped three feet; and so did I. I had never even seen her curl a lip before, much less snarl; I didn't think she had it in her. The men carefully put the pup down on the driveway and crawled into the pickup. "We're going to the bank and we'll be back with the cash," the one who could still drive said defensively. They didn't return.

This cooled us on advertising coonhounds for a while. We decided that beagles would attract a more genteel customer.

The next ad went out:

CHOCOLATE BEAGLE PUP.
Yummier than candy, glossy coat,
sparkling eyes, exquisite head. $10

We had a two-on-a-match idea in mind for this one. If they wanted a female, we'd show them the chocolate puppy, who, although she had the head of a Weimaraner, could pass in a pinch for a beagle. If they wanted a male, we'd show them the burgundy male, who had the coat of an Irish setter but had a few beagle characteristics.

No inquiries on this one until early Sunday morning, when a distraught man called and said his children's puppy had accidentally been killed the day before, and it would assuage the grief if they could find another one. That chocolate beagle sounded mighty good to his kids. Was it male or female? I took a long breath. Caught in my own trap.

Male, I said. Good, he said, that's what they wanted. A station wagon drove in with four sad-faced kids hanging out of the tailgate. They passed the burgundy puppy gently around between them, with each child getting a few minutes to cuddle the pup. When the four-year-old's turn came, he wrapped his arms around the pup, climbed into the station wagon, sat down, and turned his back on the rest of the world.

"Either we take the pup or you take the kid," his father said, and handed me a ten-dollar bill.

We received one more call from this ad, from a young working girl who said she was scared and lonely living in an apartment and wanted a dog to keep her company. She said she was allergic to chocolate but she was calling on the hunch we might have another color. We did, we did. We sold her the second bluetick puppy.

Four down and six to go, and then there followed a month during which all the prospective dog buyers within our reach resisted every blandishment we could come up with. We tried everything. We advertised the big black puppy as a "rare black beagle," as a "part bloodhound," and finally and desperately as a "big black puppy." Not a nibble. We advertised Chocolate as a "small Weimaraner, no papers," as an "aggressive lady's watchdog," and full circle back to "delicious fudge beagle." None of this was the ticket.

So we turned to signboards, which turned out to be one of our more imaginative phases of sales promotion. We went to the lumber company and bought a piece of 12″ × 24″ plywood, which we painted bright blue on both sides. On top of the blue we painted COONHOUNDS in brilliant yellow with letters six inches high. We hung this sign below our WELSH PONY sign along the road.

When this failed to bring even one automobile in off the road, we replaced it with another sign, this one in red and white, which read BEAGLES on both sides. I got fanciful and drew in one corner an outline of an appealing little beagle with his tail up in the air. Still no traffic up the lane. Stoyer suggested that we put the signs back to back, with COONHOUNDS for the eastbound traffic and BEAGLES for the westbound. No interest there, either. Stoyer thought again and came up with the perfectly obvious answer. It was apparent, he said, that the eastbound traffic wanted beagles, and the westbound traffic was interested only in coonhounds, so what we had to do was switch the signs. We switched. Still no parking problem with the traffic driving in. As a matter of fact, not a single motorist ever drove in as a result of those signs.

Occasionally, though, we did get a telephone inquiry from someone who had seen our newspaper ads and wanted to come out to look at a puppy. If they were interested in coonhounds and were coming from the west, Stoyer raced down to the road on his bicycle to take down the BEAGLE sign. If they wanted beagles and were coming from the east, the COONHOUND sign would come down posthaste.

To keep up our spirits, the kids and I indulged in a bit of fantasy that always threw us into fits of laughter. Just about the only thing we hadn't advertised those pups as were "Alaskan malamutes"—who don't bark. What if we were to run an ad for malamutes, we theorized, and as a result a car drove up the lane and into the driveway. We tried to imagine the looks on the faces of the persons in the car when they heard the horrendous yipping and yapping of all those puppies! When Witt came home from work at night and found us rolling around on the driveway screaming and laughing with tears rolling down our faces, he always said with an injured air, "God! Don't you have anything better to do than sell Alaskan malamutes?"

The signs weren't going to sell any puppies, so back to the ads again. I decided that the copywriter, to wit, myself, had failed to elicit any real desire on the part of the reader to own a puppy. I would correct this fault at once. The pale blond female was the only puppy who had not been given a turn in the ads, so she was to be the benefactress of my new philosophy:

MINK BLOND CHARMER
Give your wife the mink she's always
wanted: an exquisite beagle puppy,
diamond-blue-eyed female $15

I could have spared my brains and my words. On the day the ad ran in the newspaper, the Mink Blond Charmer became unsalable. When Stoyer was helping Liz and me put the puppies back in the pen after cleaning it, Mink accidentally slipped from his hands, and although she only fell a few feet, her leg hit a small, sharp rock. She yelped with pain, and as I scooped her up in my arms she began to tremble uncontrollably. Even though Stoyer was white with remorse, I railed at him for being so careless, as I wildly wracked my mind for what the first-aid books said to do for shock. *Was it hot or cold liquids?* I told Stoyer to bring a saucer of cold water. Mink lapped a few drops and shook even more. *It must be warm liquid.* Liz rushed in the house to heat up some milk, The puppy lapped a little of the warm milk and stopped shaking. She lay very quietly in my lap. Stoyer called Dock, but he was gone for the day. We took her in the Jeep to an animal clinic near Peatville. The X-ray showed she had shattered the bone in three places. The doctor at the clinic set the bone and kept her overnight, and when we picked her up the next day I expected to see a weak, wan, pitiful little puppy. Instead she came out with eyes blazing, already hopping around with considerable skill on her splint, which was really a long crutch attached to her leg. The only place we had available to isolate her was an empty partition in the granary.

She almost went wild with loneliness, after having spent all of her young life romping with nine brothers and sisters. Several times a day I sat down on a small stool in the middle of her tiny room. She raced around and around me endlessly, yipping and barking, chewing at my arms and legs, trying to pull my jeans off, ripping the buttons off my shirt. Occasionally, I carried her into the house, where she whirled around the coffee table like an agile Long John Silver, tore up the newspapers and hid behind the sofa when she knew it was time to go out. Two months, four trips to the clinic, and sixty dollars later, Mink was as good as new. But it was too late for the MINK BLOND CHARMER ad, and, besides, with the kind of worry and care I had invested in her, no one was likely to get her away from me at any price.

In the meantime, we still had five puppies to sell, and they weren't getting any younger, or any cuter. They were getting houndier looking by the day. We still had the big black bloodhound, the twin beagles, the black-and-tan coonhound, and the chocolate Weimaraner. The cool fall winds were blowing and we faced the dreadful possibility of having to go into winter with seven dogs, counting Dewbug—two males and five females, which meant "mixed company" and no quarters in which to separate them. In desperation we printed up small cardboard COONHOUND FOR SALE ads and put them up on all the bulletin boards of the neighborhood grain elevators. We ran two ads a week, in two different newspapers.

Just before Thanksgiving, our luck broke. We sold three puppies in two days. A man and his sad-faced wife, who had been carrying our "aggressive lady's watchdog" ad in her purse for weeks and had "finally talked the mister into it," came out and bought one of the twin beagle females. The next day I went to the grain elevator for oats, and the boy who sacked my oats said he'd seen the coonhound sign on the bulletin board. He came out and took the black-and-tan coonhound puppy. That same evening the teenage son of the man who bought the first bluetick pup drove in with a five-dollar bill clutched in his teeth and said he wanted a hound of his own and if I'd take the fin he'd take any puppy I had left. I pressed the big black bloodhound pup into his arms.

Things were looking up. We were down to three pups, all females. Mink Blond Charmer had completely recovered from her break, so we reunited her with her sisters—the remaining twin beagle and the chocolate Weimaraner.

Now a running feud began between Witt, Liz, and me, about which pup to sell next. Stoyer was away at school, so he didn't enter into it. Witt, who up to now had ignored the entire dog operation with a fine nonchalance that was irritating at best, suddenly came up with the astounding news that he had secretly become so fond of Chocolate that he didn't want to part with her! As for Liz, somehow, despite the house rules that none of us was to become attached to any individual pup, the remaining twin beagle (Twinsy) had become *her dog,* and she felt no impulsion to part with her while we still had other pups for sale. For my part, I was stalling on Mink. Didn't I deserve at least one pup out of that litter, after all *I'd* been through, weeks of sleepless nights, dispensing milk and walking the meadows with bleeding feet in the wee hours, ministering to Mink in the intensive care unit in the granary?

Stalemated, we kept all three pups for awhile, until it became apparent that it was an impossible situation. They weren't pups anymore, but fifty-pound hounds. They leaped over Stoyer's puppy pen as if it were a croquet wicket. The moment we let them out of the shed, they took off for the neighbor's woods like three fast shots, chasing anything on four legs that crossed their paths. They would show up hours later, mud encrusted, lathered, and limp, but with "Wow, that's the life out there!" looks on their faces. We were finally forced to keep them locked up twenty-four hours a day, except when we exercised them on leashes. Liz voiced the opinion that this was no time for sentiment, because more pups had to go, any reasonable person could see that.

Witt, not for nothing a public relations man, now saw that he was going to get fingered and decided he might as well get credit for it. He nobly offered to put Chocolate up for sale. Chocolate was a stunning dog, whatever she was. She had a beautifully chiseled head and a sleek body, with a coat that glowed. What's more, although she had a sweet temperament, she would make someone a good watchdog, because she could scent a stranger, man or beast, a mile away, and she had a perfectly frightening low, gravelly bark. We now advertised her in rapid succession as an "ideal lady's pet and watchdog," as a "rare mocha beagle," and as a "handsome Weimaraner female," and we couldn't get a living soul to come out to look at her.

Christmas was bearing down on us. Liz, who often ends up making the sensible decision while her parents are engaged in flights of fancy, now announced that she had decided to sell Twinsy as a Christmas gift for a family—if she could find just the right family. We advertised Twinsy as a "classic tricolored beagle," and a portly stockbroker driving a long car came out and said he wanted her as a Christmas gift for his five children. After checking out his credentials by having me drive her past his big two-story colonial in a fashionable suburb sixteen times to view his situation front, back, and sideways, Liz let him have Twinsy.

But our problem still hadn't been solved. Let Chocolate and Mink loose together, and they still took off like two liberated females in hell. Let just one out, and you couldn't get her far enough off the back step to open the door. There was nothing for it but that another pup must go.

"I sacrificed Twinsy," Liz said to me. "Now is the time for you to sacrifice. Since we can't sell Chocolate, then Mink must go."

Liz suggested we run the old Mink Blond Charmer ad,

"Give your wife the mink she's always wanted," from which we had received several inquiries during the week Mink had broken her leg. I telephoned it in to the *Peatville Daily News*. I had to delete the "diamond-blue eyes" because her eyes had changed to a more common brown. "Mink blond" didn't exactly fit anymore, either, because if one were to be absolutely truthful about it she was now more of a coonhound yellow.

The News hadn't even landed in the mailboxes before I received a call from someone wanting to come out to see Mink. When a Volkswagen drove in, I told Liz I would take care of the customers by myself, since she had a cold. A zesty young-married couple alighted, who said they had just bought "their dream house with ten acres in the country" and they wanted just the right dog to go with it. The "Mink Blond Charmer" sounded like just the quality dog they had in mind. I told them that, although we had advertised only one dog, we actually had two for sale, and that they could take their choice of either one at the same price.

I went into the shed and snapped leashes on both Mink and Chocolate, and brought them out on the driveway for inspection. Fresh from confinement, both dogs were really too much for one person to handle. Mink lunged to one side and broke away from me, running behind the barn. I shoved Chocolate's leash into the man's hand and ran behind the barn to retrieve Mink. She had already managed to get her leash entwined in the barnyard fence wire, and it took me awhile to extricate her. When I returned to the driveway with her, the young couple had Chocolate between them, stroking her glowing brown coat, crooning over her finely chiseled head.

"Perhaps you don't know it," the man said, "but this is much the finer dog. We're going to name her Genevieve."

They put Genevieve firmly in the front seat between them before I could change my mind about letting them have their choice, and drove away, a tight, smug threesome in the Volkswagen.

"Ha!" cried Liz, opening the back door wide for me so I could enter more quickly to her wrath. "I saw the whole thing from the window! A trickier switcheroo I never saw. You're not one of those slippery Geminis for nothing. I should have known you'd find some way to keep *your* dog."

To this day I've never been able to convince her that Mink pulled away from me accidentally. She's talked about it so much that even I don't know the real truth of the incident anymore. *Did I or did I not hold onto Mink as tightly as I might have done?* The more she talks of it, the more uncertain I get. Perhaps five years from now I will be admitting to full complicity in the affair.

With only one puppy left, Dewbug's maternal instincts, which had cooled to the onslaught of ten vigorous puppies, came to the fore again. Once more Mink became her baby. Although her last pup was now bigger than she was, she would grab her daughter's head in her mouth, spin her over on her back with a sort of jujitsu twist, and then clean her up with her tongue and bite hard into her throat, just as she did the day the puppies were born. Mink loved it. She lay perfectly still, groaning ecstatically in her throat while her mother worked her over.

Hunters often drive in wanting to hunt in our fields, and their eyes always pass unseeing over Mink. But their eyes get a peculiar gleam as they settle on Dewbug—this sleek, mostly bluetick hound, who is obviously quivering for the hunt as she smells their clothes and their guns. And they often say, "I wouldn't mind taking this hound off your hands."

And I always reply, "No hunting, and no hounds thrown in, either."

As for Dewbug herself, she knows she is here to stay. She

feels her position is secure enough now so that she no longer
has to "watch the door." She spends most of her time in the
back meadow, loping and whirling, lifting her nose to the
wind, on the scent of one rabbit or another. But when she
comes to our line fence, she twirls on a dime and races back.
She isn't crowding her luck.

14

The Rover Boys

*I*f you live on a farm, and your husband isn't handy, you are constantly scheming for ways to get things done.

Take the case of my white board fence. I call it mine, because the two-year scrounging struggle to get it was all mine, and when I look at it I feel the fondness for it that only a mother can feel who has brought a problem child through a difficult time.

When we bought this place, a hard-bitten board fence, which must have been twenty-five or thirty years old, separated the house and the farm buildings from the rolling front meadow below. It had survived when the old house burned down. Each section of the fence had four straight boards, two crisscross boards, and one set flat, with a slight angle, on top. It was already wobbly when we moved here and, after a few years, with the ponies itching their backsides against it and reaching their necks through the boards to get the more succulent grass on the other side, it reached the point one spring where we would look out the window almost every morning to see that another exhausted post had bitten the dust.

"Just call someone," said Witt grandly. "Have the thing torn down and replaced."

This is what he always says. "Just call someone." If I had to choose the three most futile words uttered on a farm, they would be, "Just call someone."

Many repairs needing to be done on a farm—especially an older farm—require skills no longer widely practiced or popular. Fence-making is one of these. There were only two fence-makers in our area, and they were booked up by farmers for months, sometimes years, ahead. First I called Ferbie, the little old man who had put up such a tight wire fence for us when we first moved to the farm. Ferbie was booked into the Second Coming. It was just as well. His wire fences were the best in the country but, as everyone knew, his wood fences sometimes crumbled if you gave them a cross look.

So I called Blue, the *other* fence-maker. Blue, I was delighted to learn, was booked only months ahead, and said he could possibly get to me in September, if I could wait that long. I could wait. In that case, Blue said, he'd just come right on over and give me an estimate, because he'd just returned from a funeral and it didn't pay to get his boys on the job for the rest of the day.

Blue soon drove up the lane in his blue pickup, with the blue horse riding on the hood. The horse was his trademark; a farmer who wanted to run down Blue in a hurry would go to town and start asking at the feed store or the lumberyard, "Any you guys seen Blue's horse parked around?" I once overheard two farmers having a heated argument as they were leaning on Blue's pickup in front of the Western Auto. The argument concerned whether Blue's horse was a stallion or a gelding. Neither farmer could point out any real evidence to prove his case. I thought this would be a good chance to find out for myself, so I asked Blue about it when he got out of his truck.

"Tell you the truth, never thought about it one way or t'other. I usual call him a 'she'—particular when she starts listing to the wind and I got to weld the damn thing on again."

A reedy giant of a man, with shoulders stooped from years of bending over four-foot fences, Blue's cheeks were purpled from wind and sun, but his eyes had the healthy transparency of an April sky after a rain. We stepped off the required distance of fence together, and Blue sounded relieved when I told him I wanted the old one replaced with just a simple straight three-boarder. "A feller can grow old setting a fussy stretch of fence like you got here," he said. "And that ain't the worst of it. Nobody but a crooked bank examiner with his near hand in the cash bin has got the kind of money it takes to put seven pieces of lumber, two of 'em crissy-crossed, in one section of fence anymore."

Blue recommended cedar posts set eight feet apart, instead of the usual twelve, since I had "all them contrary ponies," and he would procure rough white oak lumber straight from the sawmill. It was the only thing that stood up for farm fence, he said, not to mention the fact that it was considerably cheaper than finished lumber purchased at a lumberyard. He would have the sawmill cut the boards in sixteen-foot lengths, which would span two sections of fence and also cut down the cost of labor.

I appreciated all of these money-saving devices, especially after he handed me his estimate. The time was closing in, I thought, when only someone with free access to the cash bin could afford a straight three-boarder.

Did I know, Blue asked, that cedar posts were scarce as mutton chops on a bald eagle? He happened to know a lumberyard that had just received a shipment. He said we'd be smart to grab them up while they were available, and he offered to haul them for me, since he wasn't working that day. He returned in a couple of hours with sixty-eight gorgeous, sweet-smelling cedar posts on his flatbed trailer. He stored them in one side of the corncrib. I paid him for the posts, and said, "See you in September."

All summer we coddled the old fence, with the thought that if we could just hold out until September we'd be home free. In normal times (I don't remember any, but I suppose there have been some) we kept our for sale mares out in the front meadow so they could more readily be seen and admired by pony-lookers, but now we chased them back into the woods herd and brought in the nonpushers.

Some ponies have greater itches than others, and will stand for an hour just pushing against a fence—itching, pushing, itching, pushing—until something, usually the fence, gives. Other ponies are seldom seen itching. So Liz and I went out into the woods and neck-roped a half-dozen ponies that, in our best judgment, were nonpushers, and we brought them into the front meadow. The worrisome thing is that, in the middle of the night, or any other time, for that matter, a nonpusher can, for reasons known only to itself, suddenly turn into a pusher.

When this happened, and we woke up in the morning to find yet another section of crumbled fence, Liz and I would go out front to do our detective work, while Stoyer got out the used lumber and nails to try to patch up the hole. Paint flecks and rubbed-off hair on the rump generally identified the culprit, and she was banished to the woods, to be replaced by another nonpusher.

September finally rolled around; but Blue did not. He telephoned and said he had been in the hospital with a bad back, and he was way behind on his orders, and he couldn't possibly get to me until spring. He said he was sorry as hell. I knew he really was, because Blue took great pride in keeping his commitments. I accepted the news as gracefully as I could, and said I would see him in the spring. The ponies didn't worry me so much, because soon we would be putting the entire mare herd out on the back hayfield for the winter, but now I had a new problem.

Those gorgeous, sweet-smelling cedar posts that had been resting in the corncrib all during the humid summer were sprouting fungus and showing wood-rot in a few spots. So Stoyer and I dragged all sixty-eight of them out on the driveway, lined them up and painted them with Woodlife to kill the fungus and seal out the moisture. Then *I* went to bed for a week with a bad back.

The crocuses were just starting to come out when Blue drove up the lane one cool April morning and announced that he was about ready to start work on my fence. But he had a little problem; because of the abnormal amount of rain that spring, the sawmills couldn't get their equipment into the woods to get their lumber out, and he hadn't been able to round up that first stick of wood for me. Maybe, he said, I knew somebody he didn't know and I could scout around and find me some, seeing as how I had a lot more time than he did.

"Just keep askin' around," Blue said, "and you could possible come up with something." Meanwhile, he had a good stretch of wire fence jobs to keep him busy.

Right here is where I might have thrown in the sponge and said, "Okay, put *me* up a wire fence. It'll look ugly in front of the house, but anything to keep the ponies from trampling on the front lawn." And then I remembered those sixty-eight cedar posts resting in the corncrib, which had cost me $148.44 plus a week's worth of bad back, and I decided I'd try to find the lumber.

By now the old fence had reached the point where even a cat walking on the top board would send it waving like a conga line. It would not contain even the best nonpusher. It was breeding season, and with Bean running in the woods with his mares, we had been planning to isolate the yearling fillies in the front meadow; but now we had to put them in the stallion run behind the barn instead. That left no place to exercise the three young stallions who occupied box stalls in the barn.

We decided to try the front meadow as a stallion-run, and it worked surprisingly well. Every stallion we put out there stayed away from the old board fence like the plague, because he was too busy down at the other end of the meadow ogling the mares in the woods. So every four hours during the day we put a different stallion out front. Our only problem was getting him back in the barn; he hated to come in and leave all those luscious mares who were just out of nose reach in the woods. First I gave Stoyer the job of bringing in the stallion, but Stoyer didn't think there was a pony worth getting in who couldn't be chased in with a bicycle. This provided a lot of exercise both for him and the stallion; but it didn't get either of them in the barn. So Liz and I spent most of the summer catching stallions: a handful of oats in one hand, with the other hand concealed under it that held the snap of the lead rope, the end of which was draped out of sight over the shoulder; at the moment the stallion's lips curled over the oats, the hidden hand stealthily slipped the snap into the halter ring. We weren't strong enough to hold the stallion if we grabbed his halter, because he would rear back suddenly and break away.

In the hours between rotating stallions, I was on the road trying to track down fence lumber. Blue had spoken true, all right. The wettest spring in years was giving the sawmills fits. Trees already felled were lying awash in the woods, with no way to get them out until the ground dried. But, after traveling miles and miles, just "askin' around," as Blue had suggested, I finally struck pay dirt. I found a quaint little sawmill tucked up behind one of the small towns up the pike, with the nicest man running it you would ever want to meet. He was a huge, bald-headed man, with muscles out to here, and what struck me at once was that he used excellent grammar, compared to the other sawmill operators I had met, who mostly grunted, and he was so graceful and light on his feet, despite his tremendous bulk. Yes, he said, I was "truly fortunate" because that very day he had managed to bring in from the woods some beautiful white oak lumber. He showed me a sample of it. It looked lovely. I immediately placed an order for 201 boards to be cut into sixteen-foot lengths. He said it would take him several weeks to get it ready, and then he would be "most happy" to deliver it.

I came home and told Witt and the children that night that I had never met a lovelier man, lumberman or otherwise, in my life, and that my troubles were simply over. In fact, I raved so much that Stoyer finally said, "He sounds more like one of those old-fashioned dancing masters than a sawmill operator."

That did it, of course. For the next two weeks all I heard was, "Hey, when is the dancing master going to deliver your wood?"

The day he came with the lumber, I didn't even hear him drive in, because the children were in the basement playing caroms and screaming at each other. By the time I noticed his truck, he was just stacking the last of the lumber in a high neat pile at the side of the driveway. I went out to greet him, and ran my hand over the top board. "It's just lovely," I said, and gave him his check. When he thanked me, I thought for a moment he was going to click his heels together; but he stopped just short of it. He got in his truck and drove swiftly away.

Witt drove in early from work not long after that, and got out of his car to look at the lumber. "It looks fine," he said, and flipped the top board over to look at the one underneath. He picked this one up, and it broke in his hands. Insects were crawling out of it. He flipped another board; and another one. The entire pile, except the top board, was rotten to the core. It must have been cut a hundred years ago. The wind went out of me, and I sat down hard on top of the pile. Another board cracked.

"The moral of the story," Witt said, "is never trust a sawmill operator who uses excellent grammar and bows from the waist."

He went into the house and telephoned the dancing master, who was now back at his mill. "This is the husband of the lady on whom you unloaded the rotten wood."

There was a long pause at the other end of the line. "I didn't know she had a husband."

"It's quite obvious that you didn't," Witt said, "and I want you out here no later than tomorrow morning to pick up this kindling." When Witt gets angry, he talks extra soft and laughs a little, which can be very sinister, especially over the telephone to someone who's never seen him.

Midmorning the next day, the man returned with his truck to pick up the wood. I hid in the house, ashamed at having been so taken in. It took a long time for him to load the lumber, because the long pieces kept breaking off in his hands as he threw them in the truck. I thought how embarrassing it must have been for him, because he probably knew I was watching from the window. He swept up some of the crumbled chunks on the driveway with a quick scoop of his hands, and then started for the back door. I knew I would have to face him when he rang the bell. But he was the dancing master to the last. He didn't ring the doorbell, but very softly opened the screen door and secured my check between the door and the frame. Then he soft-footed it out to his truck and drove away.

I should have spent a few hours, at least, licking my wounds, but I didn't have time; I had to run down some fence lumber. Just on a hunch, I revisited a small lumber company up in a far corner of the county. The men there were just unloading a fresh shipment of some finished lumber in sixteen-foot lengths, which they called "batten." It was made from spruce and often used for barn siding, as well as fence. As Blue had said, it was considerably more expensive than rough lumber straight from the sawmill, but now I was willing to mortgage the homestead for a good piece of lumber. Besides, it would be easier to paint. I ordered 201 lengths, and when it was delivered I made the delivery boy wait while I went over the entire pile, board by board, before I gave him his money. "You don't trust people, ma'am?" he said plaintively, as he got into his truck. "You know, that can get to be a bad habit."

I couldn't wait to telephone Blue that evening to tell him

the good news. He had said that whenever I found the lumber, he would finish the job he was on, and mine would be next. But when he heard my voice, he groaned. He had lost most of his boys, he said, some to the Draft and some to the Open Road, and all he had left was a high school boy who was, he was sorry to say, just a little better than nothing. What's more, his back was acting up again, and for two cents he'd retire and live off his Social Security. He didn't see how he could possibly get to me until spring. If it would make me feel any better, he said, he knew a farmer with a hundred Herefords just "bustin' out" for lack of fence, who was in much worse shape than I was.

The hundred stampeding Herefords didn't make me feel a whole lot better, considering the hard fact that I was left with all that beautiful batten spread out on the driveway, vulnerable to be warped by the first rain; and fresh out of fence makers. The calendar said September 24. Even tomorrow the fall rains could start and there might be no good dry days left to dig a posthole. The corncrib was already bursting with cedar fence posts; there was no place to store the wood over winter.

Desperate people do desperate things, so I did something I don't usually do: I answered a blind ad. It was in the "milk paper," which is what the farmers call the small weekly tabloid that is distributed free to rural mailboxes and subsists on advertising alone. The ads pull extremely well. Farmers love auctions, and this is like a mail-order auction. They sit down and comb the ads for "something they could want." I once advertised my old wall-to-wall carpeting and I got at least a hundred calls. The first man who came out to look at it bought it on the spot; I was redecorating my living room, so I threw my old sofa and draperies in on the bargain, and we were both the happiest people alive. What a surprise *his* wife got that day, when her husband came home!

The blind ad said simply, "Fencemaking," with a telephone number. I called the number, and a man's nice young voice answered. I explained my needs and asked the voice if he would like to come out and look over the job. Not long afterward, a purple Porsche 911 tooled up the lane, and pulled up in front of the barn with quite a purr.

A young man jumped out who looked to be about seventeen or eighteen. This was in the late sixties, when long hair still brought the word *hippy* to mind. I was both shocked and enchanted with his long ash-blond brushover, which glimmered in the sun. If he *was* a hippy, I thought, he was the most antiseptic hippy I'd ever seen. His faded blue jeans were immaculate, and his shirt looked as if it had been purchased with the jeans as an outfit, not just thrown together. The fine film of dust on his jodhpur boots couldn't conceal the spit-and-polish. What's more, he was enormously courteous. He "ma'amed" me at the end of every sentence. We walked along the old falling-down fence, and I told him what I wanted. Everything, absolutely everything, was all right with him. Yes, ma'am, he could do, and he would do. When could he start? Tomorrow, ma'am. He and his brother worked together. Yes, tomorrow would be just fine.

I asked him to give me an estimate—for the finished job. He pulled out a piece of paper and did some scribbling. Would I like the posts set in cement, he asked, with a bit of a gleam in his eye? No, I said, absolutely not. This seemed to disappoint him, but he finished his estimate, and gave it to me. It was much less than Blue's. How about references? Well, they had done a *lot* of work, but not too much around here, ma'am. I must have at least one reference, I said firmly. He gave me the address of a woman who lived in Peatville. I told him I would check his reference and give him an answer that evening. He thanked me, gave me a dazzling smile, jumped in his Porsche which made a growling purr as it rolled down the lane.

If only he hadn't been so courteous, I thought. So polite. I could never live it down if I were stung by another dancing master routine.

I drove to Peatville to check out the reference. The house

was on the outskirts of town—an old southern-colonial mansion with tall white columns and groomed to the teeth. The only fence I could see was a small white two-board about a rod long holding up a row of rose bushes. The strange thing about it was that the posts—which couldn't have been more than two feet high—were set in cement!

A very brisk little old lady, who looked as if she had just come from the beauty salon, answered my knock, and she was eager to talk. "Well, you know how *difficult* it is to get anyone to do anything these days and the neighborhood children, God love them, were simply running *rampant* through my rosebushes, and I thought if I could just get a little *something* to deter them. So I answered this ad, and this *lovely,* beautifully mannered boy came out, so I just said, 'Go ahead.'

"The only thing I *didn't* like, they insisted on setting those posts in cement, and I'll be perfectly candid about it, I don't think I'm going to live that long. What's more, they spilled cement all over my veranda, and you know you just don't *wash off* cement." She fluttered a manicured hand at the evidence on her porch floor, which *was* a bit of a mess. "But they apologized so prettily I forgave them and said to myself, '*C'est la guerre.'* After all, at my age, fretting will get you nowhere except a fast trip to the cemetery." She giggled a little and gave me a genteel poke in the ribs.

Not much to go on there. But I had already kayoed the cement, so I wouldn't have that to worry about. On the way home, I went over my options: either take a chance on these boys, or leave $524.61 worth of lumber out on the driveway to warp until spring. Any fool could plainly see that the smart thing would be to grab the boys.

Any fool except Witt, who was going to give me trouble. If I could just remember not to mention the lovely manners.

"You mean you answered this ad with just the telephone number, and the only reference he can give you is this two-inch fence in Peatville, and now you're going to hire him, just like that?"

"What other choice do we have? I'll tell you what other choice we have. We can store the lumber in the garage, and you can let your new Thunderbird sit out in the weather all winter."

I knew I had hit him in the midsection; but he took the blow admirably, with only a slight lowering of the eyelids. "At least with teenagers," he said, "you won't be blinded by the hand-kissing routine again. I suppose it wouldn't hurt to give them a try."

Witt reminded me that I would have to go it alone for several weeks, because he was leaving in the morning for Utah. It was a trip to which he was really looking forward, because after his business in Salt Lake City was completed, he was going out to visit his old friend Robert Hinckley, who had a fabulous 400-acre Welsh pony ranch nestled in the mountains near the small town of Eden. The ranch, appropriately enough, is called "The Garden of Eden." Witt had been waiting for years for an excuse to go out West to see it.

I dropped him off at the airport the next morning; I didn't wait for the plane to take off, because I thought I had to hurry home to greet my newly hired fencemakers. I could have seen the plane take off and gone shopping in South Metropolis to boot. It was eleven o'clock before the purple Porsche came growling up the lane, followed by a brilliant orange Austin-Healey Sprite that still smelled of fresh paint.

My friend of the previous day, with the beautiful head and manners, introduced us all around. He was Rick, and he presented his brother, Robby, also with a beautiful head and manners, so much a carbon copy of Rick that in all the time they were here I would never have bet money on who was who. And then there was Gary. Gary, it turned out, was the owner of the Sprite, and was not "in the business." He was just a hired hand. He was going to be the "carry boy." That is, carry the posts from hole to hole, and carry the lumber from post to post.

Gary appeared to be about sixteen, and was a splendiferous dude. He, too, had a flowing ash-blond brushover, which looked as if it had been shampooed twice and rinsed three times. He was turned out in spotless soft gray jeans tucked into equally soft leather boots that must have cost him folding money, topped by a soft orange shirt that complemented his Sprite, without in any way stealing the thunder from it. Considering the fancy turnout, I thought, boy-oh-boy, "carry boys" must be at a premium these days.

Gary and I did not hit it off right from the start. When Rick introduced us, I thought he said Clary instead of Gary.

"Clary?" I said.

"Jesus, no!" he said. "Gary!"

That finished me off in his book. He never spoke to me again. Whenever he saw me after that, in the days ahead, he just turned his head with the injured air of one who has been insulted to the point of no return.

I made the mistake of telling the children about it when they came home from school. From then on, of course, he was Clary.

Rick said he had business elsewhere that day, and he would leave Robby and Clary to start the fence. Before he left, we discussed the job at hand. The old fence was to be taken down section by section, to be replaced immediately by a new section. The cedar posts were to be placed eight feet apart, on which were to be nailed the three sixteen-foot boards of new lumber. The old fence could not be used as a guide, because the old posts were twelve feet apart.

Rick jumped in his purple Porsche and purred off, and I went into the house, leaving Robby and Clary to the job. I took the precaution of looking out the window to see how the job progressed. Clary reached into the Sprite and produced the fanciest transistor radio I'd ever seen, pulled out the antenna that reached to the sky, and set it on the roof of the car. The voice of Johnny Cash chanting "A Boy Named Sue" came booming into my open windows. Out of the trunk of the car they produced a slim-line shovel, a wrecking bar, and a hammer.

Because that's where they happened to be standing, they

started at the edge of the barn, where the fence makes a sixteen-foot jog. Robby used his wrecking bar to tear the rotten wood away from the posts. Clary stood by with folded arms, and whenever a piece of wood hit the ground, he picked it up and threw it away a little, after which he would pay attention to brushing off his pants until the next board fell. The posts were easy. They were already rotted off at ground level, with only a prayer holding them up, and a good kick of Robby's boot sent them sprawling. An hour's labor netted them two posts down and the boards in between. Robby spent another hour digging two postholes, which wasn't easy considering the fact that he didn't have a posthole digger. Clary stood off picking lint and turning the knob of the radio until he found another station playing "A Boy Named Sue."

When the postholes finally seemed to satisfy Robby, Clary went to the corncrib and obtained two posts, one at a time, being careful not to hold them against his body, and set them in the holes. Robby spent a lot of time filling in the dirt and doing a lot of stamping. Then he came to the door, gave me a dazzling smile that showed a lot of even white teeth, and asked if he could borrow a saw. I told him to look in the toolshed. He came out with a straight saw, and Clary dragged three of the sixteen-foot boards from the driveway to the place of business. After that there was a great deal of sawing and hammering, which made me very nervous, but not nervous enough to embarrass them by going out to see what they were doing. At two P.M. "A Boy Named Sue" was giving me a headache, and I went into the kitchen to fix myself a cup of coffee. Suddenly Johnny Cash's voice was shut off as if his throat had been cut, I heard a roar, and saw the Sprite taking off down the lane with gravel spattering in all directions. When it turned onto the road, the rate of acceleration was magnificent. Again I marveled at the material success of "carry-boys."

Assuming they were going out for a late lunch, I hurried

out to see the results of their labors. They had completed one section of fence, all right. The two posts were set, perhaps a bit on the wobbly side, but not really wobbly enough to complain about. But the strange thing was that the sixteen-foot boards had been sawed in two to span the eight-foot length. Why had they not waited until they put up another post, so they could have spanned two sections with the sixteen-foot length, and saved themselves the labor of cutting the boards in two? This I was determined to ask them about when they returned from lunch, but the Sprite must have accelerated too fast and taken them too far, for they did not return that day.

They didn't return the next day, either, and after sitting down and computing how long it would take them to build the fence with no more equipment than a slim-line shovel, a wrecking bar, and a hammer—not to mention the three-hour day—I began to think that their permanent disappearance might be a blessing in disguise.

The next morning at eleven, however, just after I had written them off forever, a caravan came up the lane that knocked my eyes out: Rick was driving one of the biggest, newest red tractors I'd ever seen, with a posthole digger mounted on the rear; followed by Robby in a new red truck, not a pickup truck but a high-bed farm truck that could haul a dozen steers to market; and Clary in the orange Sprite bringing up the rear.

For better or for worse, we seemed to be in business again.

I was so impressed by the display of grandeur that I forgot my intention to go out and query them about why they were sawing the sixteen-foot boards in half.

The first thing they did was to set up Clary's radio on the high cab of the truck, with the antenna reaching to heaven. "A Boy Named Sue" instantly boomed down on them like Moses from the mountain. This spurred them on, and soon dirt began to fly as if they were building the Grand Coulee Dam. Robby started swinging the wrecker bar to loosen the old boards from the old fence. Rick wound a big chain around the old posts, goosed the tractor, and out they came.

I had taken the precaution of telling them that I didn't want the old fence leveled all at once; that they must tear it down and rebuild it, section by section. I used the excuse that I couldn't take the stallion out of the front meadow. But my real fear was that they would level the old fence, weary of the job, and leave me high and dry.

After an hour, they had about six sections of fence cleared, and then they started to dig the postholes for the new ones. The posthole digger, with its great steel auger, was something to see. Robby and Clary thought so, too. They just stood and watched in admiration as Rick worked. His beautiful hair bounced up and down as the tractor roared and the twisting steel wound into the earth. He was driving a chariot with six white horses.

This frenzied activity went on until my kitchen clock chimed two, and in the time it took me to leave my vigil at the window, go into the kitchen and pour a cup of coffee and come back, the entire caravan was taking off down the lane, spewing gravel from right to left, first the tractor, then the truck, then the orange Sprite.

It was then that I started calling them "The Rover Boys." I knew they wouldn't be back anymore that day.

I went out to survey the situation. Most beautiful postholes I had ever seen. Several looked like they could reach to China. That should have told me something, but I had my steel tape measure with me, and I was more concerned that all of the postholes were over eight feet apart. That meant that my sixteen-foot boards would not span two sections, and my precious lumber would be wasted.

It also came to me, as a gleeful stallion galloped past me through the new-found gap, that the boys had not closed up old fence with new as promised. I was glad Witt couldn't see Stalwyrt Beau chewing on his prize rhododendron at the corner of the house. As I neck-roped the stallion and led him into the barn, I vowed that no fancy caravan, or shining hair or dazzling smiles or any amount of ma'ams, was going to keep me from having a serious talk with the Rover Boys.

When the caravan showed up at the usual eleven the next morning, I was out at the postholes waiting for them.

Rick had already noticed the absence of a stallion in the front meadow. "I sure want to thank you, ma'am," he said, "for getting that horse out. Now we can let her rip straight through."

"I didn't have much choice, did I, since you left a hole big enough to let a herd of elephants through sideways when you left yesterday. Now, about these postholes—"

"Aren't they beauties, ma'am?"

"I've never seen prettier. However, I happened to be out here with my rule last night, and all of them are over eight feet apart. How do you expect to bridge a seventeen-foot span with a sixteen-foot board?"

Rick's eyes flickered. "Yes. Well, you see, ma'am, we thought we would just cut the boards to fit as we go along. You know, this is a custom-made fence."

"I know that. But I also want you to know that I custom-ordered the lumber. There are 201 lengths, exactly sixteen feet long, which is exactly what it takes for the job. And if you custom-fit *all* the sections at over eight feet, then you are going to have lumber enough for only half the job. What's more, each of these lengths cost me $2.61, and if you cut off eight and a half feet and throw away the rest, you are throwing away half of my money. I'm not going to take kindly to that."

The eyes flickered again, and I wondered whether he was saying "Goddamn witch" to himself.

"We'll do it any way you want, ma'am," Rick said. "We want you to be happy, ma'am."

I returned to the house and told myself I wouldn't look out of the window any more that day. I went into the back bedroom, closed the door, put cotton in my ears, and reclined on the bed. Even through the cotton it sounded as if they were razing the Taj Mahal. Finally I was aware of silence. I jerked the cotton from my ears, heard the clock strike two, and then a crazy swoosh of gravel, and I knew the Rover Boys had knocked off at their usual hour—perhaps to take siestas, or to go to rendezvous with flashing-eyed ladies; or, more likely, to jump on motorcycles and career to the next county and back, their ash-blond brushovers waving in the wind.

When I looked out the window, I knew I had burned my bridges behind me. The entire stretch of old fence lay flattened on the ground, as if a tornado had come through and leveled it with one fiery blast: each post lying where it fell, like a dead body, the boards resting over it.

For one thing I was thankful. Witt was safely tucked away in the Garden of Eden.

When the children came home from school and saw the wreckage, they were awed. Liz said, "It looks like when you line up a whole set of dominoes and then go, splatt, with your hand!"

Stoyer said he thought someone should play taps over it.

I spent the weekend trying to achieve a deadly calm, a stoic attitude about the whole thing. But when the caravan rolled up the lane at the usual brunch hour on Monday, my stoicism was shattered. I would never have recognized the Rover Boys except for the flair. The colors had changed; a new green tractor instead of the red one, with an even more formidable posthole digger: an enormous green truck to match, this time with a flatbed; and bringing up the rear, Clary in a new mustard-colored Sprite with the price list still hanging on the back window. Attired, of course, in a soft canary shirt that complemented his car without in any way stealing the thunder from it.

"I hope they put in a stock of new tape measures while they were at it," I thought grimly.

After Clary's transistor radio had been suitably perched on

top of the truck cab, large-scale maneuvers began immediately. I'd have to say one thing for them, I thought to myself as I watched them work, they didn't waste much of their three-hour day once they got here. With a great, grinding roar, Rick began to dig more postholes, with Robby and Clary setting the posts.

Clary's job was to run to the side of the corncrib, drag out a post, bring it to the posthole, set it in the hole, then hold it at the top until Robby got it anchored in the dirt. Clary stood as far away as he could so dirt wouldn't be spewed on his soft grey jeans. His long brushover kept falling in his eyes when he leaned over to brush the dust off his pants, so then he would have to stand up straight and give his head a good fling to get the hair back, all the while holding the post.

A carry boy's job was not an easy one, I could see that.

In no time at all, Robby and Clary, with much help from "A Boy Named Sue," had set a half-dozen posts, and something just didn't look right to me. Two of the posts were reaching for the sky, but the other four looked like pygmies with their heads cut off. I checked my measurements, which I had gone over so carefully with Rick. The posts should measure fifty-two inches above the ground when the fence was completed. Since I had purchased seven-foot posts, there was plenty of post with which to work.

Now I knew why some of those postholes I had examined looked as if they went to China. They really did go to China!

I grabbed up my steel rule and went out to have another little talk with the Rover Boys.

It took a good deal of waving and shouting to get Rick off the tractor. He was clearly enjoying his work. But he finally noticed me and turned off the tractor. There was an unaccustomed silence as the four of us stood over one of the shrunken posts.

"Rick," I began, "remember when we went over the specifications we decided that all the posts should be fifty-two inches from the ground?"

"Right, ma'am," he said, and there was quiet patience in his voice. "We don't bother too much about the exact height when we put the posts in. You see," and he made a grand, leveling gesture with a sweep of his arm, "when we are all finished, all the boards on and everything, we come through with an electric circular saw and level them all off the exact height you want them just like that, in one fell swoop."

Rick gave me his dazzling smile. I looked at Robby. He was smiling, too; a great, open forgiving smile. I looked at Clary. His lip was curling.

I pulled out a stretch of steel rule from its case, and measured from the ground up the post in front of which we were standing. It measured forty-three inches. "But Rick," I said, "unless you know something about stretching wood that the rest of us don't, how are you going to level off a forty-three inch post to fifty-two inches?"

A pony whinnied in a far corner of the woods. Another pony answered it. Three sets of legs in soft jeans shifted stealthily in their jodhpur boots. The Rolling Stones suddenly came to life after the station break, and the "Honky-Tonk Woman" cut raucously into the silence.

"We want you to be happy, ma'am," Rick said. "And if you are not happy with these posts, why, we'll just get in there and tear 'em out and reset them, ma'am. Right, ma'am?"

And tear them out they did, with a log chain on the tractor, and by that time it was the usual two-o'clock quitting time and the Rover Boys, with their caravan of new tractor, truck, and brand spanking new Sprite careened down the lane in a screech of what little gravel there was left.

"They're always fast," I sighed, "but never as fast as when they're leaving."

I had developed a fatalistic attitude about the span between the postholes. The boards would stretch or they wouldn't. One thing was certain; I couldn't stand out there as they worked and measure the distance between every single post. Each afternoon after they left, I went out and started measuring. Some posts were as much as ten feet apart, and others were as little as six feet apart. I became so nervous in trying to figure out some pattern to what they were doing that I finally just threw up my hands. Well, I had warned them. If the lumber didn't last out, I would have those shiny brushovers on my silver-plated platter. Some way, I would.

At last they had all the posts set, and now the crunch would come, I thought, as I ground my teeth and stood sentinel at the window. Now they would start nailing the boards to the posts. And how simple it would have been if the posts had been exactly eight feet apart, and they could have taken a sixteen-foot length of board and nailed it across two sections.

But, no. As they said, this was a *custom-made* fence.

First Clary dragged three sixteen-foot lengths to the work area. Then Rick and Robby cut three lengths to fit between the two posts of the section on which they were working. While they were nailing the three boards to the posts to complete the section, Clary grabbed up the three amputated lengths of board and ran up and down the battalion of posts until he found a span that would fit this length. When he did, he dropped them there.

Someone up there, someone high in the sky with a slide rule, must have been looking out for the Rover Boys, because when they finally were through cutting all the boards, they had miraculously found a span of post to fit every board!

My specifications said that the top board was to be forty-eight inches from the ground, and there were to be ten inches between each board. But from my vigil at the window, I could see that when Rick and Robby had finished nailing all three boards to the first section, they had left enough space between the bottom board and the ground so that a suckling foal could walk straight through.

This called for another trip out to the mound.

"Yes, *ma'am*," Rick said with a here-she-comes-again glint in his cool grey eyes.

"Rick," I said, "I'm not coming out here to complain. Far from it. You'll remember I told you I wanted ten inches between each board. But I trust your judgment so much that with the land sloping up and down the way it does I'm going to let you have a little leeway with that. Before you drive the final nail in any board, I just want you to ask yourself one thing: are you leaving a space so large that a small pony can crawl through, or a space so small that a big pony will get his head stuck? Other than that, be my guest. Be an artist!"

My new strategy was: if you can't lick 'em, join 'em.

I think I struck a fine chord. When I looked out the window an hour later Rick was squatted on his haunches at the bottom of the hill and looking speculatively up at the fence while Robby and Clary moved a board up and down, an inch this way, an inch that.

Several more full three-hour working days, and the fence was beginning to take shape. I went down to the bridge, and looked up the hill at the fence, and I was surprised to see that it had a graceful curve to it. Rick had used considerable art in deciding when to lower or raise a board to fit the dips and slopes of the hill on which the fence was set.

It was just about at this point that we lost Clary, and I was sorry, because the truth is that I was beginning to feel a certain fondness for the Rover Boys. I was beginning to think how dull it would be when they left. I was even developing a live and let live relationship with "A Boy Named Sue" and the "Honky-Tonk Woman."

As I was watching the boys nail the boards one day, it came to me that when I got to painting the fence, I would not be able to reach the spots on the post where the boards were nailed to it. So after they had left for the day, I got out a bucket of white paint and a brush and swished down the front of all of the posts to which boards had not already been nailed. The next day I looked out the window and saw Clary running up and down the fence trying to find a space to fit an especially short board, when suddenly he stopped, and looked down at his soft gray jeans. There was a spot of white on them, where he had brushed up against a post. He looked absolutely stricken. He dropped the board, ran to his Sprite, and careened down the lane. He was just a streak of mustard going down the road.

The next morning's caravan didn't include Clary.

"I'm sorry about Gary," I told Rick. "I really am. I should never have painted those posts."

"It's all right, ma'am," Rick answered. "He'll get over it. It will take time, but he'll get over it."

There was only about a day's work left anyway—a three-hour day, of course. Rick finished the fence, while Robby started to pick up the old fence that still lay prone where it had been felled. Robby brought a little old beaten-up pickup to haul the lumber away. I suddenly wondered why, on every other day, they had brought the huge new truck with the flat-bed that could haul a house, and they had never used it for anything but—yes, that must be it! It came to me in a blinding flash of intuition that they had brought the big truck to have something high on which to perch the transistor radio.

Finally the fence was finished, except for sawing off all the posts to an even length. I had my heart set on having them on a slant. When I told Rick how I wanted them, I thought he said, "Yes, ma'am, if that's what you want," a bit uncertainly. When he was through sawing the first post, it looked like a jagged breadknife had tried to go through a loaf of hot bread. Then I remembered Hervey Hake saying once that it was harder than it looked to cut off a post on a slant with an electric saw.

"Rick," I said, "I don't know why I wanted these posts slanted. I don't even like the looks of it. I've decided I want them cut straight off horizontally."

And I really did like the looks of the posts cut off straight. It looked more rustic. More *custom-made*. In fact, the more I looked at the fence, the better I liked it. No one else had a fence like it in the whole country. You could stand down at the bridge, and look and look, and you knew there was something different about it, but it just didn't quite come to you that perhaps it was because there was no post in it that was the same distance from his brother. It was really quite intriguing.

It was time to pay my bill. I had Rick's check in my hand while I watched him make out his receipt on the hood of the purple Porsche.

"I think you boys did a good job, all things considered," I said, "and you can use me for a reference if you need one."

"Now that's mighty nice of you, ma'am," Rick answered. "You'd never believe this, but fence-making is kind of new to us. What we really want to get into is cement. Setting the posts in cement, you know? That's where the real action is! Now if you know anyone who—"

Just then Liz ran out from the house and cried in her clear child's-voice, "Daddy's calling from the Garden of Eden and he wants to know are the Rover Boys still here, and is it all right if he's gone a couple more days?"

My face grew hot as fire.

"Tell him he can stay as long as he wants. Hurry now! Don't keep your father hanging."

I stole a look at Rick. His head was down, still writing, still making out his receipt. He looked up and said soberly, "That's what I call tough luck. Your husband living it up in the Garden of Eden and you stuck back here riding herd on the Rover Boys."

I searched his face. There was no guile at all. And then his eyes began to dance. "I guess we *have* been pretty hard on your gravel—going in and out."

"You're not angry?"

"Heck, no. We might even take the name. I can see our

new ad. 'Rover Boys have posthole digger, will travel.' " He threw back his head and laughed, and I laughed with him.

I gave him the check. "Spend it all at once, Rick. And have fun."

"Will do, ma'am." He gave me one last dazzling smile, jumped in the Porsche, and accelerated. He was just a purple streak going down the lane.

When Witt came home from Utah, several days later, he liked the fence, too. He said that when he first drove up the lane he thought it had a certain charm. He couldn't quite put his finger on it. It wasn't until the next spring, when he mowed the lawn for the first time, that he put his finger on it.

He came into the house, rather excited. "Do you know there isn't one section of that fence that measures the same length as any other section?"

I had had a long time to prepare my case. "So what else is new? Don't you know that is a *custom-made* fence? If you were getting dentures, you wouldn't want them all even, would you, like cheap store-bought teeth?"

Witt stared at me. "Sorry I mentioned it," he answered grimly, and went back to his mowing.

15
Delila

The first year we had ponies to sell, I couldn't understand why we were having such a difficult time selling ours when all the other breeders with whom I talked seemed to be doing a booming business in ponies—couldn't keep them in stock and were charging what the traffic would bear.

That was before I learned the two basic hanging-in-there rules you follow if you stay in the pony business for any length of time. The first one is that even if you haven't seen the whites of a pony-looker's eyes for thirteen months, much less sold a pony, you always give the impression that if business gets any better you are going to have to put up a padlocked gate at the end of the lane to keep the buyers out. The second rule is that you do not come out and tell another breeder—cold turkey—how much you get for a pony. Instead, you say, "I did all right, that's for sure," or "I got top dollar, you can bet on that," or "Any more like that and I'm going to have to get me some more broodmares!"

There is only one exception to this rule. In the highly unlikely event that you actually receive a decent price for one of your ponies, it is perfectly all right to be very, very specific. Such as: "Do you know I pocketed $435.50 for that damn filly?" If this elicits a dubious stare, you quickly add,

192

with disarming honesty, "Of course, that *is* counting what I got for the halter, you understand!"

A dozen or so pony breeders lived within visiting distance of our farm in the early years. Not all of them raised Welsh ponies. Some were still trying to hang on with Shetlands, especially those who had been well stocked in the business when Shetland prices had gone wild. A few of these breeders had made some money and were hoping that lightning would strike again. Other breeders had "grade" ponies— duke's mixtures of everything—and had acquired a registered stallion, usually Welsh or Hackney, with which they were trying to upgrade their herds. There was much visiting around from one breeder to another. Everyone was lonesome for pony talk. Hours were spent in the fields kibitzing each other's ponies. The only taboo subjects were: how many are you selling, and for how much?

At least half the pony breeders I knew were women, many of whom had taken over the family pony business of necessity; doing it, as I did, while their husbands toiled elsewhere to support the family and the ponies against the day when the pony-breeding operation would begin to show a profit.

One of these women was Delila McBrood.

Our first meeting did not lay the groundwork for a budding friendship. I had come out to the barn on an early May morning to find that Egrett had given birth to her third foal, a huge black filly whom we named—I'll never know why—Hummingbird. In later years we let our mares foal out on clean pasture if the weather was good; it lessened the danger of navel-ill in the foal, and the mare snapped back faster if allowed to run freely. But in the first years, when we had only one or two mares foaling every spring, we put them up in box stalls at night when foaling was imminent. This particular spring morning was so calescent I decided to put Egrett and her foal in the barnyard to bask in the sun. As I watched the filly staggering on long, shaky legs after her dam, I saw a red pickup coming up the lane. Halfway up, the pickup jumped the lane, careened across the front meadow, and came to a stop at the barnyard fence where I stood.

A well-muscled little woman in jeans leaped from the pickup, vaulted over the barnyard fence as if she were born to it, and landed resiliently on the balls of her moccasined feet. As she sailed over the fence she reminded me of a redwinged blackbird: she wore a red flannel shirt, and her hair, black as a bird's wing, was parted in the center and cut off straight all around at chin length. She had snapping black eyes that blinked rapidly, as if fighting back the sensations surging in on her own personal antenna. Her face, creased in multitudes of tiny wrinkles, was saddle-leather brown from the sun. She ignored me and squinted at the foal.

"See you got a foal down in the pasture," she said in a high, bell-like voice that could have cracked iron.

"No," I answered. "You saw wrong. We have no foals down in the pasture. This is the only one we have."

The woman gave me a sharp look out of the rapidly blinking black eyes. She grunted. Even her grunt seemed to have a piercing quality.

"This one sure looks down in the pasture to me!"

"How can you say that when she's right up here in the barnyard?" I asked incredulously.

"Get one thing straight," the woman said, shaking her head belligerently. "This foal may be up in the barnyard, but she's sure as hells bells down in the pasture!"

We glared at each other for a moment, and then she threw back her head and broke into such wild, pealing laughter that Egrett leaped high in the air, setting her foal to quivering.

" 'Stead of standing here jawring," the woman said, "I better introduce myself. The name's McBrood. Delila McBrood. Me and Cloyd, that's my husband, has got us a dandy little pony farm just this side the county line. I've gotten shed of them durn Shetlands and gone into the Welsh all the way. Figured I'd just drive over and size up the competition!"

And then she threw both arms in the air and gasped, "Hells bells! I left Melissey tied to the bedpost!" Back over the fence she jumped, landing again buoyantly on the balls of her feet; threw herself into the pickup and was off in a screech of gravel.

That evening after supper, as I finished telling Witt and the children of my peculiar-to-say-the-least, early-morning visitor, I was idly paging through my veterinary handbook in the hope of picking up some new pointers on how to handle fresh foals. Something on the page stopped me cold. The doctor was saying that it was not uncommon for a large, ungainly foal to be born with weak leg muscles, causing him to walk for several days on the back of his pasterns, with the tip of the hoof pointing upwards. This condition, he wrote, almost always rights itself without treatment, and is known as "down in the pasterns."

So that was it! She wasn't crazy after all. She was trying to tell me my foal was "down in the pasterns" and I, in my monumental ignorance, had thought she was saying "down in the pasture." My face burned. I was certain I wouldn't be getting another visit from Delila McBrood.

I was wrong. The very next Saturday morning, early, the red pickup appeared again, and this time Delila had brought her husband Cloyd. She was full of smiles and high, pealing laughter. "Didn't get to finish jawring last time on account of that durn Melissey I left tied to the bedpost," she said.

"How did you find Melissa?" I asked cautiously.

"Right as rain," Delila answered. "Wasn't even foaming at the mouth. I want you to see her soon's you can get over that way."

I couldn't wait.

"I'm sorry we had that misunderstanding about the foal when you were here the other day," I said. "I realized later that what you were saying was that the filly was 'down in the pasterns.' "

Delila blinked her snapping black eyes rapidly at me and said cheerily, "Son-of-a-gun, girl! I knowed you would finally come to see for yourself that filly was down in the pasture!"

I quickly changed the subject.

I asked the McBroods in for coffee; Witt was at home, and the four of us sat around the kitchen table, as Delila said, "jawring," and soon the house was vibrating with the peal of her laughter. Cloyd was a broth of a man, not much taller than his wife, and wiry, with an exquisitely ruddy pink skin pulled tautly over high cheekbones and just a shred of soft black hair lying around on a skinny head. His gentian-blue eyes sparkled on and off, intermittently, like the lights on department-store Christmas trees. He had a low pleasing voice that leaned precariously toward laughter. He and Delila settled immediately into a quarrel as to how many grandchildren they had. Delila said twenty-three and Cloyd said twenty-six.

"Now, Cloyd, honey," Delila said, "you know good and well Marilyn's got five and Randy's got four—that comes to nine—and Bonnie, poor thing, had eight 'fore she even knew where babies come from, that's seventeen right there. And Linda's got one by that snot she married—she'd of been better off if she'd of thrown names in a hat. That's eighteen, and Buck got five with that lollapaloozy grass widow he harnessed up with, they ain't even ours but we throw 'em in on the count anyways. And that makes twenty-three, so there, Cloyd, I knowed I was right!"

Delila's triumphant laughter rattled all the windows in the house. Cloyd just sat there, his eyes sparkling on and off, the pink coming and going in his cheeks. Suddenly he grinned, and said softly, "What about Donna?"

Delila's chin dropped a little. Her black eyes blinked furiously. "What *about* Donna?" she demanded contentiously, trying to stare Cloyd down.

"Donna's got three," Cloyd said, and all the Christmas tree lights flashed on full battery.

Delila jumped up from the table, headed for the door. "What I come to see," she said, "is the rest of your ponies, and not to set here jawring on crap that don't amount to a hill of bush beans."

I followed her out. Witt and Cloyd elected to stay in the kitchen for another round of coffee.

I took Delila out into the front meadow where Stalwyrt Beau was grazing with his three mares and the new foal. It was breeding season, but Widowbird was already serenely pregnant from the previous autumn (with some help from Dock and Normal Hayes) and due to drop her first foal in September. Egrett would be coming into foal-heat in a few days, during which time she would be bred back to Beau to produce next year's foal. Mourning Dove, now a two-year-old, was in the breeding field for the first time.

It was the kind of May morning on the farm that always reminds me of an impressionist painting. The leaves on the giant old silver maples that surround the house were half-way out, dainty and shimmering in the damp of the morning. The short bluegrass on which the ponies were grazing still held the brilliant yellow-green of early spring. At the bottom of the hill, a fine mist was lifting up from the creek. Killdeer were skimming along the rocks of the creek bed, purring roughly as they bobbed along looking for insects, taking off with a shrill cry. As they flew, the salmon-pink in their tails glimmered through the mist.

We walked through the wet grass to the low corner of the meadow where the ponies were grazing. Delila said she couldn't wait to show me the outstanding Welsh breeding stock she had picked up by scouring the country. She had come up with, she said, some *whales* of individuals. And she had just last year brought in from the West a *whale* of a stallion she had acquired through secret channels, the nature of which she wouldn't discuss, should I probe her.

I was somewhat crestfallen then, when Delila began to

look over *my* small Welsh herd and didn't seem to find any *whales*. She prowled around Beau, opened his mouth, checked his teeth, then went around behind him, lifted up his tail, squatted down, and carefully observed all appendages she could see from this angle. After a long moment of deliberation she dropped the tail, clucked her tongue and exclaimed, "Son-of-a-gun, girl! If the front end of this stud was as good as the back, you'd be onto something!"

Treading buoyantly in her Indian moccasins on the springy wet grass, she circled around Egrett and Widowbird, evaluating, comparing, her blackbird eyes blinking so rapidly I could envision the judgments coming in almost too fast to take care of on one antenna. "This Widow mare is holding up a dandy bunch of bones," she said, her bell-like voice cutting through the crisp morning air. "It's a durn shame she had to sacrifice her tail set for that good flat croup!"

Her tanned face tautly wrinkled in concentration, Delila turned toward Egrett and ruminated further. "I don't know but what if I had my druthers," she concluded, "I wouldn't take 'em a mite swaybacked like this other good cobby mare you got here."

This pretty well took care of my two fine imported broodmares. As we walked down to the creek's edge to look at Mourning Dove, who had separated from the other ponies to get herself a drink of water, I thought rather grimly to myself that if Mrs. McBrood didn't like this one there might soon be an outsize, muscular, redwinged blackbird in Indian moccasins with some ruffled feathers. Because it was hard for me to fault Mourning Dove anywhere. Delila gazed at the young chestnut mare, her eyes snapping and batting furiously as she circled and judged from every direction. I held my breath for the final verdict.

"Now *there*," she boomed, "is a whing-ding of a pony!"

I sighed, rather mollified, although I suspected that *whing-ding* was just a mite lower than *whale* in Delila's book. When, after further inspection, she said that she would like to load up Mourning Dove and take her home with her, I promptly forgave her for all remarks to date. But then she added darkly, shuddering a little, "A perfect animal like that. It gives me the edgies. You know something's bound to happen to her sooner or later!"

We walked back up the hill and perched on the board fence, watching the ponies graze, and Delila told me she had started in the pony business about ten years ago, when they had moved to the old McBrood place after Cloyd's father died. She had started out with grade ponies, had worked up into registered Shetlands, realizing too late that the "durn shaggies was no account." So she sold out the Shetlands and went into Hackneys. That was before she discovered that "their bones was too brittle and their blood was too hot," a combination she considered dangerous in the same animal. The Hackneys subsequently were moved out, and now she was into the Welsh *all the way*.

"Whatever else I done," Delila concluded, "I always sold my ponies for top dollar." She indicated that it was a good thing she did, because Cloyd foundered on and off in the family shoe business and had to be bailed out every now and then. When she heard Cloyd revving up the pickup as a signal that it was time to leave, she made me promise that I would try to get over to her place on my first free day.

"Now there's a woman," I told Witt as we watched the red pickup bounce over the bridge and turn onto the road, "that seems to make money in the pony business no matter what she turns to. Maybe there's hope for us."

Witt laughed. "That isn't the way Cloyd talked. He told me that over the last ten years Delila has spent almost eighteen-thousand dollars of his hard-earned shoe money—he's in the children's shoe business, you know—by switching from one pony breed to another. 'You have to sell a mess of booties to net eighteen thousand,' is the way he put it. He said she always buys high and sells low. And she always becomes disenchanted with a breed just as she's got some stock to sell—and then goes into something else."

Witt laughed again. "Do you know he calls her Deli? I'll bet no other human being alive could get by with that without getting smacked to the ground."

"I feel kind of sorry for Cloyd," I mused.

"I wouldn't feel too sorry for Cloyd," Witt answered. "He thinks Deli is funny as heck. By the looks of his eyes he's had more jolts of enjoyment and burned up more batteries than a dozen men his age. Maybe Deli's got him jumping through hoops, but it's a different kind of hoop every day, and he considers it a challenge."

I restrained myself into the middle of next week before I returned Delila McBrood's visit. After seeing the children off on the school bus on a hazy spring morning, I drove toward the county line to seek out the McBrood spread. As I drove past Normal Hayes' place I was surprised to see Melody high up on a ladder against the barn wall with a can of paint. She was touching up the large white letters that read: HAYES ACRES. NORMAL AND MELODY HAYES. Her presence up on that ladder meant one of two things, and I idly wondered which it was: either Normal had confessed to his fear of heights—or the honeymoon was over.

Delila had given me directions: "Turn right at the durn trailer camp, left at the Duroc pig farm—you'll smell it 'fore you see it—then keep barrelin' along until you see a *whale* of a bunch of good ponies."

I followed directions, kept barreling along until I saw ponies grazing in a large field along the road. A long lane, flanked by Lombardy poplars, led back to the farm buildings. An old Federal-style farmhouse, a two-story brick with a chimney at either end, was connected by a graveled driveway to an old unpainted barn that winged out in a right angle to make a cozy courtyard with the house. As I drove in, the mystery of Melissa was instantly revealed to me. Standing in the corner of the driveway where the barn wall angled out was a handsome palomino Welsh mare. She was tied to an antique Victorian bedpost sunk in the driveway. The post was resplendent with swirls, scrolls, and curlicues from which the sun and rain had washed layers of varnish in varying degrees.

When Delila came out of the barn, I called, "That's some hitching post you've got there!"

"Solid cherry!" Delila answered with a shrieking laugh that didn't stir a muscle on the palomino. "Mother McBrood give us her fourposter when Cloyd and me was married. I said to Cloyd, hells bells, it takes a fancier lady than I am to sleep in a bed like that, and besides, I didn't have no Irish lace on my nightgown. I stored the durn bed up in the attic until Cloyd's mama passed on, and then I got the idea to make a hitching post out of one of them posts. There's three more where this one come from when it busts."

"And I suppose this is Melissa?"

"And what a *whale* of a mare she is." Delila answered. "I bought her off a chicken farmer out of Sioux City, Iowa. Week before last me and Cloyd was hightailing it out of Sioux City on U. S Twenty 'bout four o'clock, hell-bent on makin' it to Waterloo 'fore dark, when I seen this mare pokin' her head through the fence to get at the road grass, and I said to Cloyd, I said, 'Whoa there, buddy!' The upshot of it was I made the Leghorn man an offer. He'd picked up this mare on a notion at a dispersal sale—didn't give beans about her. We was driving the Volkswagen bus with the back seats out, and we just run the mare up in the bus and took off. Never did get to Waterloo. We backtracked to U.S. Fifty-nine, hit right for St. Joseph, Missouri, picked up Thirty-six, drove all night, streakin' for home. Never had so much fun. Melissey stuck her head right over the front seat twixt me and Cloyd, and ever' time we met a car, the headlights picked up her face. Them drivers gasped and stared like they'd seen the Holy Ghost."

Shrieks of laughter poured out of Delila as she remembered the incident, but Melissa, tied up short to the bedpost, didn't twitch a muscle. "I keep her tied a hour or two a day to settle her down," Delila said. The mare looked to me as if she'd had all the settling she needed. After a ride like that, she was probably immune not only to Delila's laugh, but to lesser things like bombing and strafing.

Delila took me into the barn to see her stallion. Sitting cross-legged on the floor was a small boy—an angel with gentian-blue eyes and a bob of yellow curls. He was reaching an arm up over a rubber bucket and taking out handfuls of grain and stuffing them into his mouth. Instinctively I seized the child and shook the grain out of his hand. The angel screamed in protest.

"Leave him be," said Delila serenely. "Won't hurt him a bit. I mix my own pony feed, you know. Wouldn't trust them yahoos at the feed store to make me up a pound of bird seed. I use nothing but clean crimped oats, bran, linseed meal, molasses and honey, and a few whole kernels of corn throwed in for chewing."

"But the corn," I said in alarm. "The child can't chew the corn."

"He knows he's s'posed to spit it out," Delila answered. She cupped her hand under the child's chin. "Spit out the corn for grandma, sweetheart." The child obediently popped a kernel of corn out of his mouth.

With a flourish of one who knows what she's about, Delila threw open a box stall, snapped a longeing rope on her stallion, brought him out on the driveway, and ran him smartly around in a circle so I could see him from all angles. He was a young spirited strawberry roan. His tail was set high on a good short back, and he had a beautiful shoulder, along with the short, dense cannon bones of the classic Welsh; but he was rather plain headed. A somewhat long horse head on a Welsh-pony body. I said lovely things about the body, but declined to mention the head.

When I asked her—not without guile—whether this was the stallion she had brought in from the West, she pursed her lips and looked mysterious. She put the stallion back in his stall, took her grandchild by the hand, and we went out into the back field to look at her herd of mares.

A half-dozen mares, each with a young foal at side, were grazing on about twenty acres of lush pasture that Delila identified as brome grass she had planted from a special mixture given to her in Arkansas by a quarter-horse man who had developed the seed himself and was growing it in the southern part of the state with great success, she said, on nothing but a pile of rocks.

The mares were sleek and fat; all looked to be of good Welsh conformation, but I noted that several of them, too, like her stallion, were perhaps a bit plain headed. The foals were a sight to see: racing around their mothers, putting their noses to the ground and impudently chasing the brown-headed cowbirds that were walking on the ground chirping and looking for seeds, running back to their dams and snooting ferociously for a drink of milk. I seemed to be hearing the soft tinkle of a bell, and at first I thought it was just the cacophony of birds: a flock of kingbirds, their snowy breasts gleaming in the morning sun, were flying low in the sky, catching insects on the wing, all the while uttering shrill cries as they tried to scare off a pair of crows flying higher overhead. But the tinkle persisted, and then I spotted a foal with a bell around his neck. Every time the colt leaped and bounded away, the bell tinkled and his mother—the blackest pony I'd ever seen—ran after him, nuzzled him, and went back to her grazing.

Delila laughed and said, "Makes you wonder, don't it?" She walked toward the black mare, speaking to her in a strangely soft voice, put her hand on the mare's neck and stroked her. "This is Blackfeet, my prize mare. She's blind. The bell on her colt helps her keep track of him."

The mare was a beauty, there was no doubt about it. She

had lovely liquid bones that seemed to flow one into the other with no interruption at all—a quality enhanced by her very blackness. Unlike most black ponies, she had no spot of white, neither star in her forehead nor one white foot. Against all of this blackness, her unseeing opaque eyes, speckled with prisms of blue like fine Scandinavian china, seemed to be imbedded in infinity.

"How I come by this mare," Delila said, "is this way. Me and Cloyd had run up to a pony auction in northern Michigan. This breeder—well, his heart had clean wore out and he had to get shed of his stock. Cloyd and me we sat in on the auction just long enough to know there was nothing there I give beans about. So I said to Cloyd, I said, 'You just set here a minute and check the going prices, maybe you'll learn something, and I'll take a turn around the barns 'fore we leave.' As luck would have it I found this mare all alone in the barn in a box stall, not with the rest of the herd up for sale. I took one look at her and knowed I had to have her, so I went around and found the old man and asked him why she wasn't up for auction. He said he'd raised that mare from a colt, he wasn't going to let her fall into bad hands, and after the sale he was goin' to shoot her. Well, I said, give her to me and I'll see to it she gets a good home the rest of her life.

"I give the old man my word. Paid a good price for her to boot, just to show him I wasn't no low-life horse-trader wanting somethin' for nothing. That old man cried, and then I cried, and we was both happy."

Delila wiped a tear from her eyes, and gently combed the mare's black mane with her fingers.

"She's well named," I said. "The Blackfeet Indians are known for their beautiful women."

Delila looked surprised and pleased. "Now that's one thing I didn't know," she said. A statement I had the feeling she didn't make very often.

Hoisting her grandchild on her shoulder, she invited me into the house for coffee. We had to go through the barn to get back on the driveway. As we passed the stallion's stall I asked Delila why she didn't have her stallion out with the mares now at the beginning of breeding season.

"Hells bells, you wouldn't catch me pasture-breeding," she said. "I hand-breed exclusive. Don't you know, girl, that if you pasture-breed your mares the stud carries them genes back and forth from one mare to the other? 'Fore you know it you got such mixed bloodlines you'll never get 'em straightened out. It don't matter a hill of bush beans if all you got is no-account grades, but you pay out money for good pedigreed stock, you want to keep them pure."

Delila said if I knew what was good for me, I'd take my stallion out of the field, hand-breed him in the barnyard to no more than one mare a day, and always wash his genitals thoroughly with Ivory soap before and after breeding. "Them pesky genes can hang around longer than you think," she said.

We went into the house, and Delila steered me left out of the center hall into the dining room. "The living room is over there on that other side," she said, indicating a closed door, "but I never use it 'ceptin' Christmas week and the Fourth of July for the McBrood reunion. Saves me a hell of a lot of fussy woman's work. There's not a single thing in there anyway 'ceptin' Mama McBrood's ugly antiques."

The dining room seemed to be where everything was dropped on the way to the kitchen from the barn. Red, white and blue striped wallpaper, with a full-blown rose border, was obviously a holdover from Mother McBrood. An ancient A.B. Dick mimeograph rested on one end of a massive cherry dining-room table, and a round glass bubblegum machine on the other. In between was a western saddle, bridle, bits of harness, and a large can of Neetsfoot oil resting on a lambs' wool polishing cloth. Delila's grandson ran to the cherry buffet—an elegant Queen Anne—pulled open the silver-ware drawer, took out a penny, put it in the gum machine, popped the round ball into his mouth. The top of the buffet was heaped with an assortment of pony halters and lead shanks. We continued on into the kitchen, which, I could see at a glance, was where the McBroods lived. It was a large cozy keeping room, with a fireplace at one end, a huge bright rag rug on the pegged oak floor, faded redwood cupboards on one wall, a sink, refrigerator, and range along another. A long redwood picnic table ran down the center of the room, with benches on either side. The remaining wall had a bay window through which the ponies could be seen grazing in the pasture.

Soon I was drinking coffee and eating a piece of cake so good I didn't want to swallow it, I just wanted to roll it around on my tongue forever. Delila said it was "sausage fruitcake," but there didn't seem to be any fruit in it. It was moist and tangy and tasted vaguely of sage and something else that may have been thyme or rosemary. When Delila asked me if I'd like to have the recipe, I accepted with alacrity, and she went to a cupboard drawer and pulled out a piece of paper and gave it to me. It was mimeographed.

"Ever' single person who eats that durn cake wants the receipt, so I grind out a batch of 'em every year or so. I borry the mimeograph from Buck's grass widow. She come by it in the divorce settlement."

Delila was holding her grandson on her lap; between bites of sausage cake he was covering her wrinkled face with moist kisses. He called her Gamma Brood. "The trouble with these durn grandchildren," she said, her voice suddenly husky, "is they never want to go home."

The atmosphere was pleasantly somnolent; I was staring dreamily out of the window at the foals frolicking in the meadow, when Delila said abruptly, "Did you know my mama was Shawnee?"

"Shawnee?" I asked stupidly, bringing myself in from the meadow with a start.

"Haven't you never heard of the Shawnee Indians?" Delila asked rather scornfully. "There was a pile of 'em right over there in Greene County. That's where Chief Tecumsee grew up. My mama goes right back to Tecumsee in her bloodlines. That's where this black hair I got come from."

Hurriedly trying to make up for what seemed to be my ignorance of Indians, I told Delila that I had grown up in North Dakota, where there were four or five Indian reservations, and that when I attended Minot State Teacher's College, one of my best friends was an Arikara girl from the Fort Berthold reservation.

"Well, what do you know!" Delila said. She heaped another piece of sausage fruitcake on my plate and filled my coffee cup.

"Yes," I said, pressing my advantage. "There were quite a few Indians at college, and a handsome Sioux from the nearby Fort Totten reservation had a bit of a crush on me. He looked like Clark Gable, only swarthier, of course. He asked me for a date one Saturday afternoon, and took me to see a movie. I even remember the name of the movie. It was called *Cherokee!* with an exclamation point. When he tried to hold my hand, I became slightly panicky, and as soon as the movie was over I cut and ran."

Delila's eyes were snapping, and she said suspiciously, "This isn't just a big story you're telling me, is it?"

"Every word is true," I said. "You can call up my sister Gladys in Idaho and ask her. She knows. She was there at the time."

Delila looked relieved. "This Sioux. Did you ever go with him again?"

"No. Every time I saw him in the halls after that I ducked. Just before school was out that year, he called me, late one Saturday night, on the dormitory telephone. He wanted me to meet him in downtown Minot. It sounded as if he'd been drinking. Anyway, it was after hours and I couldn't go. The women's dorms in those days were locked up like fortresses at eleven on Saturday night. On weekdays it was ten-thirty. I was glad to have the matter decided for me. I couldn't handle a sober Indian, much less one in his cups."

"I see what you mean," Delila said, nodding wisely.

I couldn't help noticing that Delila was suddenly treating me with a new deference. She wrapped up a piece of sausage fruitcake for me to take home to my children, and when I left she told me that I shouldn't worry for one minute if any more of my foals were born down in the pasture. "It don't amount to a hill of bush beans," she said. "It's something them durn horse doctors come up with to jawr about and take a five-dollar bill away from you for when they get a foot on your place."

Soon there was no doubt in my mind that my Indian connections were at least partly responsible for my burgeoning friendship with Delila McBrood. It was no time at all before we were visiting back and forth several times a week, and having long telephone conversations in between. Her attitude toward me had turned unmistakably benign; she stopped running down my ponies, at least to my face, and occasionally she even sent a spare pony-looker my way. In the pony world, this was carrying friendship to ridiculous extremes. She was more fun than a dozen picnics running concurrently, and news and gossip from near and far flowed from her as water drawn from a bottomless well. She had visited almost every pony farm in Ohio at one time or another, as well as scores of others in all parts of the country. Most of them, if her reports were true, did not have the quality of breeding stock to make it worth the time and effort to set a foot on their farms.

One day I stopped in at Dock's office to pick up some worm medicine for my ponies, and I asked Dock if he knew Delila McBrood.

"You mean Old Broody?" Dock answered. "You bet I know the old girl, but she don't have much use for me. To hear her tell it, she knew more about horse doctoring the day she was born than any DVM running up and down the roads today. Last time I remember being out to her place was five o'clock in the morning four, five years ago. Old Cloyd he come a 'hammering and a' beatin' on my door before the sun was up and said Delila's Shetland stallion had jumped into a bob-wire fence and tore his shoulder open. Said a flying saucer had spooked him. Said Deli had got up to put the cat out, had seen this thing flying low in the sky, and then heard her stallion crashing the fence.

"Well, I grabbed my bag, jumped in the pickup and Cloyd drove like holy hell back to the McBrood place. We'd a done better to stop in town for a soda pop. Old Broody come meandering out of the house calm as a cucumber."

Here Dock raised his voice high in a good imitation of Delila.

" 'Now, Cloyd, I wondered where you streaked off to. There wasn't no need to drag Dock out of bed at this hour when I've took care of everything!'

"And you can bet your liver she had, all right," Dock continued, laughing out loud as he recalled the sight. "She'd stitched that stallion up neat as you'd ever want to see with some kind of quilting-bee cross-stitch. Said she'd soaked a rag in chloroform and give it to the stallion out of a can to quiet him. And then she give him a good shot of penicillin after that."

"Where on earth does she get her drugs?"

"You and a few other people would like to know that," Dock answered. "I asked her and she just pressed her lips together and looked smart. She asked me in for coffee and some of that sausage cake of hers and offered to teach me how to make that cross-stitch. I declined. I wouldn't take her money for the call neither. I could just hear her spreading it through every barn in three counties how she'd taught old Dock everything he knows about surgery. No way."

"She certainly has an outgoing personality for being half Indian," I offered, thinking that I should contribute something to the exchange myself. "Every other Indian I've known has been the taciturn type."

"Indian, my ringworm!" Dock snorted. "If there's a drop of

Indian blood in that old girl I'll eat my stethoscope. Seldom use it anyway. Why that there is just some old story she come up with because her mother was left at an orphanage and didn't know who her people were. My father knew Old Man Fleagle—that was Broody's father, who was a blacksmith over in Greene County. Had his shop on a small farm somewheres not too far from where that Shawnee chief Tecumseh was supposed to have grown up. That's where old Broody got the idea to instill herself with a little Indian blood. She's been spreading that story around since she was a little girl. Dad said Old Lady Fleagle had black hair but her skin was white as cake flour. He said Broody's father was the dark-complected one in the family. He always had a horse or two around back. That there is how Broody comes by her full and complete knowledge of the equine."

I asked Dock if he'd ever heard Delila's theory about how pasture breeding mixes up the mares' bloodlines. Dock threw back his head and roared. "You mean how the stallion carries the genes back and forth from mare to mare? There's so many Broody stories going around the barns, but that's my pick of them all. First time I heard that one, I figured it was worth the price of the call right there.

"But you know," Dock said, sobering up, "Broody might not be as dumb as she sounds on that one. You'd be surprised how many horse breeders I know believe in telegony. That there's a fancy word that means a stallion who's gotten a mare in foal is able to pass his characteristics along to later offspring she may have by other stallions. If anyone can believe that, maybe Broody's theory isn't so farfetched, after all. Maybe Broody is just ahead of her time."

Ahead of her time or not, Delila knew things that other people didn't. She was always coming up with enticing morsels of information that no one else was privy to. Like the time she came up with the demise of Luther Humsucker, for instance. . .

She telephoned me one day and said she'd heard "over

town" that the old pony breeder had unexpectedly passed away. Luther was one of the oldest breeders in the area; had been one of the few who had made some money, having been fortunate enough already to have been in the business with a good supply of stock in the early years, when the pony boom hit. He raised both Welsh and Shetlands, in addition to grades, and was a horse trader to boot. He was not the most endearing man in the world. "Let the buyer beware" was not only his favorite axiom, it was his creed. There was scarcely a pony breeder in the state who, at one time or another, had not come under the spell of Luther Humsucker's super-salesmanship. In more barns than one would care to count, there was evidence of the Humsucker charm: a stallion that proved infertile; a bred mare that never foaled; a harness pony that kicked over the traces; a "child-broke" riding pony that bucked into the next county. At a public auction, all some mischief maker had to do was whisper, "I half believe that's a Humsucker pony," and every live bidder in the barn became a deaf mute.

So when Delila hit me with the news of Luther Humsucker's passing, I hesitated for a moment—whether to be a hypocrite and say, "I'm sorry to hear that."

But Delila didn't wait for me to answer. She said, "I know what the old goat should have on his tombstone. 'Three foot in the trailer and he's yours!' "

A few days later, she called with more details. Yes, it had been a heart attack. And she had heard "over town" that the Humsucker family couldn't wait to get rid of every pony and horse on the place. "Old Luther wasn't even cold in his grave," she said, " 'fore they was offering everything on the place for pocket money."

Every day or so she called with more interesting details. She had just heard that the entire four hundred acres was going on the block next; the widow was shopping for a big house in town. She had heard it whispered around that she already had her new husband picked out.

We spent many happy times on the telephone discussing

circumstances evolving out of the demise of Luther Humsucker.

And then, a few weeks later, I received an early-morning visit from two area pony breeders, Honey Free and her friend Beatrice Framson. Honey had been one of those who had been burned badly by Luther's spellbindery, having purchased from him a supposedly bred Welsh mare that not only did not produce a foal, but cribbed on the fences day and night. Honey, a tiny woman with red-brown eyes and straw-colored hair, was bringing up four children alone since her husband was killed in a tractor accident, and she was trying to raise a few ponies to augment her income from her corn and soybean crops. Honey was tough, and she never gave up. She had been squabbling with Luther about that mare for years; but Luther had so far refused either to take back the mare or give her a price adjustment on the almost thousand dollars that she had been hypnotized into paying. As for Mrs. Framson, she was an elegant, generously endowed older woman in her seventies, who always wore a cornflower silk dress, whether to church, a pony show, or while milking her prize Jersey cow. She was the only pony breeder around who had been in the pony business longer than Luther Humsucker; had, as a matter of fact, sold him his Shetland foundation stock—an act she was on record as regretting from that day on.

As the two women stepped out of their car, I said, by way of conversation, "I suppose you know that Luther Humsucker passed away several weeks ago."

Honey looked at me sharply. Something very much like hope gleamed in her eyes, then faded.

"I'm afraid you're wrong," she said. "I was talking to the old son of a bitch just yesterday."

Silence fell like a heavy fog on the early morning air. I stared disbelievingly at Honey, then at Mrs. Framson, both of whom stared disbelievingly back at me.

"But, but Delila said—" I murmured.

"Oh—Delila!" said Honey grimly. "Delila hears things the rest of us don't."

"But he's been dead so long—weeks," I said.

I felt a small tickle coming up into my rib cage, and then a wave of laughter welled up into my throat and choked me and I sank down on the driveway and began to sob. The women stood silently by for a moment, and then Honey gave a great shout and started to laugh uproariously. After a few minutes, trying to get control of myself, I became aware that I wasn't hearing a thing from Mrs. Framson. I didn't know her at all well. What she must think of us. I mopped at my eyes with my sleeve, looked up, and saw Mrs. Framson standing with her back turned. Her head was down, and the cornflowers on her silken shoulders were shaking convulsively.

Later that day, when I felt confident I could talk with some degree of sobriety, I telephoned Delila and told her that "we" had been mistaken; that Luther Humsucker was still with us. I thought if I shouldered some of the blame it would soften the blow for her. I wondered what her explanation would be. Silence fell over the wires for a long moment. Then I heard a long, hissing, between-the-teeth whistle. Then a low "son of a gun!" Then another long silence. Then such wild peals of laughter rippled into my ear that I hurriedly held the telephone away and let the sound diffuse through the house. I waited and waited for the noise to subside, but I couldn't have said anything anyway because I was out of control again myself. Finally Delila gave out one last short shriek, sobered up, and said indignantly, "Hells bells! It just goes to show you can't take stock in one single, solitary thing you hear over town no more!" and she hung up.

Wherever she went, Delila McBrood made her presence felt. If you couldn't see her, you could always hear her. Nowhere was this more evident than at the county fair.

A rumor floated persistently around the country for years that secret bounty money was available out of the fair office to anyone who had the temerity to sneak over to the McBrood place under cover of darkness and deflate the tires of Delila's pickup the night before the judging of the pony-halter classes at the county fair.

Seldom showing any of her own ponies, Delila chose instead to sit and pass judgment on those of others. She traveled to the fair with her aluminum camp chair, starting early in the morning and moving from class to class. The pony-halter classes were all held in small, intimate, roped-off, open-air rings on the turf. Delila's *modus operandi* was always the same. She seated herself in the back row where she could keep an eye on spectators, judge, and ponies alike. She remained silent and unobtrusive until the pony she had preselected as the blue-ribbon winner came up for judging. Then suddenly all hell broke loose. She whistled through her teeth, yelled, "Hooray, team!" and beat her hands together in such wild applause you would swear there was a cheering section of ten instead of one middle-aged woman in Indian moccasins.

After this initial outburst, she remained silent until the judge had picked *his* winner. If he agreed with her choice, she again went through the whistle-and-applause routine, and all was sweetness and light in camp. But, dear God in heaven, if the judge disagreed with her, she set her teeth together and gave out a hissing "sheesh" that descended on the gathering like a pall. Then she arose and, folding up her camp chair with a tremendous clatter of gnashing aluminum, she stalked from the scene, leaving the spectators tittering, the judge apoplectic, and the unfortunate winner gloomily clutching his blue ribbon as he led his tainted pony out of the ring.

On July 21, 1969, I drove into the McBrood place in the middle of the morning to find Delila dejectedly kicking a stone around the driveway with her moccasined feet. Her shoulders had an unaccustomed, alarming droop. I asked her what was wrong.

"Hells bells and bells hells and throw 'em back!" she cried, viciously kicking the rock so that it skipped across the driveway and landed with a thunk against the barn wall. "I would have give everything I ever had or ever hope to get to be the one that made that moon landing yesterday!

"Let me tell you something," she said, "I was so jealous of that Armstrong fellow, my stomach twisted up in a knot harder'n this fist. I finally had to turn off the durn set!"

If only she could have been a man, she stormed, she would never have stayed in the same place very long, but would have been off to conquer new worlds—like her brother Darrel. Delila had told me of Darrel before; he was almost twenty-five years younger than she, was a test pilot for the Air Force and did so many exciting things that Delila's voice actually quivered when she spoke of him. She seldom mentioned her own sons, who, she felt, had gone into mundane occupations: Randy worked in a factory and Buck ran a western sports shop. But Darrel—Darrel was different.

"Ever' single time I see one of them Army planes up in the sky," she said, "I wonder if it's Darrel, and I wish I was in his shoes, and if I was, I'd like as not just keep going, maybe 'til I got to the moon."

The first moon shot hit Delila hard, but a few weeks later she suffered a much harder blow. Darrel was killed in an airplane crash in testing grounds over Texas. When she called to tell me, her rage had momentarily overcome her sorrow. "There is all kind of people walking around on this earth that don't amount to a heap o' horse droppings," she cried. "Why couldn't the good Lord have taken one of them 'stead of Darrel?"

She asked me if I had a hat that I could lend her to wear to the funeral. She had never owned one. I had stopped wearing hats myself after we moved to the farm, but I rounded up five of rather ancient vintage and took them over to her place. I thought the black cloche that fitted snugly over her straight black hair looked well on her, and told her so, but she looked in the mirror, grimaced, and blurted without thinking, "It makes me look like I'm going to a goddam funeral!" Then broke down and wept. She decided to wear the floppy brown Leghorn straw with ribbons streaming down the back, which I had bought in a fanciful moment and never had the occasion to wear.

For months after that, Delila dragged around, and I could see that her enthusiasm for her Welsh ponies was subtly on the wane. She began to complain that she got nothing but fillies from her Welsh mares; a strange complaint, indeed. Every other pony or horse breeder in the country would have gladly taken a second mortgage on the homestead if it would have given him a better ratio of fillies to colts. Unlike the rest of us, who were constantly fighting the plague of too many stud colts, Delila had had the amazing good fortune to acquire a stallion who produced a filly about four times out of five; in only a few years she had amassed a herd of several dozen beautiful young Welsh mares, most of whom she bred back to the sire to get more fillies. Compared to the rest of us, she was sitting pretty.

But one stormy day in January she drove in to see me, as bouncy and excited as I'd seen her in a long time. So much snow covered the lane that even the United Parcel man had given up and backed out. But Delila put on a tremendous burst of speed and came plowing right up in her red pickup. She said she had just returned from visiting a pony breeder in Iowa who was raising Appaloosa ponies. Called POAs, they were produced by crossing good quality ponies of any breed to a small Appaloosa stallion. It could work the other way around, too. The only requirement for registering an animal was that it be under fifty-four inches and that it have the physical characteristics of an Appaloosa—such as a blanket of spots on the back and croup, and sclera around the eye.

"What a *whale* of a using pony this POA is," she cried. "Why your average a-hunnert-fifty-pound man who don't eat too much can ride him from sunup to sundown without winding him. And disposition? Man! You can set under that durn pony ringin' a school bell and he'll go to sleep on you."

I didn't see or hear from Delila again until spring. Witt became suddenly and violently ill with a kidney stone; I had to call out an ambulance in the dead of night to get him to a South Metropolis hospital, where he stayed for several weeks. I had no more than brought him home to convalesce, than Liz stepped in a hole in the barn while doing chores and broke her foot. With a cast to her knee, she couldn't manage the school bus. It snowed every other day and the snow piled up so high in the lane that even the Jeep had difficulty negotiating the hill. Stoyer spent every daylight hour when he wasn't in school shoveling snow so we could get in and out. With running liaison between Witt's office and Witt at home, taking Liz to and from school, and keeping the ponies fed out at the barn, I was totally absorbed in trying to maintain some sort of holding pattern. It was the end of March before I got squared away enough even to think about catching up on the gossip out there in pony world.

When I dialed the McBrood number, the operator said the number had been discontinued. Mystified, I telephoned Honey Free.

"For heaven's sake, where have you been?" Honey asked. "Didn't you know the McBroods had an auction the second week in March? They sold out lock, stock, and barrel including the shoe store. Bought a small ranch up in somewhere. Delila is up there raising POAs."

"POAs! In Montana? I can't believe it. How could it happen so soon?"

Honey laughed. "You know Delila. When she wants

something, she wants it fast, and there's no stopping her. She latched onto the idea she's going to sell POAs to the Indians up there. You know, she's always had this Indian hang-up. She though it was time to get next to her brothers and sisters!"

Honey said that Delila had sold all of her ponies except a half dozen of her best two- and three-year-old Welsh mares; that she had hired a big national horse-van outfit to transport them up to Montana for her; that she was planning to find a small Appaloosa stallion in the West somewhere to cross with the mares. She said that Delila had taken a beating on the ponies she had sold at auction, because she hadn't taken the time to advertise the sale, and what is more it had snowed, then rained, on auction day and there was a poor breeder turnout.

"But you know something?" Honey concluded. "The antique hunters got wind of the sale, and a little sleet never stops *them*. What Delila lost on ponies she more than made up for on Mother McBrood's antiques. She really cleaned up on all that solid cherry. Even jerked her hitching post right up out of the driveway and threw it in with the fourposter."

Suddenly I thought of something. "Oh, my God," I said. "What about Blackfeet?"

"Don't worry," Honey answered. "Delila kept her promise to the old man. She took the blind mare with her. The last thing she and Cloyd did was to load her up in the Volks-wagen bus and take off. Except for the mare, they were traveling light. They'd sold everything except the clothes on their backs."

Later that spring, one day when the dandelions were sprouting yellow all over our front meadow—I remember the day because I saw a pair of bluebirds sitting in the sycamore at creek's edge (bluebirds are almost extinct here now, run off by the starlings)—I walked down the lane to get the mail and found a letter in the box postmarked Chinook, Montana. It was from Delila. I was so mesmerized by the handwriting that it took me awhile to get to the contents. Written with a felt-tipped burgundy pen on rough white mimeograph paper, the script was large and forceful, full of flourishes and splattered dots. Every time Delila wanted a word emphasized, she tailed out the last letter around the word in a great swirl. When she wanted greater emphasis she made two swirls. The letter was whirling with swirls. It read:

Hey, Kiddo!
—Sorry as heck we didn't get to say good-bye tried to call you on the phone but no answer. Where was you anyway? Even drove over to your place—boy was it quite. Even the dogs had took off.

Well here we are where the coyotes howl and the wind blows free, as the song says. Ohio it ain't. That northwest wind comes barrelin through from Canada and don't stop for us or nobody else. We got us a dandy little fifty-acre ranch up here with a good tight little barn—house not much but you know me the less housework I got hangin round my neck the better. Blackfeet come through the trip like gangbusters in the Volks sorry I can't say as much for them other six. They all had a good case of the scours when that fancy coast to coast transport unloaded them. I give them all a good dose of K.O. Pectate with their evening feed and by morning they was binding up satisfactory.

Soons we got the mares straightened around, we found an old fella to chore a couple days and me and Cloyd took a fast run up to Palloose country there where Ore— Wash—Idaho all comes together and found us a whale of a Appaloosa stud I mean this one is [swirl, swirl] TOPS!! Stands just 56″ and man what a front end on that horse. I lost no time puttin my mares to him and I know Blackfeet has took already and one or two others and I got Cloyd sayin his prayers ever night fore he goes to bed that all seven of them foals we are expectin next spring will have spots on their rumps.

What a dandy—yes I would say A-1 location we got here to sell our born and bred in the US of A ponies to the likewise Indians. We are situated dead center not more than 100 mile each way between the Blackfeet reservation to the west and the Fort Peck res. to the east—that's your Sioux—and you can throw a rock down to the Chippewa and Cree and if that isn't enough Indians for you there is more right down here to Fort Belknap.

I can tell you one thing kiddo we are onto something with this great POA breed and if you was smart you'd sell that stud horse of yours he don't have no front end on him anyways and get you a Ap.

All for now here comes Cloyd barrelin it up the road with the roll of fence I run him into town for. I been keepin him busy settin iron posts but he don't mind too much says its a change from selling booties.

Delila & C McBrood

I didn't hear another word from the McBroods for almost two years—except for the Christmas postcard with the Star of Bethlehem zeroing in on a horse of indeterminate origin drinking from a pool of water. No message. Just signed "Delila and C McBrood." The next Christmas we received the same postcard. It figured, when I thought about it: Delila disliked fuss and ritual so she did her cards up in two-year batches and had it over with for awhile.

I really missed her the first year, missed those long telephone conversations with news that had just come in on her own private teletype, missed sitting at her kitchen table and eating her sausage fruitcake. After she was gone, I dug out the recipe she had given me years before and that I had never tried. It turned out heavy and soggy, like wet sand. Maybe it was true, after all, what everyone had said, that she had, deliberately or not, left out a key ingredient.

I dropped her a note every month or so that first year; the second year, getting no response, I slacked off, too. But one dismal March day, when the rain was freezing on the windows and Witt and the children had left for office and school, I decided to write her just one more letter. That morning, we had found Mourning Dove dead behind the barn. Our first foal born on the farm. It was hard to believe she was almost fourteen years old. Dock said she must have been stricken with a sudden colic in the night, most likely from picking up a stray piece of frozen clover in the barnyard. I was lonely, and I was sad. I felt that Delila would understand.

I received an answer almost by return mail. It read:

Hey, Kiddo!

I am sorry as can be to hear about that Dove mare of yours. She was a whale of a mare if I ever seen one to tell you the truth she give me the edgies first time I laid eyes on her she was so perfect. Them are the ones that always goes first and the buck kneed jibbers stand around to a handsome old age.

Well I knowed I should have wrote sooner but I never was one to take pen to paper if anything better come along to do. I can tell you one thing we have got us a whale of a yearling crop of POA's seven in all and ever one showing spots on their rumps. We are getting a dandy bunch of visitors to the farm every day and hope to move each and every ycarling off the place for 4-H before the summer is out.

Suppose you are wondering about the Indians well I don't mind saying they have been a disappointment to me and Cloyd. The only ones in here so far was a couple of Crow who had drove all the way up from Billings. The Crow is one tribe I got nothing for sale to. Them were the bastards that threw in with old Custer prior to the skirmish out at the Little Big Horn.

As for the rest of them there is a pile of them around here and they do not seem to have two 50¢ pieces to rub together but Lord know they'd have plenty if we hadn't stole it from them and now the government in Washington is treating them like shirt-tail relatives that has clean wore out their welcome. I got to say this—from what I seen of them I half believe if they did have any spare cash they would spend it on fast cars and booze stead of your good POA's. I wouldn't say this to anybody but you besides there isn't a Indian left in Ohio in case you spill the beans so here it is. I think one of their troubles is the mixing up of the bloodlines by passing them genes back and forth.

Don't know how much longer we will be in Montana I can tell you one thing me and Cloyd has taken to these wide open spaces maybe could use a little less wind. But Ohio will never see us again just thinking about it throws us into a coughing fit.

Delila & C McBrood

P.S. Me and Cloyd run up to a horse show in Butte and seen one of those Paso horses that was brought in through Mexico from down across the border and man what a whale of a horse that is!!! I hear you can set on that durn horse with a tea cup and fly like the wind and never spill a drop.

I didn't really expect to hear from her soon again, and I didn't. As Christmas neared that year, I was in the Peatville post office one day waiting in line to mail a package to my sister Florence in St. Paul. It was a knitting-instruction book she had been trying to find for a long time and that I had come on quite by accident in a bookstore. There were many people ahead of me in line, and the man directly in front of me was pushing along a tremendous package that took my eye because it was impressively wrapped, as if it were really going somewhere. The outside brown paper wrapping was new and heavy duty and the package was tied with new white clothesline cord.

I leaned forward to peer at the address and saw that it was going to Tucumcari, New Mexico. To Mr. and Mrs. Cloyd McBrood.

I straightened up and looked at the man ahead of me. He was tall, with a formidable set of shoulders about to burst out of a western-style shirt that had a brass-studded leather yoke. I hesitated a moment and then tapped him gently on the shoulder. "Excuse me, sir, but is your name McBrood?"

The man turned quickly and replied, "You bet! I'm Morgan McBrood."

"Buck?"

He smiled, and I was enchanted to find myself looking into a familiar pair of gentian-blue eyes that sparkled on and off, intermittently, like the lights on department store Christmas trees.

"Hey! You must know my folks!"

I said I did indeed and we settled into a chat. Buck said his parents had suddenly taken a notion early that fall to pull up stakes in Montana and move to New Mexico. They had gone south on a scouting expedition and had found a small cabin with ten acres, had bought it on the spot, had contracted to have a pole barn built, and then had gone back to Montana, had an auction, sold the ponies, and taken off.

"Those two are getting to be gypsies in their old age," Buck said. "Anyone else would be looking for a retirement village. Mother should have been a pioneer. She would have loved crossing the country in a covered wagon. Trouble is, she would have been the one wanting to ride point."

We both laughed. "Anyway, last fall she got the idea she couldn't live another day without having herself one of those Peruvian Paso horses. She found one down there in southern California somewhere. I think she's already got her bred to have a foal come spring."

I started to ask, decided I didn't want to know, and then

asked anyway. "What about Blackfeet? Was she auctioned off, too?"

"Blackfeet? Nope. The folks put her in the Volks and took her right along with them. Mother says Blackfeet is getting some age on her. Likely won't be moving her again."

The line surged ahead, and we moved along with it. "You've got your father by about thirteen inches, the way it looks," I said.

The gentian-blue eyes flashed on full battery. "It was all that sausage cake that did it!" Morgan McBrood said as he effortlessly heaved his package up on the counter.

I haven't heard from the McBroods since they moved to New Mexico, and it's been a few years. But I think about Delila a lot, and there is one way I always imagine her. I imagine her riding through the New Mexican desert on a magnificent black Paso horse. The two of them are really flying, and Delila's straight black hair isn't moving at all. She is holding a cup of tea on a fine saucer, and she isn't spilling a drop.

16

The Cats:
The Williams Dynasty

*F*our volatile cat lovers try-
ing to live in the same household, even on a farm, is not an
easy situation. Everyone wants the best for *his* cat, often at
the inconvenience of someone else's cat. Turbulence among
both cats and people is inevitable.

Strangely, none of us knew how fond of cats we could
become until years after we'd moved to the farm. We had
inherited from the previous owner a young spotted tom, a
free-lance Lothario who came and went on his nocturnal
rendezvous, stopping only long enough in the barn for a
change of clothes and an occasional saucer of milk. He
brooked no interference from us and gave none. One winter
he was caught in a steel leghold trap. He simply chewed his
foot off and went about his business on three legs. In the
year of the great Cat Epidemic of 1960, which killed most of
the feline population in the county, we found him dead in
the barn one morning. His funeral cortege was a slow ride in
the coaster wagon from the barn to the edge of the orchard,
with four-year-old Liz walking solemnly behind. It had
dignity and dispatch. He would have liked that.

We were without cats for a year or two and never missed
them, never dreaming that the great *Williams* dynasty was
soon destined to spring up on our farm. It began with a fey,

225

utterly aloof and untouchable long-haired feline—big, beautiful, and black, with a feathery expanse of white on her breast—whom we found waiting at the back door one day. She slipped inside, floated around all of the rooms with an eerie will-o'-the-wisp grace, then skimmed out the door as suddenly as she had come. She flatly rejected any proffers of food or affection. She was just looking, thanks.

This intriguing routine went on for months, until one cold spring morning Witt found her in the haymow with four new kittens. Only then did she graciously accept food for herself and her family.

The children went wild to think that our housing facilities and possibly even we, ourselves, had passed her rigid code of acceptance. They gave her the most glorious name they could think of—Queen of Sheba—and took her kittens to their bosoms. They each chose a kitten for their own. Liz took the languorous pure black female and named her Blackie, which shortly became Bla'. Stoyer claimed the snapping-eyed live-wire spotted female and named her Footer. They gave away the male, and tried to give away the remaining female, but she was so irascible and downright evil-tempered that she had no takers, and she stayed by default. They called her Peewee, always with the intention of some day finding a better name for her, but none ever surfaced.

As for the Queen of Sheba—that name didn't take at all. None of us could ever think of it. She was usually called What's-her-name Famous, until the children decided they wanted their kittens to have the dignity of a surname, even though the sire was out there in the woods somewhere—unknown, promiscuous, and probably indigent. They tried out and discarded dozens of surnames, but always came back to one—*Williams*—it seemed to ring so true, so right, so *legitimate,* for a respectable cat family. So the Queen of Sheba became Famous Williams, and thereafter all the cats or kittens either born or adopted on the farm would bear the name of Williams.

In no time at all, the beautiful Famous and her three daughters, who were all short-haired and obviously not carrying quite the royal blood of their mother, had infiltrated into the house. Stoyer and Liz spent hours making elegant sleeping boxes for all four cats out of cardboard grocery cartons. Each box was wallpapered with construction paper, further enhanced with intricate crayon scrolls, and each, of course, with its own name tag. Each cat knew its own box, and if one decided to try out another's box, the fur would fly. Footer, the live wire, went through a period of reducing her box to shreds, and after every demolition Stoyer made her yet a fancier one. The most splendid one he ever constructed was out of cardboard pieces the laundry put in Witt's shirts. Stoyer glued and molded dozens of pieces into a mod round swirl that exactly conformed to Footer's body. She didn't appreciate the work involved, for she eventually tore this one up, too.

When the kittens were seven months old, it dawned on us that both mother and daughters were getting uncommonly plump. One day in early fall, when Liz got home from kindergarten, she and I packed up all four cats, two to a cardboard box tied down with string, and drove to Dock's office. We both agree it's one of the most exciting rides we'll ever hope to have. I had one box on the front seat with me, and Liz had the other one on the back seat with her. Halfway to town, on the busy state highway, cats suddenly started clawing out of boxes. I was driving with one hand while frantically stuffing heads and paws back into ever-widening cardboard holes. Liz was screaming in the back seat that she was losing the battle. Soon there was so much black fur floating around my head I could scarcely see to drive, and then there were cats flying at every window, clawing and yowling. We got some curious looks from motorists passing us on the highway that day!

Dock did a mass spay job on the entire Williams family. He said each cat would have reproduced herself six times in another two months. Somewhere out there in the woods, in the dark of night, the ubiquitous seducer whose name was Williams had led not only the willing Famous down the primrose path again, but all of her (and possibly their) daughters as well.

A strange thing happened when the four arrived home from their three-day incarceration at Dock's. Although Famous had weaned her daughters months before, she now took them back to nurse, and nothing we could do could stop her. It was almost more than we could bear to see them cozily bedded down in front of the fireplace on a cold winter's night: Famous stretched out luxuriously full-length, while her three daughters, who were as big as she was, gorged themselves on her milk, all four of them setting up a roaring purr of unashamed bliss.

The maddening thing about cats is that they are unequivocally their own free agents. Ponies can be compromised and bribed. Dogs will sell their souls for a pat on the head and a stale biscuit. But cats will say to hell with you and you know where you can put your piddling tidbits. *Give it to me straight or don't give it to me at all.* They can be housetrained not because of anything *you* do, but because they are usually neater than you are and can't stand a mess.

As the Williams family matured, their personalities solidified. Liz's Bla', a true Sybarite, spent most of her day languishing on the foot of Liz's canopied bed, reveling in the silky feel of the quilted comforter. Early dawn on a summer's day would find her walking along the gabled roof under Liz's second-story window, scratching to get in. If she scratched long enough—and her patience was endless—Liz would wake up, and lift the screen out a few inches so Bla' could crawl in.

Stoyer's cat, Footer Williams, always the secretive one, became more and more mysterious with the years. Footer was spotted black and white. On her face, the white ran flush to the inner rim of her eyes, and the black ran flush to the outer edge, which meant that her eyes, starting at the inner edge from the starkest white, ran to the outer edge into darkest infinity. This gave her a look of pure enigma, and she had the personality to go with it. She took to traveling, and after she had been gone several days Stoyer would spend hours hoarsely calling for her from all edges of our fifty acres, trying to bring her back from her wanderings. Once she was gone for three weeks, and came back looking amazingly sleek and well fed. The suspicion arose in Stoyer that the bed and board were of better quality in someone else's house. He made her ever-fancier boxes and gave her tidbits of "people" tuna on her cat chow. This did not keep her at home.

After six years of mournful calling at dusk and frequent joyful returns (scratching on the door in the middle of the night), Footer packed her bags one night, headed into the woods, and never came back. Stoyer stoically accepted the inevitable. It had been like a stormy marriage bound for the rocks and held together too long with string. It was a relief when it was over.

It is difficult to pinpoint just exactly when it was that Stoyer and Liz and I became aware that Peewee, the Irascible; Peewee, who had stayed because no one else would have her; Peewee, who could take your foot off at the ankle if you were naive enough to turn your head—had become Witt's cat. After years of being mostly a barn cat, she was suddenly sleeping on the sofa in the master's study, with no interference from the master at all. The day he came home and found her furring up his desk chair—the one with the solid orange-linen fabric that shows *everything*—and he only smiled benignly while he tenderly lifted her off to place her on the sofa—this was when we knew that Witt had officially taken possession of Peewee.

It hasn't been easy—this relationship. As long as Peewee kept her choleric temper outdoors most of the time, there was room for her to explode. But after she became a house cat, and a precious one, too, well, danger lurks around every corner. She'll crouch behind the door between the kitchen and the living room for the pure joy of clawing a lady's legs—especially if the lady is wearing hose. If you're sitting on the floor watching television, she'll come purring and cozying up to you and lie down snug against you, as sweet a cat as you'd ever want to see. Temporarily mesmerized, you stroke her fur. She purrs even louder and snuggles up closer and, encouraged, you scratch her playfully under the chin. Pow! She has drawn blood on your arm. *"Take that, you brazen hussy,"* she yowls as she stalks off into the master's lair.

"What have you been doing to my cat?" Witt yells from the study. "The poor thing's fur is standing on end."

For years Peewee hunted every night in the neighbor's woods contiguous to our orchard. But one night during hunting season her luck ran out and she came staggering home with a wound in her head. Witt rushed her to the vet, and there was a battle to the finish between her and Dock, after which Dock retreated to a neutral corner to bind up his lesions, while he pronounced his protagonist fit as a fiddle, with just a shallow scratch that would heal itself.

The little head wound did heal in several days, but Peewee herself went into a swift decline and wouldn't eat a bite, and Witt wouldn't take her back to Dock. He said he just couldn't stand to put her through that ordeal again—she was so terrified of Dock. Liz and I snorted privately to each other, "Poor Dock's the one who's laying his life on the line."

We shamed Witt into taking her back to Dock by telling him she was too good a cat to let die. This time Dock took no chances. He anesthetized her before she could join the battle. On a bit closer examination, he found she had been shot straight and clean through the jaw. He washed out and cauterized the wound. With her kind of spirit, Dock said grimly, she'd pull through.

After that, Witt refused to let her out at night, ever again. She's been roosting in the garage ever since. Our cars are unique in that they have cat tracks running up one side and down the other. The first five miles we drive, the fur flies.

The second sequence of the Williams dynasty began when the calicoed and cross-eyed Miss Tabatha Williams came meandering up the lane, fresh, no doubt, from one of those invidious drop-offs. For Miss Tabatha, however, it turned out to be a most fortuitous time. She was pregnant with kittens that could fill the void of Footer's departure. When Stoyer opened the back door one evening, she darted in, lifted her head to him and gave a plaintive meow, while one eye looked at the west wall and the other eye looked at the east wall. Stoyer was hooked. As fast as you could say, "Cut up a grocery carton," she was installed on the back porch with her own sleeping box, sixteen saucers of milk, and a smug expression. No abandoned cat had ever made it so fast, or so good.

What is it about a cross-eyed female—woman or cat—that makes her utterly irresistible, especially to members of the opposite sex? Is it her vulnerability, or that she is a congenital woman of mystery? Whatever it is, I have known at least a dozen cross-eyed women, and every one of them—whether their eyes were crossed to the limit or had merely the fleeting shadow of a list—had male admirers standing up one aisle and down the other waiting their turns to proffer them lifelong protection and devotion.

As for Miss Tabatha, what a sire, what a Williams, she must have lured with that cross-eyed bait of hers! She subsequently gave birth to three of the biggest, most voluptuous kittens we had ever seen. There were two incredibly beautiful longhairs, male and female, and a flaming orange short-haired male. Stoyer went for color and immediately stamped the orange one for his own and named him Pumpernickel. Liz took the female, Gingersnap, who was an ethereal vision of sinuous fluff, with a face so sweet one could sit and cry just looking at her. By default, and what a cat to be left by default, the long-haired tiger male became mine, and I named him Gemini, for my sun sign.

Gemini grew up to be a huge, lissome, floating froth of a cat, against whose wiles I was utterly helpless. No mistake about it, I was a fool for that cat. When he came toward me undulating under the full fall of tiger fur, with his bushy tail held straight up, as happy cats always hold their tails, I dissolved into warm butter. The thing about Gemini, he *knew* he was devastating. He could never stand to have me read the newspaper. Soon after I'd picked up the evening paper, I'd feel a soft jump on my shoulder and then a body softly slithering down into my lap, and soon the newspaper had been ever so subtly pushed away, and Gemini was having his stomach rubbed instead. His favorite spot was on a kitchen chair with the tablecloth completely covering him except for the tail dropping off almost to the floor. From this position he would peek out just long enough for his huge soft eyes to see in mine how enchanting he was.

Like most devastating males, Gemini had an exception- ally roving eye. When he was six months old he stayed away for three nights, loping home one morning dusty and scruffy, with a pad missing from one of his feet. I straight- away sent him, along with Pumpernickel, to the vet to be neutered. The timing was bad. I didn't know that a lethal cat virus was epidemic in the neighborhood. Several days after they came home they became acutely ill. It was a raw, cold December and we were forced to keep them in the basement for warmth and to quarantine them from our other cats. Dock gave us antibiotic tablets, which he said they must have every day.

I'd rather fight a lion bare-handed than try to get a pill down a cat. A dog is duck soup to pill. You just fold his lips over his teeth with one hand and shove the pill down his throat with the other. You don't need to be afraid he'll bite you because he won't bite his own lips. But a cat is a horse of another color. You must hold the pill in a pair of long tweezers with one hand while you try to wedge open the mouth containing all those sharp, snapping teeth with the other hand. In the struggle, it's ninety percent certain you'll either lose the pill out of the tweezers or get scratched or bitten in the process. If you enlist someone to open the mouth for you while you poke down the pill, the opening of the mouth never seems to get exactly coordinated with the poking down of the pill, and the pill ends up getting lost on the floor while your assistant gets roaring mad because he held up his end of the bargain and you were sleeping in the crunch.

We managed to get the antibiotics into Gemini, but the first time we tried to get a tablet down Pumpernickel he went into shock and fell over dead. He just stopped breathing. I looked at Stoyer's stricken face as he stared down at his orange cat, the fur suddenly looking strangely pale spread out like a rug on the cold concrete floor. In desperation I grabbed the cat up around his front legs and pumped his body furiously with my hands. The air whistled emptily in and out of his lungs. Then the cat began to breathe. Stoyer and I stared at each other in disbelief. The cat struggled to get free, then dropped over lifeless again. Once more I pumped his body between my hands, and again he breathed, struggled, and collapsed. On the third try, I quickly laid him flat on the floor when he resumed breathing, and held him down so tightly he couldn't move. He slowly relaxed under the pressure of my hands and went to sleep.

We watched Pumpernickel sleep for half an hour, after which he yawned, stretched, got up and walked around as if nothing had happened. But we never tried to pill him after that. Stoyer and I agreed that Pumpernickel must recover without benefit of medication. Both he and Gemini did get well, but not until they were ghosts of their former selves. They ingested nothing for weeks except water and an occasional lick of mackerel. Dock said the only thing that saved them was that they both started out their illness at a hefty twelve pounds and were able to live off their fat.

I never realized until it happened to me how short the life

of a heroine is. Not long after the cats had recovered and gained the run of the house, I was baking cookies in the kitchen one day, and put Pumpernickel rather unceremoniously out the back door because he was under my feet. Stoyer, who was sitting at the table eating burned cookies, said quite seriously, "You know, I don't think you like my cat." I stared at him in disbelief, then burst out laughing. My illusions of retaining permanent heroine status had just gone out the door with Pumpernickel.

Animal owners often make the mistake of thinking that the neutering of their pets will change their personalities and habits. The only thing it is ever going to change is their desire to copulate. If you have a nasty-tempered beast, he is still going to be mean as sin even though he's neutered. If he loves to travel, he's still going to buy that bus ticket to Tijuana every night, and neutering is not going to bring him home sober in the morning, either. Spaying didn't keep Footer Williams from departing on her last journey, nor did it diminish Peewee's urge to take an arm off at the elbow. And neutering didn't keep Gemini from taking off on Thanksgiving night of his second year, never to return.

I called him until my throat was so raw I could only croak. I went to every farm within a radius of five miles and asked for him. I knew he hadn't been stolen, because he was terrified of strangers; even the milkman driving in would send him cowering to the haymow for half a day. Weeks after he had disappeared, I was still looking for him. Every time I drove down the road and saw a stray cat even remotely resembling Gemini, I jumped out of the car, tore my hose on barbed wire fences and followed the stray through muddy fields until I was absolutely sure it wasn't he. Sometimes in the midst of this madness I would stop and tell myself, "For God's sake, woman, it's only a cat!" But the next time a gray tiger cat loomed in the distance, I was off on the trail again. Even today, I would mortgage the farm for the sight of Gemini coming toward me with his bushy tail waving gaily in the air, his soft eyes telling me he knew he was irresistible.

Stoyer thought it was a bit much how I carried on about Gemini, and he let it be known he thought it was rather silly how emotional we let ourselves become over our animals. But that was before Pumpernickel became ill again. He was four years old when I found him on the barn floor one hot summer morning, sprawled out limp as a wet leaf. Stoyer returned several minutes later from an early-morning bike ride, and when he saw his cat, he paled and said, "Why haven't you gotten him to the vet?"

He cradled Pumpernickel in his arms while I drove them to Dock's office. Dock sucked in his breath and clucked when he examined the cat—the ominous sign. He said the cat had uremic poisoning, and the chances were not good for his recovery. He gave Pumpernickel a shot and sent some red tablets home with us to give him daily.

Stoyer installed his cat on the screened porch in his favorite box, with a cot for himself beside it. The cat was limp and weak and would neither eat nor drink. When it came time to give him the first pill, Stoyer and I remembered at the same moment that we had vowed never to try to give Pumpernickel medication again. We took him back to Dock's. Dock told Stoyer gently to bring him back every day. He always had time to pill a cat, he said.

Stoyer sat by his cat for three days and two nights. A half hour before he died at sunset on the third day, Stoyer was still trying to pour liquid Jello into Pumpernickel's limp body.

The word came from the screened porch, gruffly, "I think he just died."

A few minutes later. "I guess I'll bury him before he stiffens up."

We heard the screen door slam and Stoyer going out to the toolshed to get his shovel. There was just enough light left in the warm summer evening to see to dig a grave under a lilac bush at the edge of the orchard. Stoyer wrapped the still-warm Pumpernickel in one of his old green striped crib sheets he found in the ragbag, fitted him snugly into a cardboard box, tied it with string, and buried him. Then he went for a stroll along the neighbor's woods, where the sunset gleamed hotly through the oaks and sycamores.

When he came back into the kitchen, I said, "Do you want some popcorn if I make it?"

"Might as well," he said.

He ate his popcorn in silence, a huge bowl of it. He swished the unpopped kernels around in the butter at the bottom of the bowl and chewed them up. "I always thought if I tried hard enough there wasn't a thing in the world I couldn't do," he said. "I was so sure I could save my cat."

He bit down hard on some more black widows. "Kinda hits you the first time you find out that isn't always the case."

Liz is really the only sensible one in the family when it comes to cats. She loves her cats as much as anyone, but she doesn't let love blot out all reason. From the time she was in kindergarten until her middle teens, she let Bla' sleep at the foot of the bed, but always put her out at night. One winter Bla' got caught in a leghold trap, and had to spend most of the winter in the basement while the foot healed. When Bla' became very old and incurably ill, Liz asked Stoyer and Witt to take her to Dock's with instructions that she was to be put to sleep if nothing could be done for her. She wouldn't go herself because several years before that she had fainted in a vet's office in South Metropolis, when we had taken our German shepherd Holbein in to be X-rayed after a car hit him. Her head had struck the doctor's instrument table, spewing instruments all over the concrete floor, and the horrendous clatter they made had rung in her ears ever since. She didn't want a repeat of that. She buried Bla' under a lilac bush next to Pumpernickel, and after a decent length of time she started to let Gingersnap sleep on her bed.

Sister to the sainted Gemini and Pumpernickel, Gingersnap is acknowledged by all to be the official house cat. Witt calls her *Special,* because she has run through so many names he never knows what the current one is. She went from Gingersnap to Dinner Nap to Nappy Night, then jumped clean to Roly Poly Williams, and seems to have settled down as just plain Polly. But there is nothing plain about Polly. Eleven pounds of gorgeous cat enclosed in a heavenly coat of orange and brown fur, she pads lissomely around the house on huge fat paws, smelling divinely of fresh air and fresh hay, and she is allowed to sleep on absolutely everything. The first person awake in the morning lets her in the house, and from there on she nags around from bed to bed, first of all to see if everyone is breathing, which really concerns her, and from then on to find someone alive enough to feed her.

She loves to sit on the living room desk and look in queenly fashion out the window over the front meadow—at the lowly peasant ponies who must feed outside on grass—and at the other cat peons who are out there hunting mice for a living. She is not without guile. She will jump on your lap to smell your breath to learn what you have just eaten. If it happens to be roast beef, she meows silently as if she is too weak to utter voice, jumps down, runs to her empty cat bowl, sniffs it, turns around, sits down, and waits for you to ante up with the evidence she has found on you.

Before settling down in the living room of an evening, she methodically jumps from lap to lap, testing the flesh for softness and warmth by hard kneadings with her fat front paws. The winner gets the pleasure of her eleven pounds of dead weight for the rest of the night.

Even Dock, a hard-headed soul, succumbed to her blandishments. When we took her to be spayed, we asked Dock afterwards if she had had any kittens in her. "Oh, no," he said, really shocked for Dock, as he lifted her gently into her box for the home trip. "That there's a juvenile."

I guess that's the secret of Polly's charm. She's the perennial ingenue.

When it comes to the cat population on our farm, we know for a fact that the Lord giveth, and the Lord taketh away. But it seems that every time the Lord takes away, he gives again in a hurry, and perhaps a bit too abundantly. Not too long after Gemini disappeared, the third, and at this writing, the last matriarch of the Williams dynasty made her appearance.

Going into the barn one night to check the ponies, I heard such a horrendous wail coming from behind the barn that I scuttled back into the house and told Stoyer and Liz that there was either an abandoned baby behind the barn or a lonesome hyena. Arming ourselves with sticks and whips, we peered cautiously around the side of the barn. I felt pretty silly when a tiny cat ran toward us. I couldn't believe a noise that large could come out of anything so small. This was an unhappy cat, no doubt about it, and she was screaming to anyone who would listen that she had been done wrong. She was tigerish gray, with big ears, and she had a malformed foot with an extra claw, and a stubbed-off tail that looked as if it had been caught in a door and sliced off. Her one good feature was her eyes, which were huge and Cleopatralike and clear. She had been somebody's cat, all right, and she was voicing her indignation a little louder than most at the outrageous way she had been treated. She was, of course, the usual starved and pregnant.

Now right here is where I made my mistake. She was just a *little* pregnant, not a lot pregnant at all, and I could easily have taken her to Dock to have her spayed, but immediately I thought of myself and how nice it would be to have a new set of kittens to take the edge off the grief of losing Gemini.

So I let Short Tail Williams have her litter, and here was a batch of five kittens that seemed to have a hex on them from the day they were born. There were pure black triplets, which Liz adored and named Tutti-Frutti, Champagne, and Teddy Bear. Teddy Bear was her favorite because he had huge glassy eyes like a teddy bear and wasn't very smart. Stoyer's favorite was a big, black-and-white spot he named Big Un, alias Bad Boy, who became such an instant brawling, roving stud we had to have him neutered at five months. Again by default, I was left with the remaining male, a gray tiger I named Popover, who was so timid that even a mouse could run him up a tree. We didn't have Popover neutered because we felt he needed all his original equipment to hold his own in the world.

At seven months, Tutti Frutti and Teddy Bear disappeared together one night, never to be seen again. Soon after that Popover developed a chronic respiratory ailment and just wasted away, drawing his last breath in his warm basket beside the furnace one windy January afternoon, as the funeral drums for Lyndon Johnson were beating upstairs from the television set. Big Un, alias Bad Boy, developed weak, watery eyes, which give him a lot of trouble—but not enough so that he still doesn't try to fight everything in the county twice his size. He is usually convalescing from a wound of one kind or another, usually severe enough to take his mind off his eyes. Only Champagne was born free of ills, hang-ups, or rotten luck—a glossy miniature panther who pads happily around the farm not rippling any waters.

Of the three Williams families, two matriarchs remain: Short Tail and Miss Tabatha. The original matriarch, the beautiful Famous, the wisest and most intuitive of them all, knew when her time had come, and she was not going to let anyone watch her die. She walked into the woods one summer night and undoubtedly went about the grim business by herself, with no onlookers intruding. That's the way she wanted it, and being the matriarch she was, she usually got her way.

I have sworn a hundred times there will be no more Williamses on this farm. That if another cat comes walking up that lane, fresh from a drop-off, I will point a straight arm due north in the direction of the county animal shelter and say, "Go. Get thee to the pound," or something of that dramatic nature.

I know I can do it if the cat is not hungry, or hurt, or pregnant, or cross-eyed or cute. I know I can do it then.

Epilogue

*A*fter vowing for years that I would never take in another stray cat, of course I did. Last summer I took in Raggle Taggle Williams. By what procedure does one go about rejecting a terror-stricken baby kitten who comes walking up your lane at midnight? I knew of none, so I fed the small black-and-brown ball and warmed her and cuddled her and put her in a box on the back porch for the night, and in a few days she thought I was her mother. Every time I came through the door she grabbed me around the ankle with all four paws and hung on.

Stoyer, who loves to figure the odds, asked me to think seriously whether I really wanted to make a fifteen-year commitment to this kitten. According to the life-expectancy tables, he said, all of our other "keeping" animals—the ponies, the dogs, and the other cats—would be gone by then, and she would be the only one left. I replied giddily, as I danced Raggle Taggle around on my shoulders and she washed my face with her long straggly tail, that if that were the case then Raggle Taggle and I would go into a happy old age together.

On a torpid, shimmering Sunday in August, two months later, Liz and I were sitting on the grass watching Raggle Taggle play. She was scampering up and down the silver

241

maple trees, doing figure eights around us, stopping on a dime, leaping at insects in the air, when suddenly she collapsed at our feet, and in minutes she was dead.

Who can accurately predict what will be a fifteen-year commitment? A fifteen-year commitment can be truncated, in the space of a bound or a leap, into a two-month commitment.

In recent years one of the biggest family arguments we can get into is *where the cats are buried*. We didn't put markers on the cats' graves, each one of us thinking that surely he would remember where his cat was buried. The cat graveyard is in a straight line north to south, just outside of the orchard fence and underneath two towering spruce trees and a row of white and purple lilac bushes. Witt knows for a fact where *his* cat lies—under the evergreen in a spot directly in line with the view from his study window. And Raggle Taggle Williams is easy; the earth is still mounded and soft. But for the others, the years have blurred the memories, and if we happen to be strolling on the back lawn of a summer evening we are soon shouting and pointing and claiming double occupancy under the lilacs and evergreens.

As for the ponies, Stalwyrt Beau, herdsire of them all, lies deep in the back meadow, where each spring the alfalfa and the bromegrass and the timothy sprout up from his bones to nurture his children and his grandchildren and his great-grandchildren, whose hooves will thunder above him for many more springs, or the number that has been allotted to them.